IMAGES
of America

ASSYRIANS OF YONKERS

On the Cover: The Assyrian National Women's Association, Yonkers, June 1943. This picture was taken in the yard of the first Assyrian National Association at 371 Riverdale Avenue in Yonkers. The women's organization was an auxiliary of the Assyrian National Association, whose leadership was male. See page 86. (Author's collection.)

IMAGES
of America

ASSYRIANS OF YONKERS

Dr. Ruth Kambar

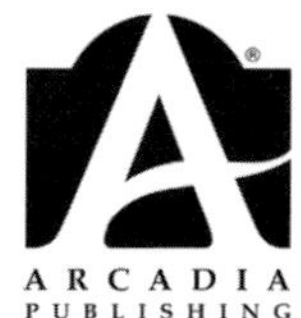

ISBN 978-1-4671-2963-3

Published by Arcadia Publishing
Charleston, South Carolina

Printed in the United States of America

Library of Congress Control Number: 2018938767

For all general information, please contact Arcadia Publishing:
Telephone 843-853-2070
Fax 843-853-0044
E-mail sales@arcadiapublishing.com
For customer service and orders:
Toll-Free 1-888-313-2665

Visit us on the Internet at www.arcadiapublishing.com

Contents

ACKNOWLEDGMENTS

I would like to thank my grandfather Nicolai (Nicholas) Benjamin, who arrived in the United States in 1914. He could often be heard commanding an audience with his storytelling. Our history did not die because Pop left me a trove of books, photographs, and stories about life in Urmia, Persia, and about the Assyrian immigrant experience. Joining him, great-aunt Lucy Benjamin, my grandfather's sister in-law, provided me with her stories and photographs.

I would also like to acknowledge my father, William Kambar, for his contributions to this photographic monument. He bequeathed to me many photo albums with pictures of my paternal family. Through him, I am able to complete my understanding of our family's immigration to the United States. My paternal grandparents, Yonan and Emma Kambar, raised a generous man who loved family, history, photography, and narrative.

My mother, Lydia Benjamin Kambar, and her sister Shirley Benjamin also contributed their photo albums, black-and-white negatives, and a suitcase of photographs from long ago. For months, Shirley arrived at my home with "a few more pictures." Many cousins also assisted me in identifying Assyrian brethren, including Elizabeth Jacobs Bender, David Benjamin Sr., Michele Yohanna, Roni Yohanna Wedig, Nancy Lee Jacobs, Emmy Aslan, and Estelle Vitti Tortora.

Rev. Adday Francis, Jacquie BabayiKunka, Nancy Mirza Multari, Rabbi Sara Akalski, and Alice Aziz David contributed images, translated, and identified Assyrians. Fred Sarkiso, president of the Yonkers Assyrian American Association, and Valeh Sarkiso hosted an event to support the record-breaking opening of the gallery exhibit Assyrians in Yonkers, a collaborative project with Assyrian artist Kathy Yacoe. Two hundred Assyrians gathered for a screening of Jordan Allot and Helma Adde's film *Our Last Stand*. Helma Adde and Prof. Sargon Donabed engaged our community in the ongoing plight and relief of the Assyrians.

Special thanks to Kathy Yacoe, Julie Cousens at the Blue Door Gallery, and Marcos Torno at Images of Old Greenwich Inc.

INTRODUCTION

The Assyrian community of Yonkers, descendants of the ancient Assyrians of Mesopotamia, initially emigrated from eastern Turkey and northern Iran, particularly from the Urmia region between the late 1800s and the early 1900s prior to and during World War I. In November 1914, a jihad proclamation against Christians was read in all provinces of the Ottoman Empire. January 1915 marked the beginning of the Seyfo (the year of the sword), when approximately 700,000 Assyrians were murdered or driven from their homes. Many sought refuge in Russia and the United States. The first Assyrian arrivals to the United States were sent to learn missionary work in the homeland of the Protestant missionaries who had resided with them in Persia and converted them from Nestorian to Protestant. Their families joined them to escape genocide and persecution by the Ottoman Turks.

In 1933, Iraqi and Kurdish leaders killed 3,000 Assyrians in the Semele Massacre in Iraq. One third of the Assyrian population fled to Syria. More recently, the Iranian Revolution in the 1970s, the Iraq War, and the Syrian Civil War have displaced additional Assyrians, many of whom survive in refugee camps in Syria and Iraq. Assyrians are the victims of ongoing genocide.

Yonkers continues to provide a home for these Assyrians in diaspora. Despite ongoing genocide, Assyrians persist in perpetuating their cultural heritage. As part of an ethno-genesis movement common among dispersed peoples, their lives are marked by a sense of place and memory. This book is a testament to the patriotism and assimilation process of Assyrians in the United States. The Assyrian community in Yonkers sustains its culture and rituals like Kha b-Nisan (Assyrian New Year), the Assyrian Aramaic language, and ethnic traditions, with pride.

In celebration of the Assyrian community's membership and its contributions to the city, Yonkers politicians annually raise the Assyrian flag at Yonkers City Hall to commemorate the anniversary of the first national Assyrian American Association, which was founded in Yonkers in 1914, and to bring in the Assyrian New Year. In 1968, Artist George Bit Atanus of Tehran, Iran, designed the current Assyrian flag. Its history is tied closely to Yonkers; in 1974, the Assyrian Universal Alliance voted in Yonkers to approve the flag as a symbol of the homeland and the indigenous people of Iraq. The community sustains itself through an active congregation at the Church of the East: Mar Mari Parish on Buena Vista Avenue, the Assyrian American Association on Ludlow Street, and through familial and social gatherings in Yonkers.

As you read the history and sense the Assyrian American culture through photos and captions, take note of the countries from which this community has migrated. Also, notice that the family names and places of origin may vary in spelling, depending on the phonetic translation and the paths of family migration.

Assyrians today still maintain hope that as the indigenous people, they will have a home in part of their ancestral lands that stretch from the region of Ninevah, today's Iraq, to the Urmia region of Iran, the Syria Jezirah, and the southeast of Turkey. Obtaining such a homeland would allow the Assyrians to protect their culture, language, history, and religion.

One

Urmia and the Presbyterian Mission

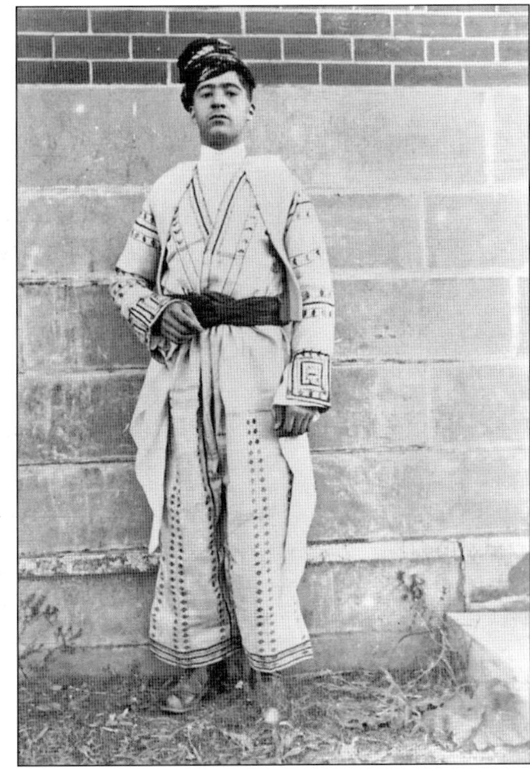

Teddy Benjamin. Theodore Benjamin (called T.D., Teedy, or Teddy) is pictured wearing traditional Assyrian clothing to preach. Teddy and his brother, Jacob, were educated by the American Presbyterian missionaries in Urmia. (Courtesy of Shirley Benjamin.)

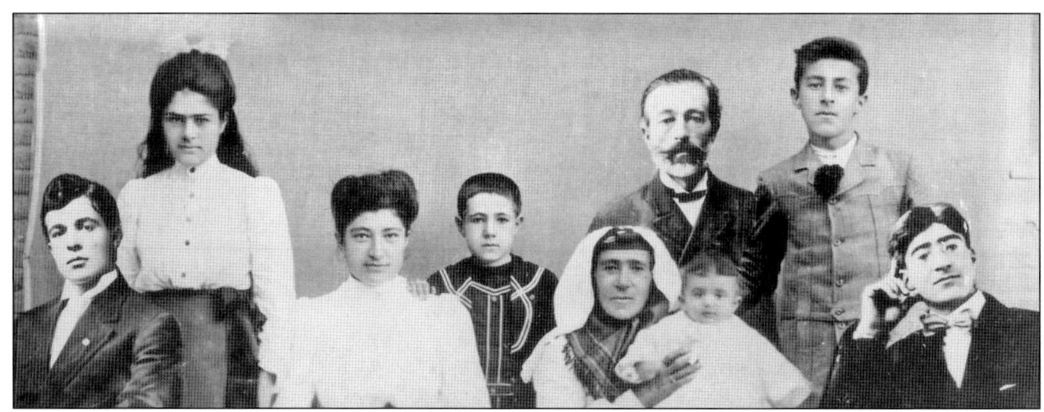

The Rev. David Jacob Benjamin and Julia Benjamin Family. This photograph was taken in Urmia around 1909–1910. From left to right are Jacob, Emma, Louise, Nicholas, Julia (Momma Juja), Katherine, Rev. David Jacob (Poppa Jura or "Big Father"), Nathan (Natan, also known as Nelson), and Teddy (Teedy). When Katherine was approximately 10 months old, she and her brother Nathan accidentally fell from a flat roof while playing in Hayderlooi. She did not survive the fall. Nathan was very badly injured. (Courtesy of Shirley Benjamin.)

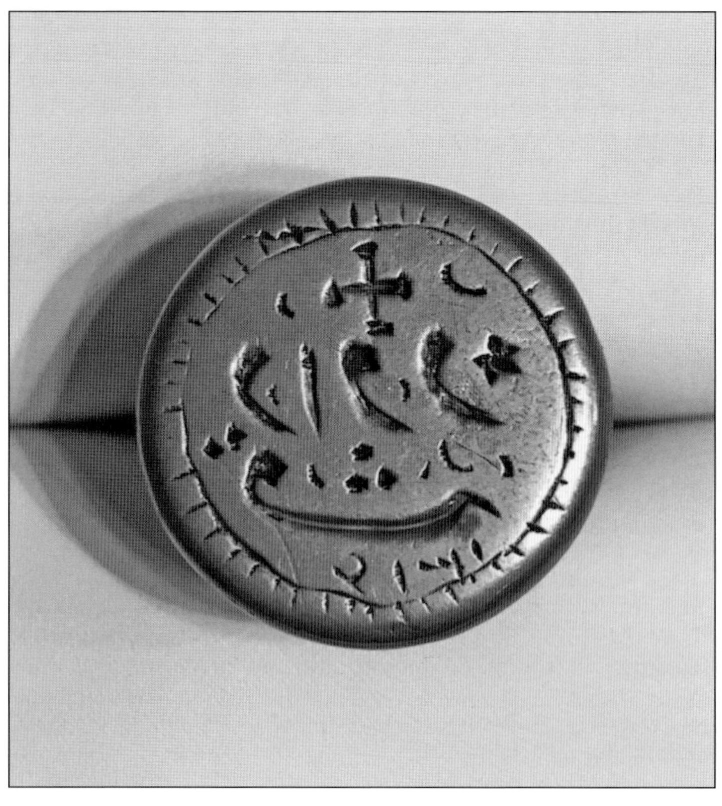

The Rev. David Jacob Benjamin's Sealing Wax Stamp. This sealing wax stamp belonged to Rev. David Benjamin Sr., father of Rev. David Jacob Benjamin, who was born in 1864. Both men were Presbyterian ministers in Urmia. The stamp contains Arabic and Farsi letters and the worn Assyrian signature of Qasha Dawud Benjamin (Rev. David Benjamin), dated 1316/1816. The Assyrian cross at the top of the stamp represents the trinity of the father Asshur, the god of fire; the mother Ishtar; and the human king. The writing was translated by Dr. Sargon Donabed. (Courtesy of Shirley Benjamin.)

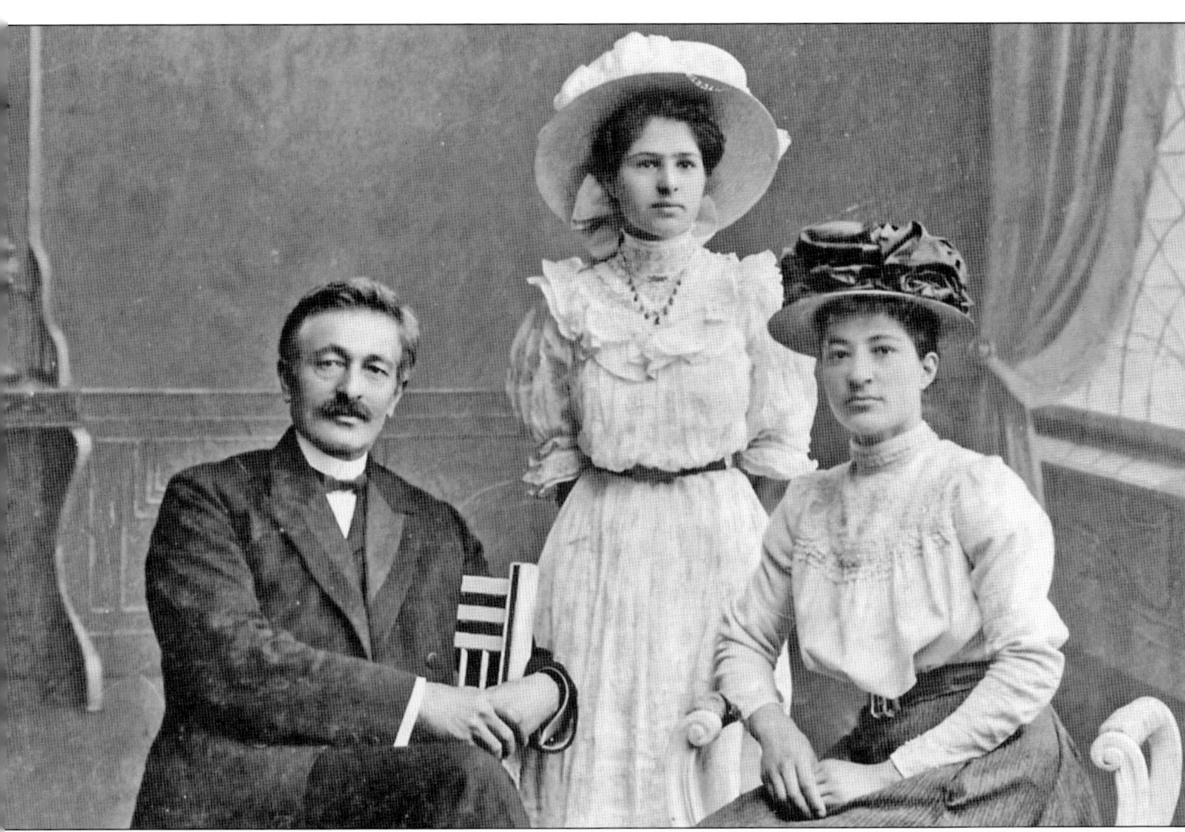

Rev. David Jacob Benjamin with Daughters Emma and Louise in Holland, 1912. David Jacob Benjamin found a welcoming home in the Netherlands with the Pieter Wilhelm van Rossem–Aleta Lamberta Gunning family, where he stayed for almost half a year in 1906. Van Rossem's family was committed to their guest, making several attempts to raise money for Benjamin's mission in the Kurdistan mountains. The family inquired about his background with the president of the Presbyterian missionary society, and his references were favorable. Benjamin had been serving this missionary society for 22 years, making him eligible for support. Together with Rev. Syb Talma, Mrs. van Rossem wrote a book about Benjamin, *Special Moments from the Life of David Jacob Benjamin, Armenian Missionary*. Reverend Benjamin's second journey to the Netherlands was undertaken from Sweden. Again, the van Rossems offered help. This second stay lasted several months. After his return home, Reverend Benjamin wrote in a letter dated March 4, 1908, that five cities in Urmia were attacked by the Kurds and during the attack, his niece had been murdered. Roughly 200 people had been killed and the survivors' homes were plundered. He wrote that his sister and her four children were living with him and his family and that the Turks had penetrated Urmia. He also wrote that all Christians in Persia were in danger. Addressing his friend Reverend Kersten from the Netherlands, he pleaded, "In this time our eyes are only focused on God. Everyone in Persia is in danger. Remember us in your prayers, if you can, help us." At this time, he made an arrangement with the van Rossem–Gunning family to allow his daughters to escape the danger imposed by bands of nearby Kurds who were killing the Christian population, before Seyfo (the Assyrian genocide in the Kurdistan Mountains). Louise and Emma studied in Holland while living with the van Rossems, as did their brother Jacob, before he left to look for work in Russia. The girls studied nursing, and in the United States, Louise served as a nurse. Upon the advice of their father, Louise and Emma never returned to Persia, eventually meeting their family members, including brothers Jacob, Nathan, Nicolai, and their mother, Julia, and father, David, who sought permanent refuge in the United States. (Author's collection.)

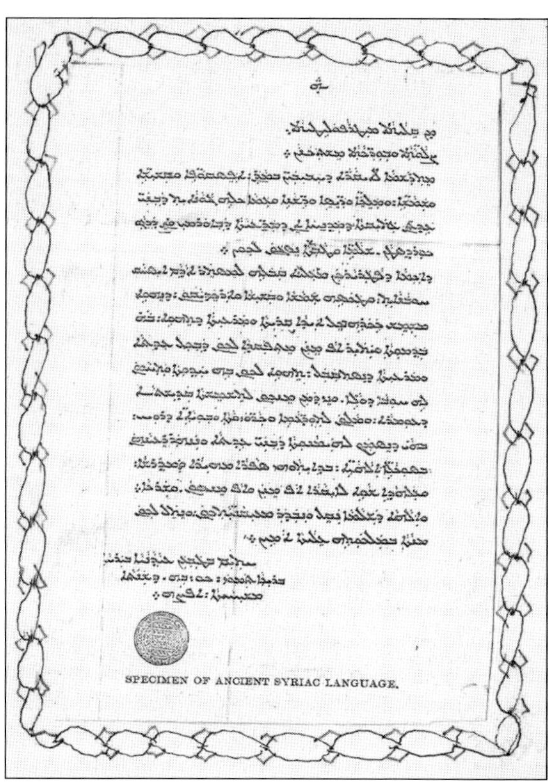

SPECIMEN OF ANCIENT SYRIAC LANGUAGE.

SPECIMEN OF SYRIAC WRITING. Rev. David Jacob Benjamin wrote: "From the office of the Metropolitan, Receive prayers and Blessings. It was written to honor our beloved in Christ: Bishops, Priests, Deacons and leaders, in general, all members of the congregation of the Ancient Church of the East, City of Urmia and Kurdistan. Peace and blessings to all on behalf of our Patriarch to receive Mr. Adam Iskhaq [Isaac] that he is elevated from deacon to priest and *archedyaqno* [archdeacon, the level below bishop, but above priest]. Receive him with honor and respect and show him necessary love to be all to serve the church and stay in the faith of the church, and to celebrate mass and *madrashe* [catechetical hymns sung in the liturgy]. God of Peace save you from your trouble, and have a place in Heaven. The year of Christ, June 26, 1895." Rabbi Sara Akalski and Rev. Addai Francis of Mar Mari Church in Yonkers provided the translation. (Author's collection.)

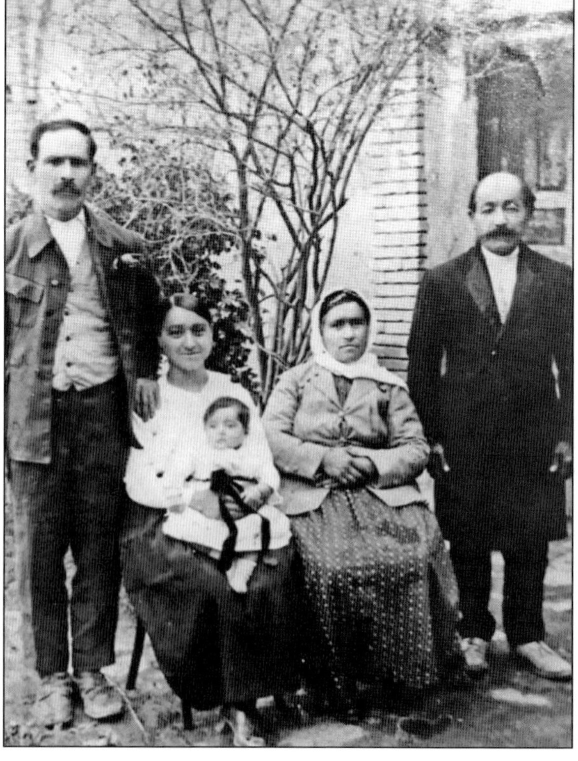

THE JERJIS/GEORGES FAMILY, 1920. Pictured here from left to right are Lazar and Nanajan Georges (holding baby Beatrice) and Nanajan's parents, Sara and Piera. Sara was raised by missionaries in Tabriz, Iran, after her father died. Her mother could not provide for her family. She studied English with the missionaries and taught the Assyrian language to the priests and orphans. (Courtesy of Jacquie BabayiKunka and Juliet Gevargis-Mizimako.)

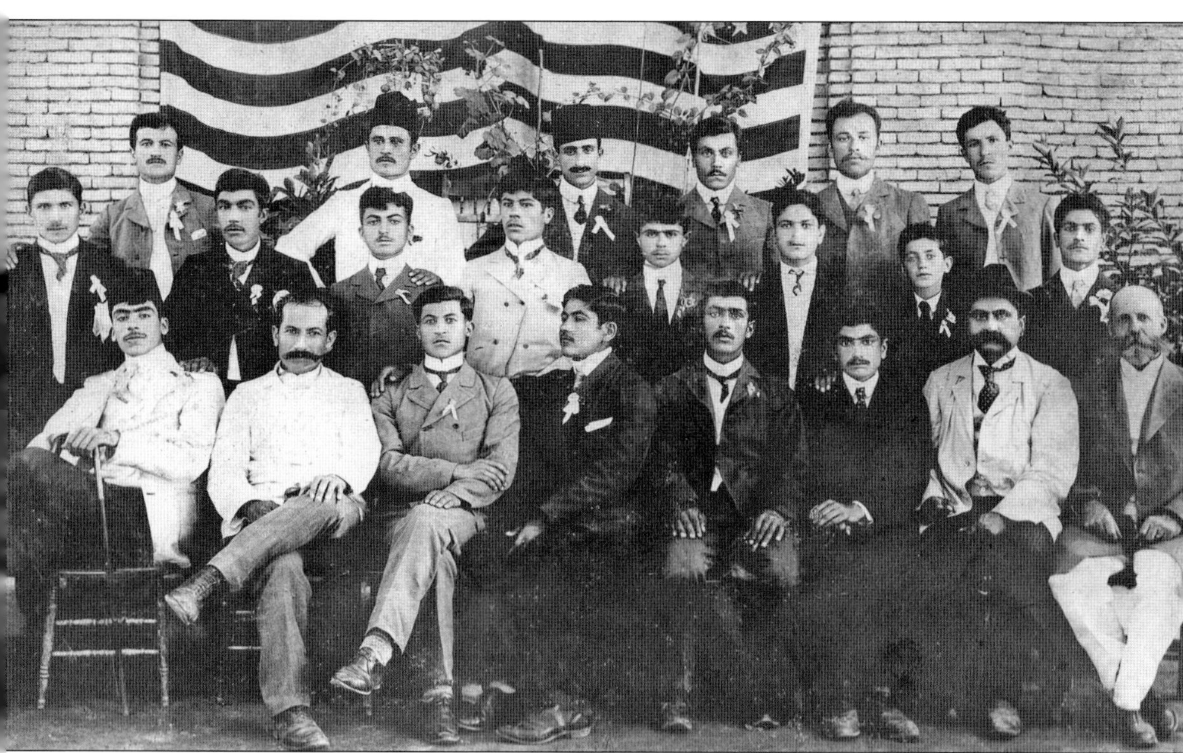

Urmia College, with the American Flag, c. 1910–1913. Westminster Medical College and Hospital was built in 1879 and closed in 1915. The students were Assyrians and Armenians. All of the missionaries' properties in Urmia were sold to the Iranian government just before World War I started, and the missionaries were moved to Tabriz. The back of the picture identifies these people and their hometowns as, from left to right, (first row) Dr. Cohn, Kasha Isaac Malik (Guitapa, uncle of George Malik Yonan in Teheran), Oner (Shemsajian, son of Kasha Yosip Avanus or Hevanus, changed to Evanns when he came to the United States, and Susanne Ameer Monasa's mother's brother), Yoel Rupus (Guitapa), unidentified (Bas-Turkish place), Mishael (Saralan, also known as Marhsall, son of Dr. Yaku), Rabbi Pera Amruchas, Rabbi Yukhana, and Kasha Keena (Bas-Turkish place); (second row) unidentified, Shmuel Mar Yukhana (nephew of Agha Lazar), David (Dizateka), David (Ardeshai, son of Rabbi Shakar), Hike (Guitapa, son of Kasha Mooshi), Yosip Mar Nuka, David (Gulpashan), and Dr. Shmuel Tamraz (Dizateka); (third row): Dr. Alkhas Amrikhas, Rabbi Isaac Urshon, Rabbi Gabriel Genesa, Rabbi Mneshi Baba (Seri), Dr. Abraham Suldus, and Kasha Khendoo. (Courtesy of Susanne Ameer Monasa.)

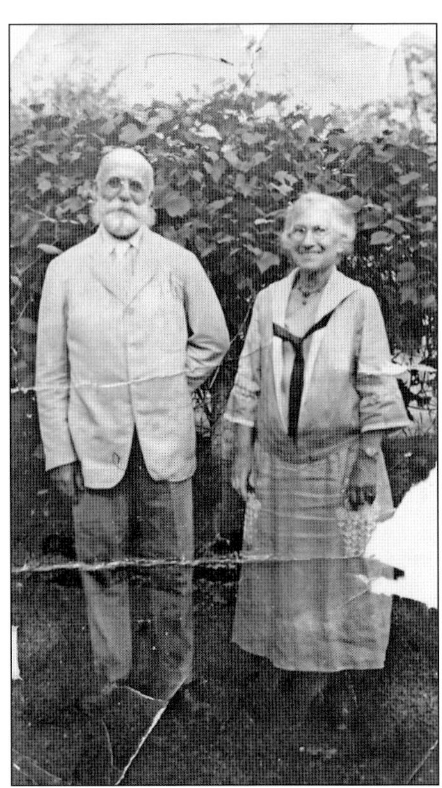

The Missionary. Pictured here during the early 1900s are Emma Cochran Ponafidine, author of *My Life in the Moslem East* (1932), and her husband, Pierre Ponafidine. She was the daughter of the Urmia missionary Joseph Plumb Cochran. (Author's collection.)

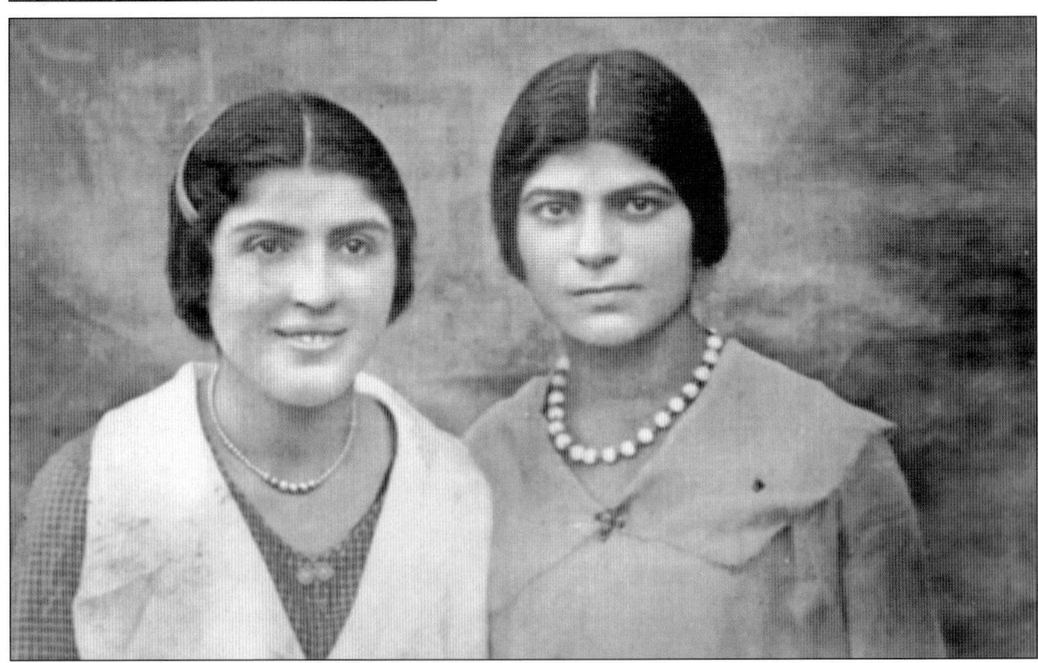

Cousins. Julia Yonan Essakhan Lazar (left) is pictured with first cousin Maria Ameer (sister in-law to Susanne Ameer). They both graduated from the American Missionary School before coming to the United States from Iran. Julia immigrated in 1931 and married her cousin, Ephraim Bob Lazar. Maria came to the United States in 1942. (Susanne Ameer Monasa.)

Two

IMMIGRATION AND LIFE IN THE OLD COUNTRY

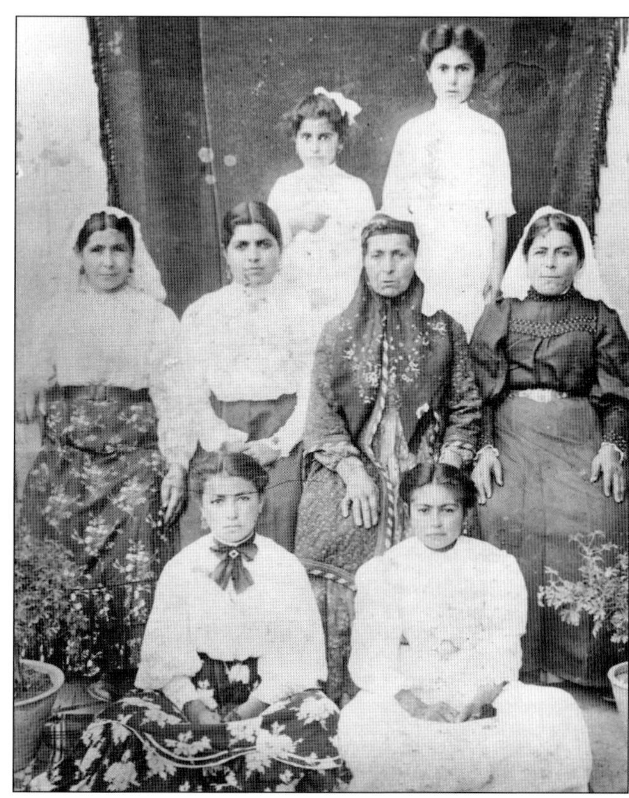

DEGALA, IRAN, 1913–1914. The younger girl in the back row is Zenhela Sargis (Vitti), and directly in front of her, second from left, is her mother, Esther Sargis. The other women are unidentified. (Courtesy of Estelle Vitti.)

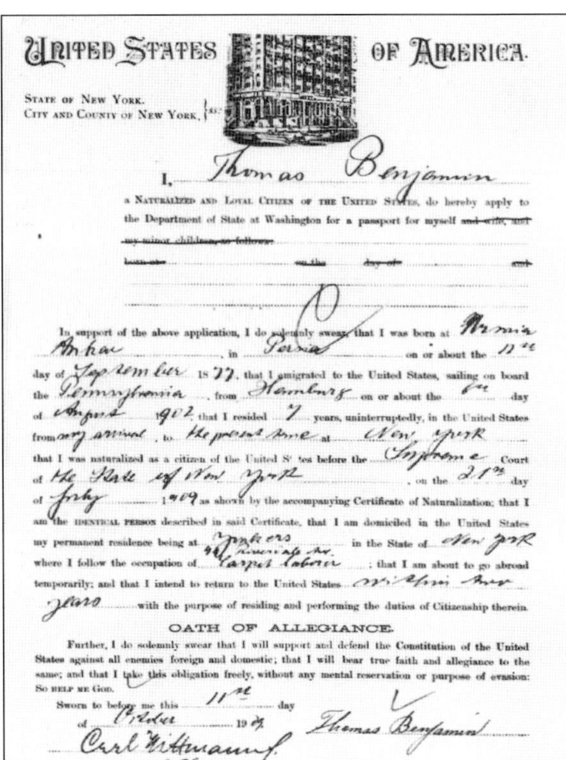

UNITED STATES OF AMERICA.

STATE OF NEW YORK.
CITY AND COUNTY OF NEW YORK, } ss:

I, Thomas Benjamin a NATURALIZED AND LOYAL CITIZEN OF THE UNITED STATES, do hereby apply to the Department of State at Washington for a passport for myself ~~and wife, and my minor children, as follows:~~

~~born at~~ ~~on the~~ ~~day of~~ ~~and~~

In support of the above application, I do solemnly swear that I was born at Urmia Anhar, in Persia on or about the 17th day of September 1877, that I emigrated to the United States, sailing on board the Pennsylvania, from Hamburg on or about the 6th day of August 1902, that I resided 7 years, uninterruptedly, in the United States from my arrival, to the present time at New York that I was naturalized as a citizen of the United States before the Supreme Court of the State of New York, on the 21st day of July 1909 as shown by the accompanying Certificate of Naturalization; that I am the IDENTICAL PERSON described in said Certificate, that I am domiciled in the United States my permanent residence being at Yonkers 44 Riverdale Av. in the State of New York where I follow the occupation of Carpet laborer; that I am about to go abroad temporarily; and that I intend to return to the United States within two years with the purpose of residing and performing the duties of Citizenship therein.

OATH OF ALLEGIANCE.

Further, I do solemnly swear that I will support and defend the Constitution of the United States against all enemies foreign and domestic; that I will bear true faith and allegiance to the same; and that I take this obligation freely, without any mental reservation or purpose of evasion: SO HELP ME GOD.

Sworn to before me this 11th day of October 1929

Thomas Benjamin

Carl Wittmann
(99) Notary Public.

THOMAS BENJAMIN'S US PASSPORT APPLICATION, OCTOBER 11, 1929. Thomas Benjamin was born in September 1877 in Urmia and immigrated to the United States on August 6, 1902. Upon his arrival, he lived at 43 Jefferson Street in Yonkers. He later resided at 44 Riverdale Avenue. (Courtesy of Joe David.)

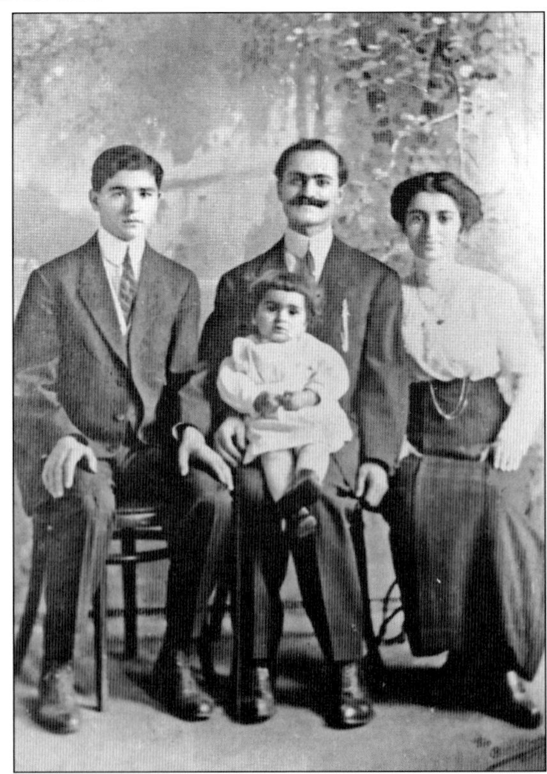

THE DAVIDS. From left to right are unidentified, Benjamin Isaac David, Batishua David, and their son, Theodore David. (Courtesy of Joe David.)

LAYA PAULUS, DAUGHTER NANO, AND FAMILY. This photograph was taken in Ardashier, Persia, in the early 1900s. Laya immigrated to the United States, but her daughter, Nano, and family were redirected to Cuba. Nano raised her children in Cuba, but eventually they were able to migrate to Puerto Rico. (Author's collection.)

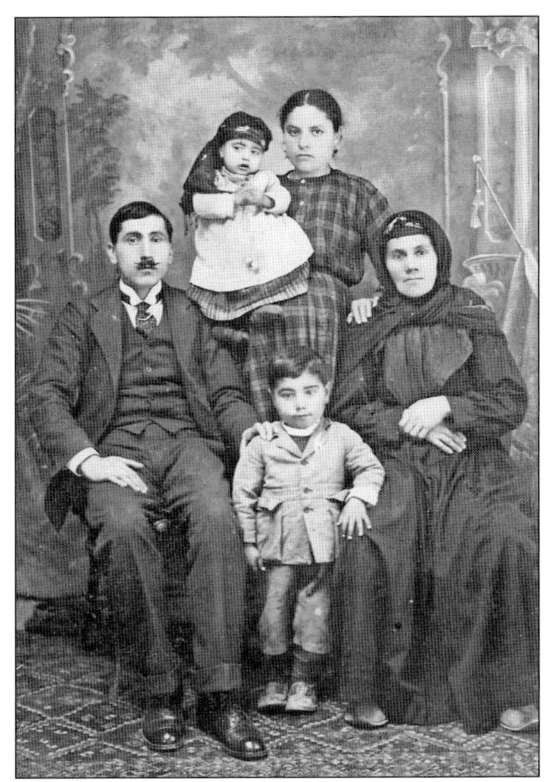

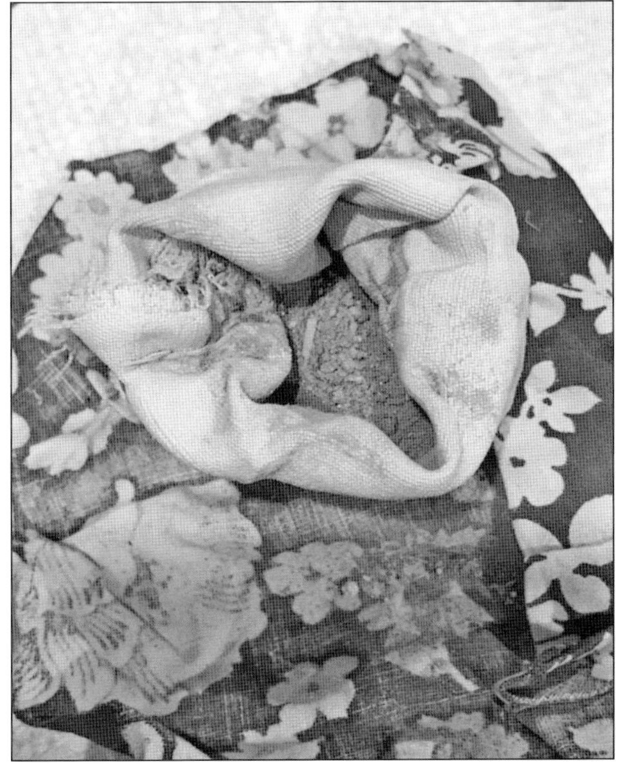

REMINDERS OF LIFE IN PERSIA. Running from her village of Ardashier to escape the Ottoman Turks and the Kurds, who had been murdering the Christians in Persia and the Kurdistan mountains for years, Blandina Jacobs Paulus joined the Christians as they desperately attempted to avoid genocide. Blandina stopped to grab part of her homeland, the dirt pictured here. Her family sought safety in a refugee camp in Iraq, Baquba. She fled with her mother, Laya, and her aunt Elishva, who carried Blandina's baby sister in her arms. Elishva and the baby were shot and killed. This dirt is the only remains of her home, a sad reminder of the Assyrian predicament as a continuously and forcibly dispersed people. (Author's collection.)

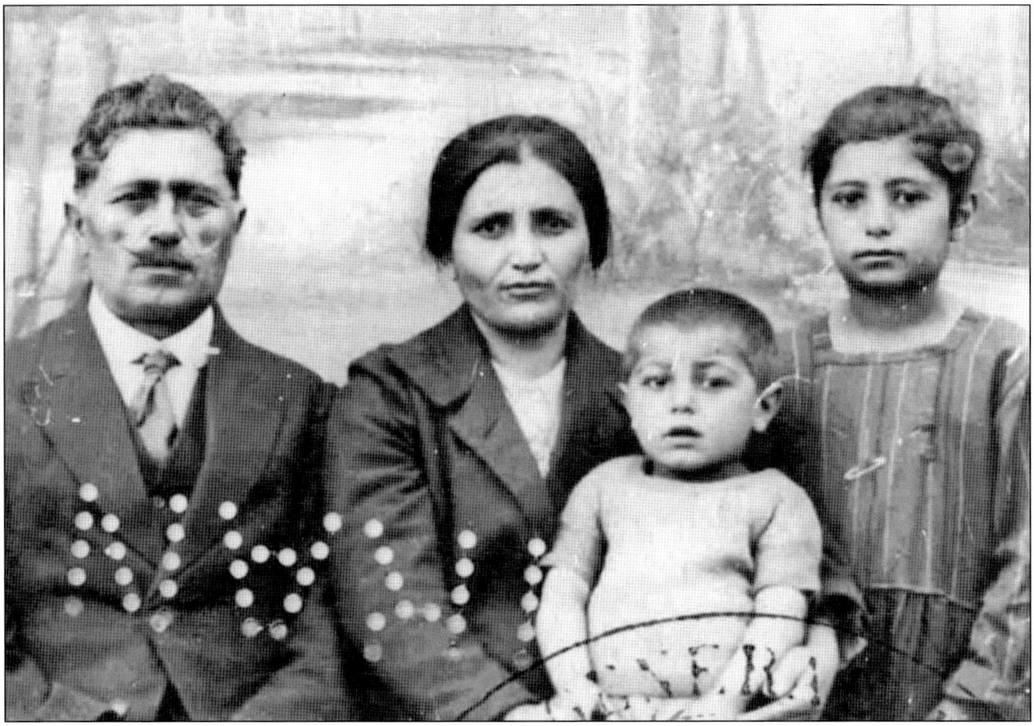

IMMIGRATION PHOTOGRAPH OF THE JONATHAN AND NAZLU JACOBS FAMILY. Jonathan and Nazlu are pictured with their children, James and Florence, in 1921. As indicated by the stamp on the photograph, they lived in Armenia, then part of Russia, but were originally from Iran. (Courtesy of Nancy Lee Jacobs.)

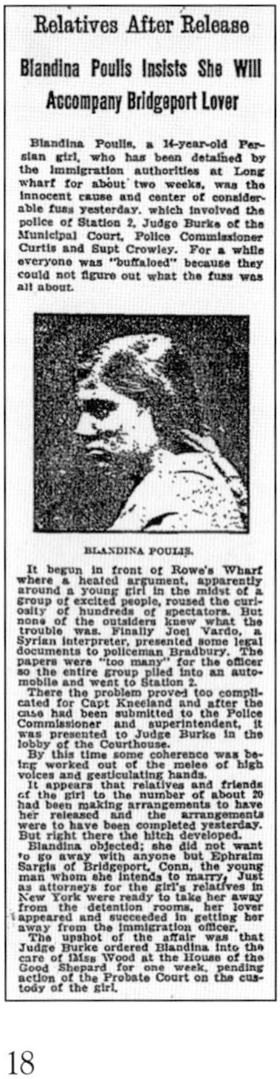

Relatives After Release

Blandina Poulis Insists She Will Accompany Bridgeport Lover

Blandina Poulis, a 14-year-old Persian girl, who has been detained by the immigration authorities at Long wharf for about two weeks, was the innocent cause and center of considerable fuss yesterday, which involved the police of Station 2, Judge Burke of the Municipal Court, Police Commissioner Curtis and Supt Crowley. For a while everyone was "buffaloed" because they could not figure out what the fuss was all about.

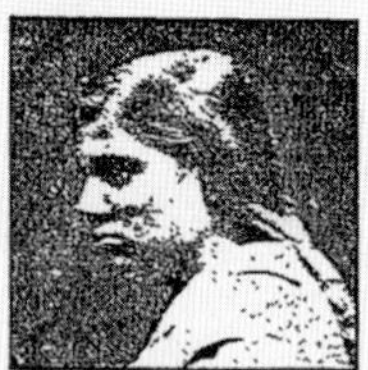

BLANDINA POULIS.

It begun in front of Rowe's Wharf where a heated argument, apparently around a young girl in the midst of a group of excited people, roused the curiosity of hundreds of spectators. But none of the outsiders knew what the trouble was. Finally Joel Vardo, a Syrian interpreter, presented some legal documents to policeman Bradbury. The papers were "too many" for the officer so the entire group piled into an automobile and went to Station 2.

There the problem proved too complicated for Capt Kneeland and after the case had been submitted to the Police Commissioner and superintendent, it was presented to Judge Burke in the lobby of the Courthouse.

By this time some coherence was being worked out of the melee of high voices and gesticulating hands.

It appears that relatives and friends of the girl to the number of about 20 had been making arrangements to have her released and the arrangements were to have been completed yesterday. But right there the hitch developed.

Blandina objected; she did not want to go away with anyone but Ephraim Sargis of Bridgeport, Conn, the young man whom she intends to marry. Just as attorneys for the girl's relatives in New York were ready to take her away from the detention rooms, her lover appeared and succeeded in getting her away from the immigration officer.

The upshot of the affair was that Judge Burke ordered Blandina into the care of Miss Wood at the House of the Good Shepard for one week, pending action of the Probate Court on the custody of the girl.

BLANDINA PAULUS, AUGUST 9, 1921. Blandina Paulus arrived in the United States in 1921 from Ardashier, Persia. The family that was paid to bring her safely to her cousin David Jacobs in Yonkers preferred that she remain with them instead of her relatives. Upon meeting her family, Blandina, according to the newspaper report, refused to go with her cousin David. The *Boston Globe*'s version does not include the family legend that Blandina was drugged, dressed like a boy, and smuggled off the ship while the transport family members sat on her to kidnap her for their son. The incident inspired a court verdict to appoint her cousin David Jacobs as her guardian. At the time, Blandina was 12 years old. (Courtesy of the *Boston Globe*.)

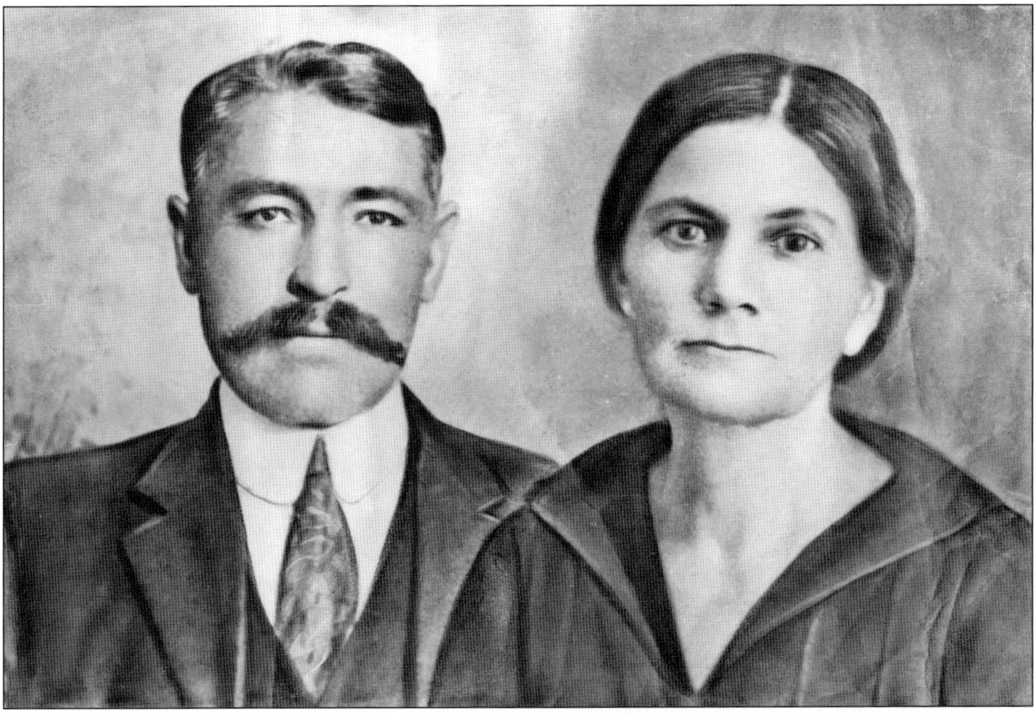

PAULUS. This charcoal sketch of Laya Solomon Paulus and her husband, Jacob Paulus, parents to Blandina and Nano, was made in Ardashier, Persia. (Courtesy of Shirley Benjamin.)

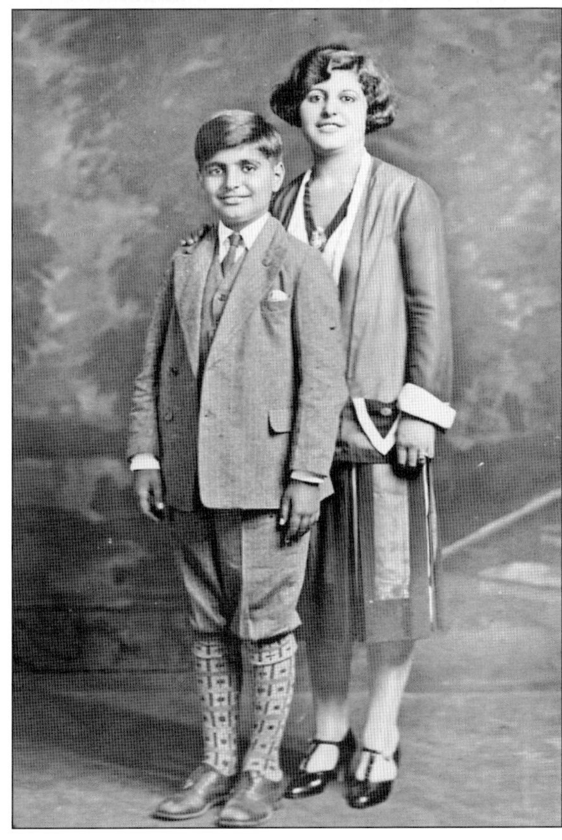

THE SARGIS FAMILY. Zenhela Sargis is pictured with brother John in Degala, Iran, during the 1920s. (Courtesy of Estelle Vitti.)

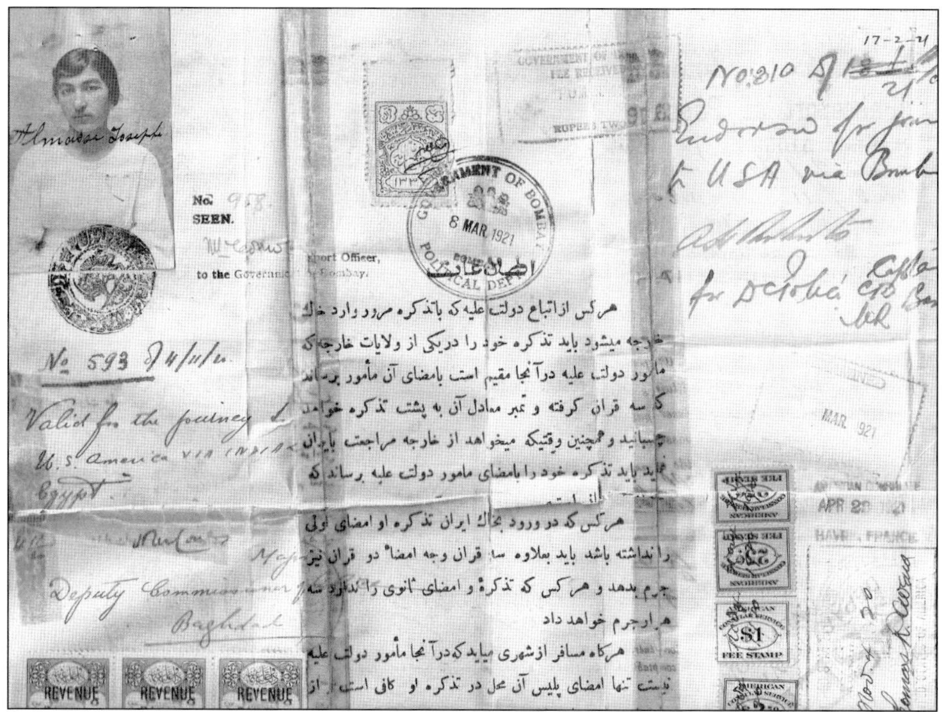

Almas Joseph's Passport. On the passport's first page (above), Almas Joseph's journey from Persia to Baghdad includes stamps from France and India. When she began her journey in 1920, she was just 12 years old. The second half of her passport (below) indicates her lengthy journey to the United States. (Both, courtesy of David Muldoon.)

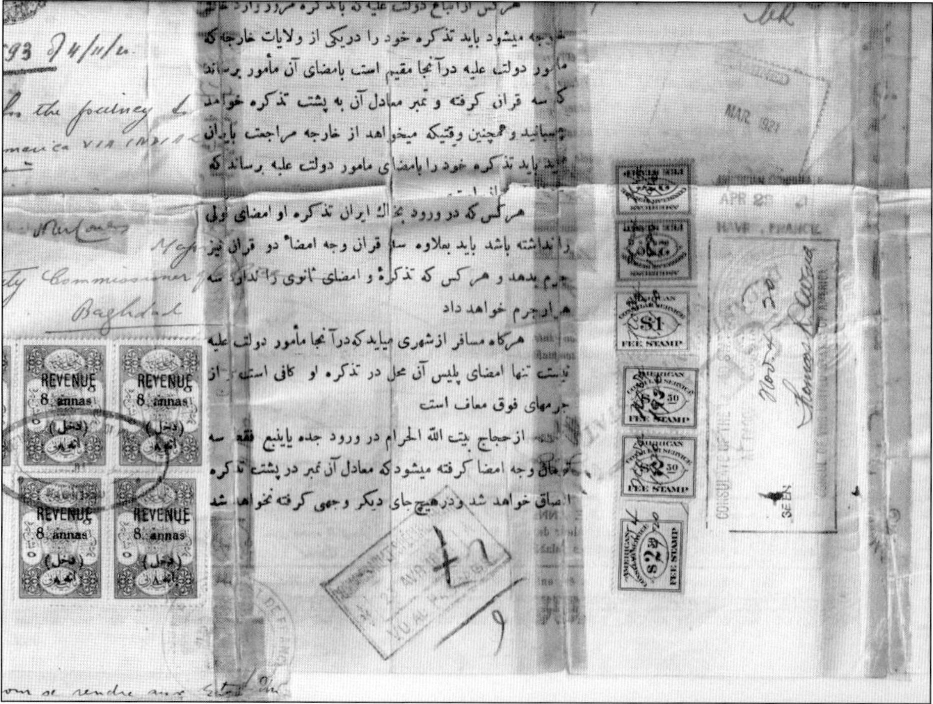

Jacob Eshmail. Pictured here is the father of Jonathan, Sam, and David Jacobs in Persia. He did not immigrate to the United States. The brothers derived their surname from their father 's first name. (Author's collection.)

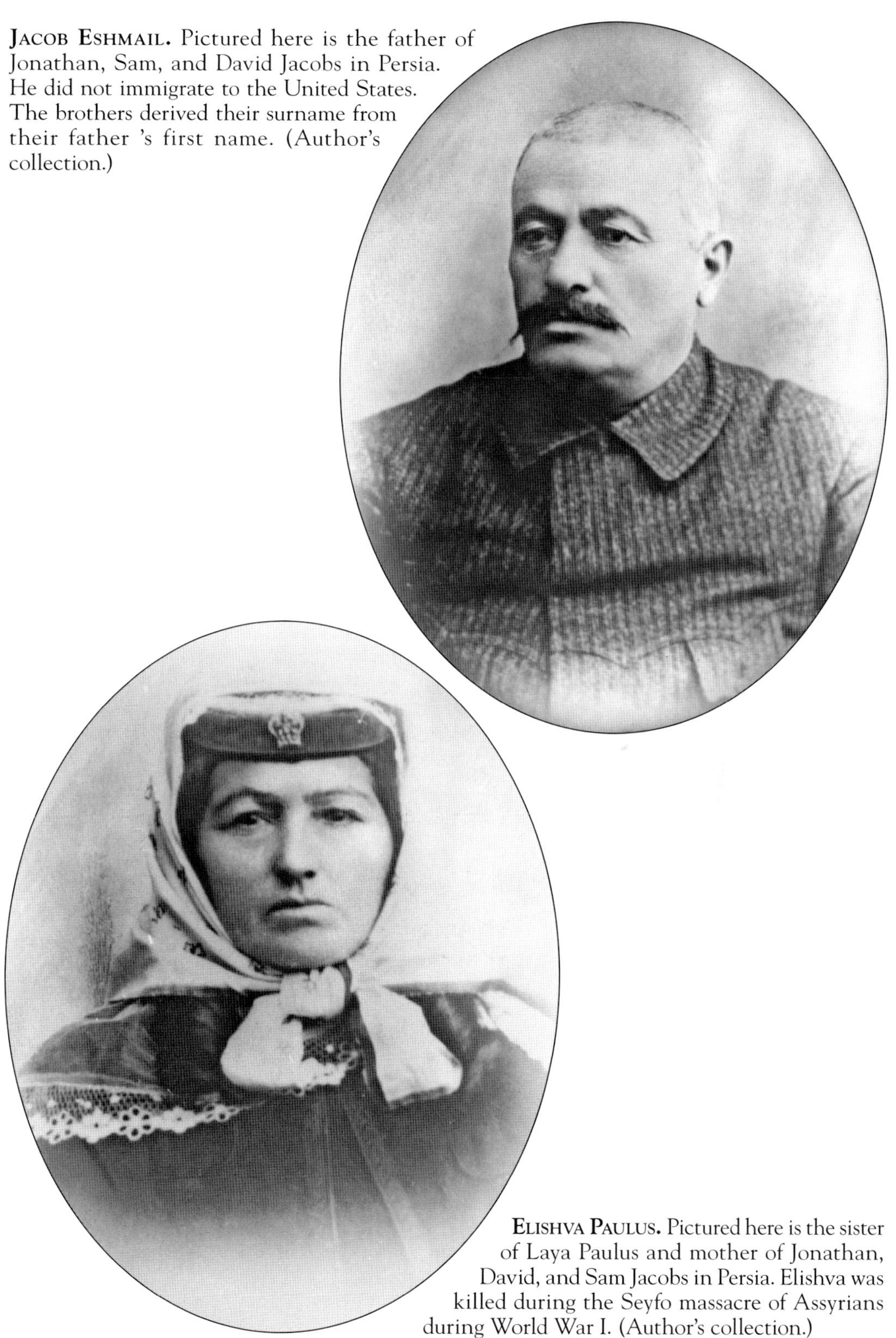

Elishva Paulus. Pictured here is the sister of Laya Paulus and mother of Jonathan, David, and Sam Jacobs in Persia. Elishva was killed during the Seyfo massacre of Assyrians during World War I. (Author's collection.)

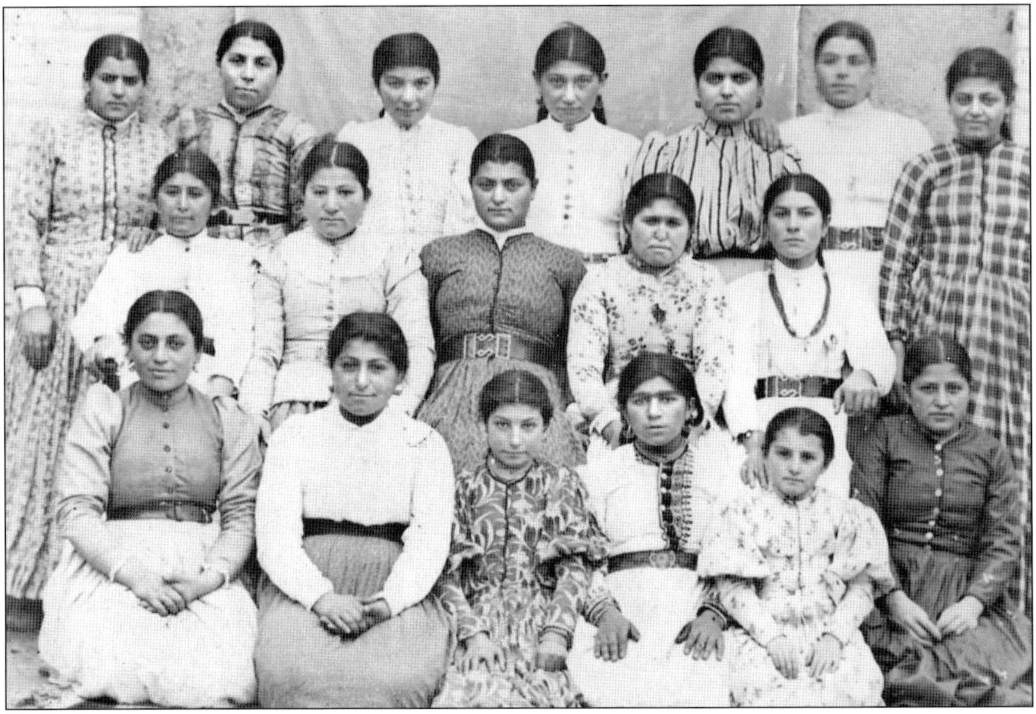

ASSYRIAN WOMEN, DEGALA, IRAN. Esther Sargis (third row, fifth from left) is pictured with her family. (Courtesy of Estelle Vitti.)

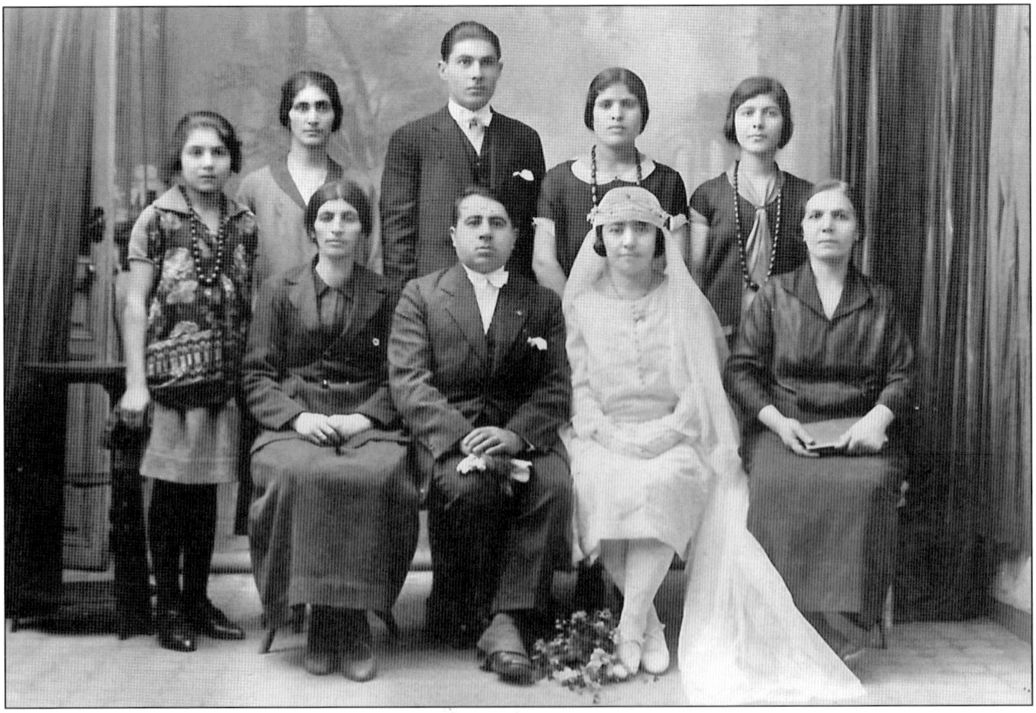

THE ODISHOOS. This photograph of Eshoo and Rosa Odishoo was taken at their wedding in Marseilles, France, in 1925. (Courtesy of David Odishoo.)

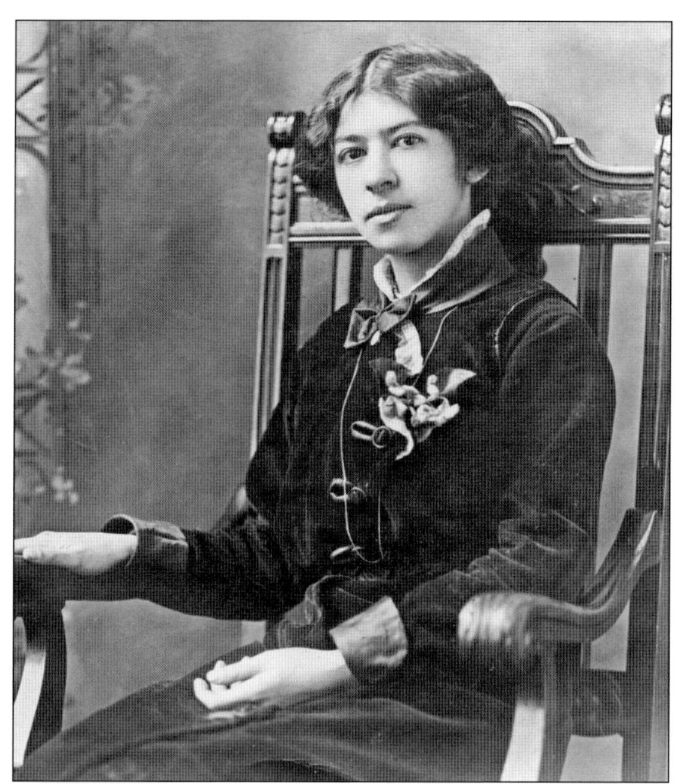

Cousin from Iran. Pictured in Urmia is an unidentified cousin of the Nicolai Benjamin family. (Author's collection.)

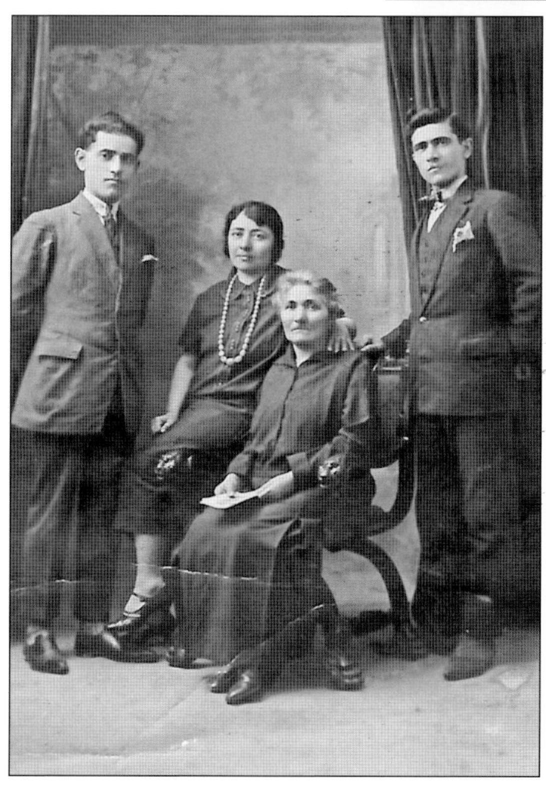

Rosa Malik Odishoo and Family. Rosa Malik Odishoo is pictured with her mother and brothers, Leon (left) and Joe, in Marseilles. (Courtesy of David Odishoo.)

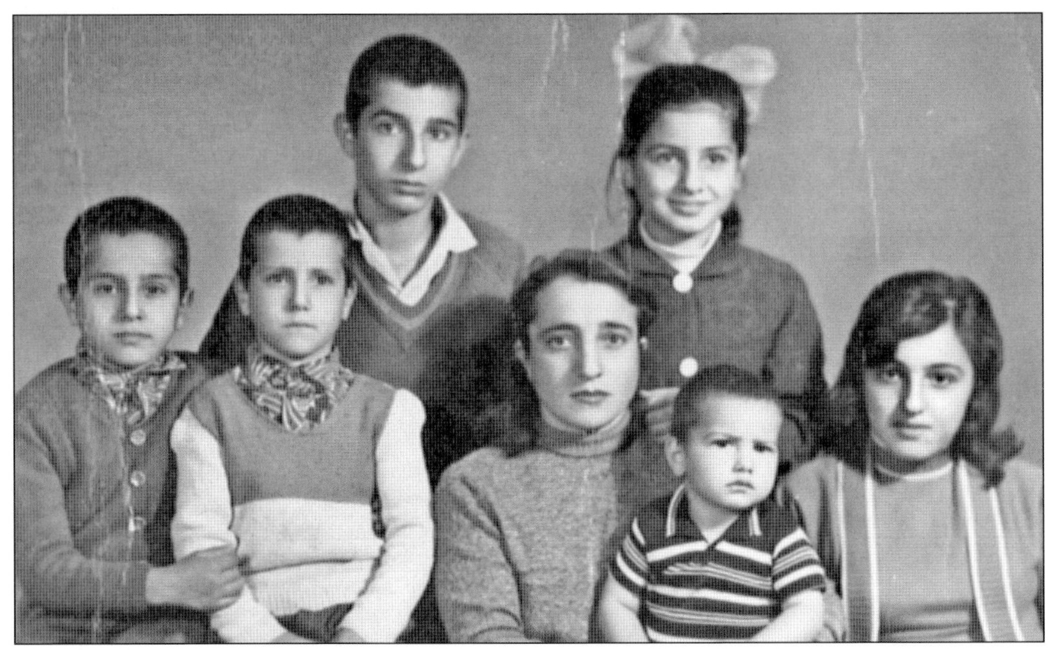

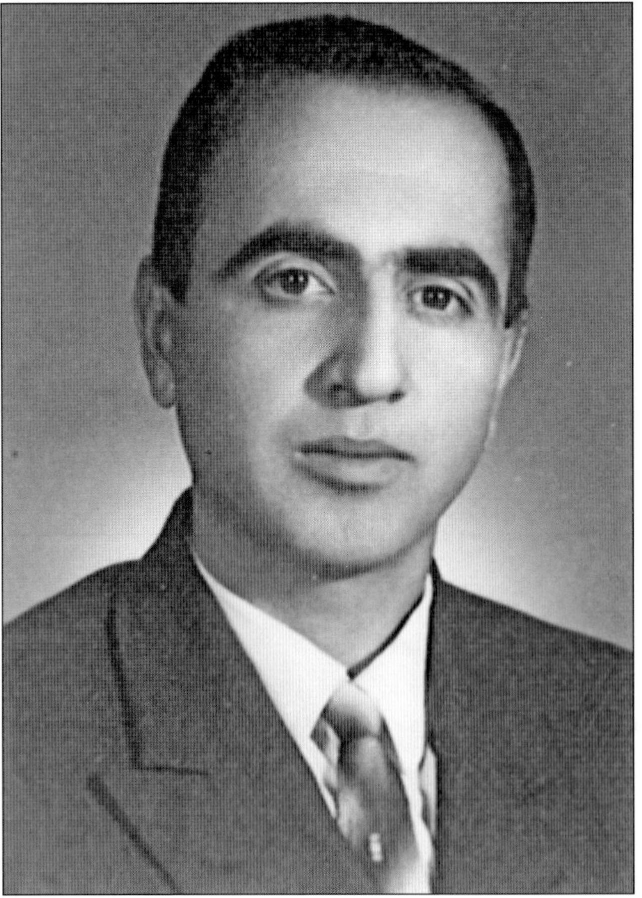

Nadia Gevargiz with Children. Leva Gevargiz and Nadia Melhampor were born in Russia during the 1930s. Prior to the Iron Curtain, their parents moved the family back to their homeland, Iran. Nadia's parents lived in Qazwin, the ancient capital city of Iran. Nadia and Leva married in the 1940s and lived in Tabriz, Iran, until they moved to Tehran in 1966. Nadia is pictured with their children in 1962 in Tabriz. From left to right are (first row): Victor, Albert, Nadia, Vania (on Nadia's lap), and eldest daughter, Mania; (second row) Issak and Najiba. The family migrated to Yonkers in 1969. They celebrated the Mar Gevargiz commemoration in Mar Mari Church. (Courtesy of Angela Gevargiz.)

Leva Gevargiz. Leva Gevargiz worked as a Russian and Farsi translator in 1949 while living in Tabriz, Iran. (Courtesy of Angela Gevargiz.)

Nadia Gevargiz. This 1940s picture shows Nadia Gevargiz as a teenager in Qaswin, Iran. (Courtesy of Angela Gevargiz.)

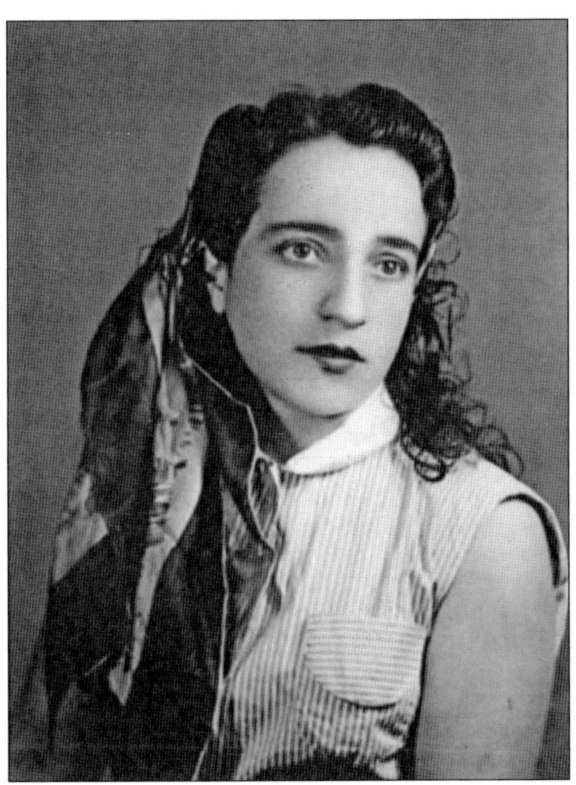

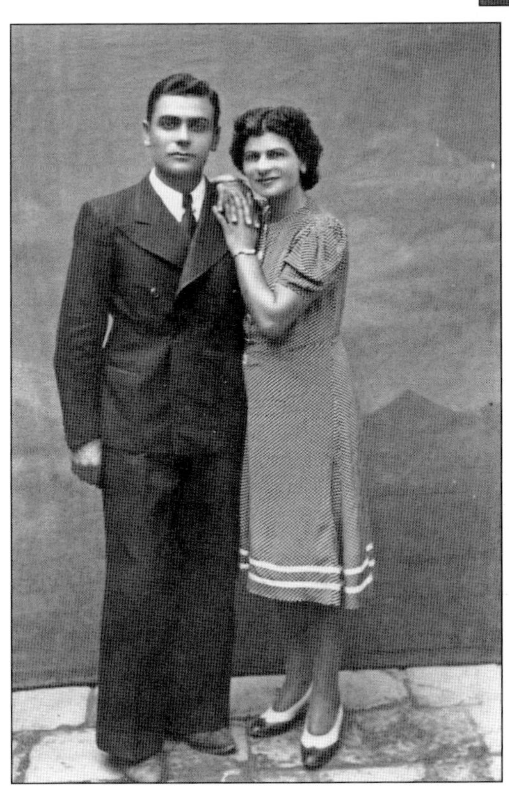

Simon Ameer and Maria Ameer. This picture was taken in Kermanshah, Iran, in 1941. (Susanne Ameer Monasa.)

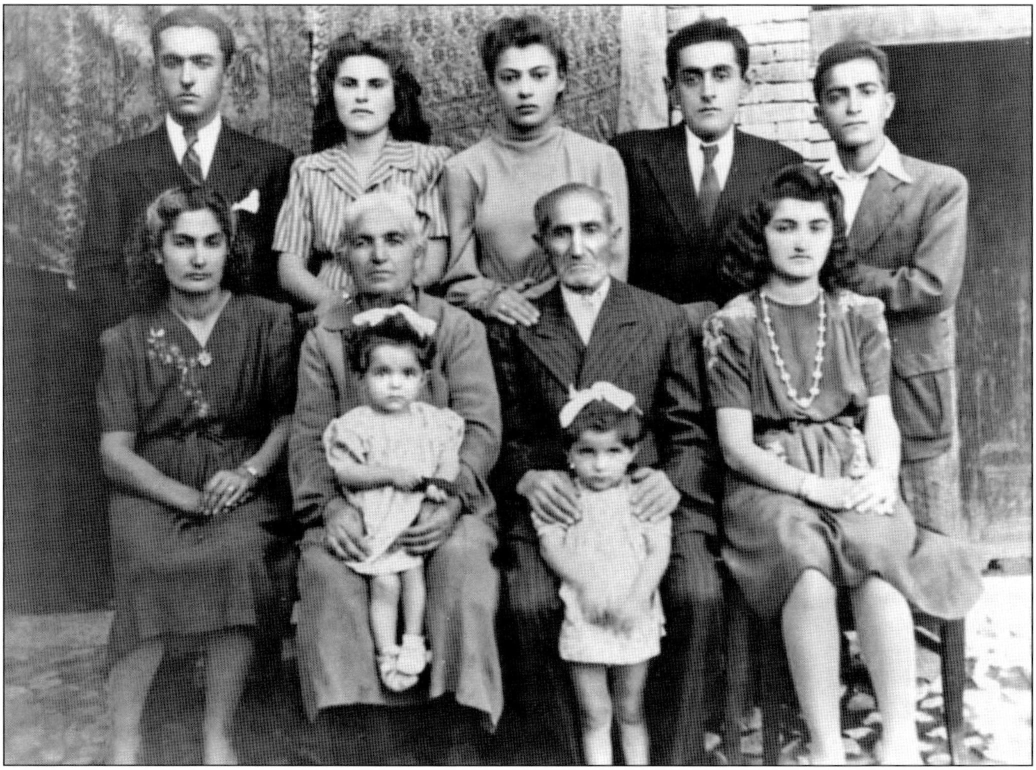

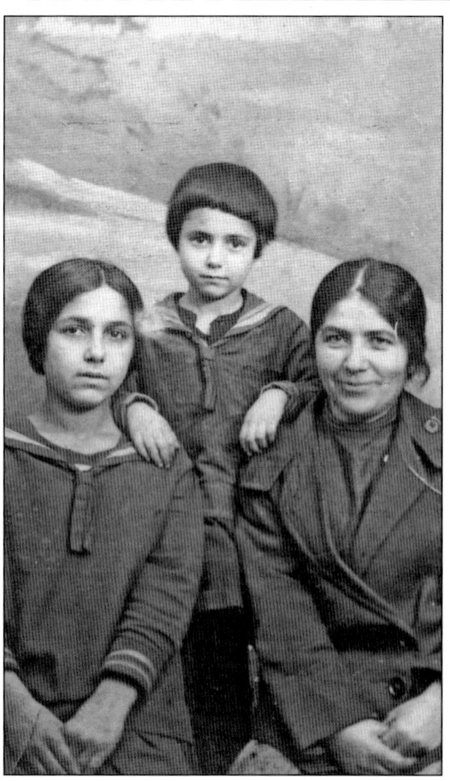

The Shmoovel and Dalia Badal Family. This picture was taken in 1947 in Hamadam, Iran. From left to right are (first row) Mariam Badal Baquse; her mother, Sabeh Badal; and father, Sarmas Badal; and Soria Badal Saraee with children Khava and Lilla Badal; (second row) Shmoovel Badal; his wife Dalila Badal; Lidia Badal and her husband Nickola Badal; and their nephew Ishalim Badal. Sabeh and Sarmas Badal fled from Iran to Russia; two of their younger children died in 1914 while seeking refuge from the Turks who plundered Assyrian villages near Lake Urmia. The Badals, from the village of Balulan, along with a large group of Assyrians from Urmia, fled to Russia. They later returned to Iran and settled in Hamadan with other Assyrians. Since the 1960s, the family has migrated, one at a time, to Yonkers and on to Los Angeles. Ishalim and his wife, Valya, took care of Sabeh (his grandmother) until September 1978. Sabeh passed away in 1979 in Tehran at the age of 100. She had been a well-known homeopathic doctor who healed many with a simple remedy like gum from a cider tree and egg yolk on a thick cotton cloth. (Courtesy of Angela Gevargiz.)

The Zaya Family. This picture of sisters Noosha (left) and Sonia (center) and their mother, whose name is unknown, was taken in Moscow in 1929. (Courtesy of Susy Gevarguize.)

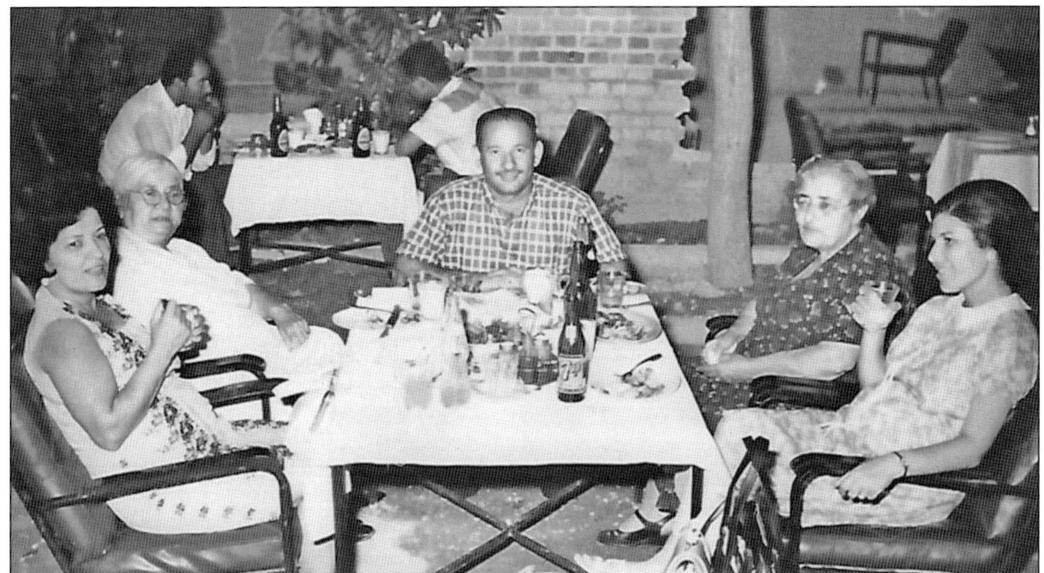

Visiting Iran for Mohammad Reza Shah Pahlavi's Coronation. Rosa Malik Odishoo (right) is pictured with her sister and sister's children. The family went to Iran in the 1960s for the coronation of the shah; Assyrians received special visas to go back to Iran for the event. (Courtesy of David Odishoo.)

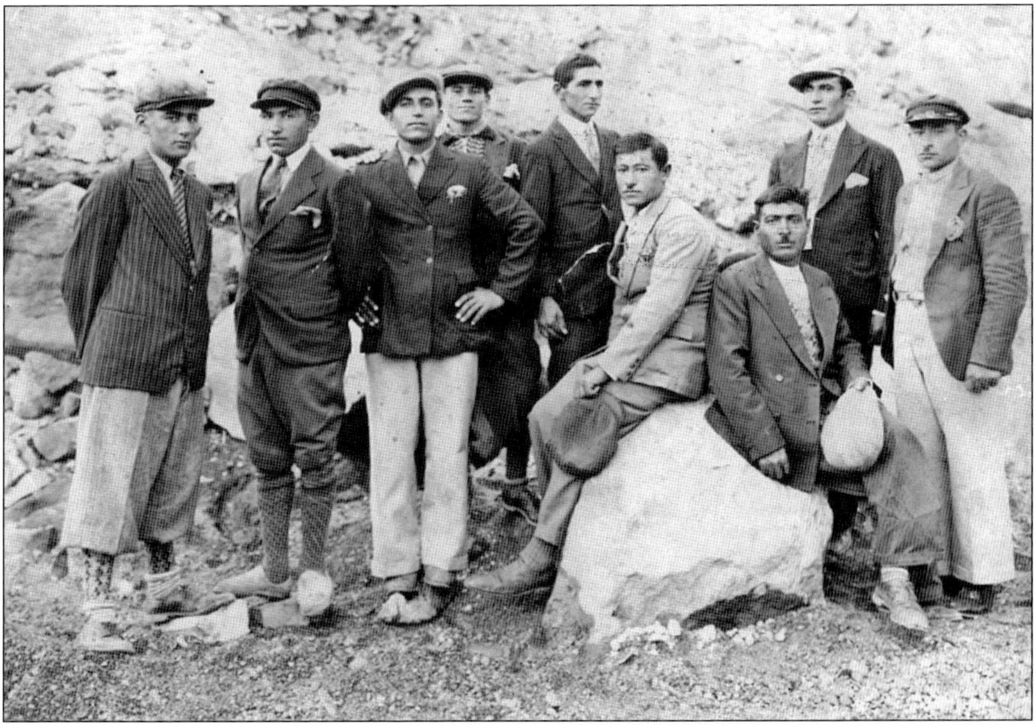

Working in Kuwait. On the left of the rock is Benjamin Gevargis, who worked in Kuwait as a carpenter in 1952. In hopes of earning money to send to their families, many men left Iran to work abroad. On the far right is Benjamin's brother, Elijah, three years younger than him. (Courtesy of Juliet Gevargis-Mizimakoski.)

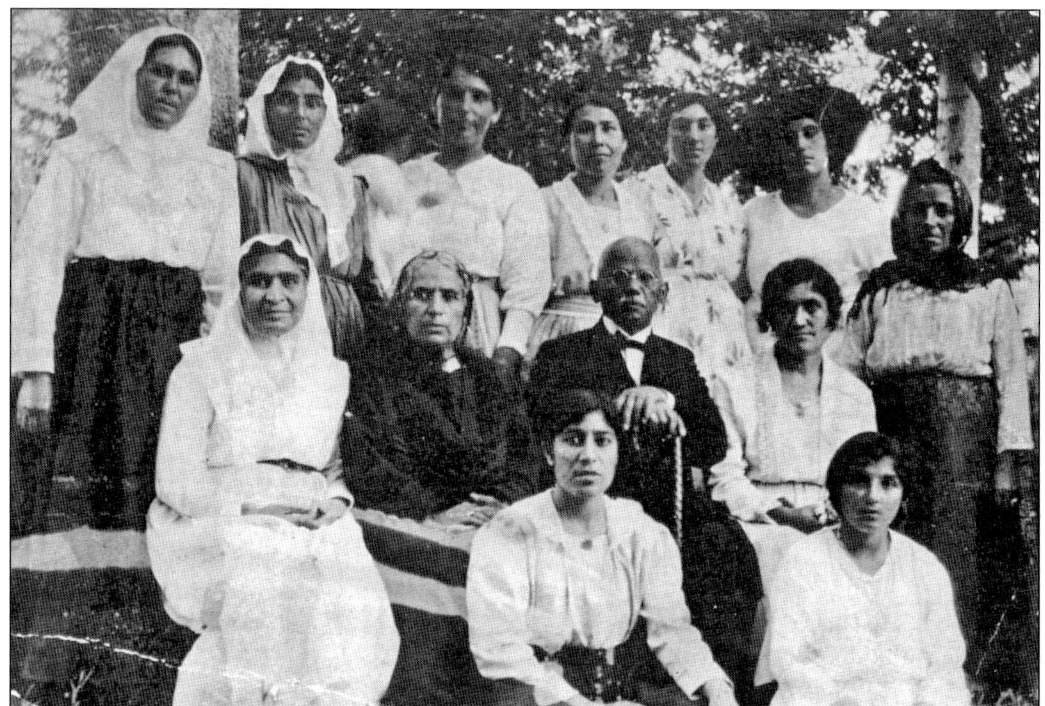

The Ameer Family. From left to right are (first row) Simon Ameer (late husband of Susanne Ameer Monasa) and Maria Ameer; (second row) Shalem Ameer, Usta Envia Ameer, and Ludia Ameer; (third row) Esther Ameer Ross, Samuel Ameer, Sadie Ameer, and Julia Ameer. The family immigrated to the United States in 1960 from Iran. (Susanne Ameer Monasa.)

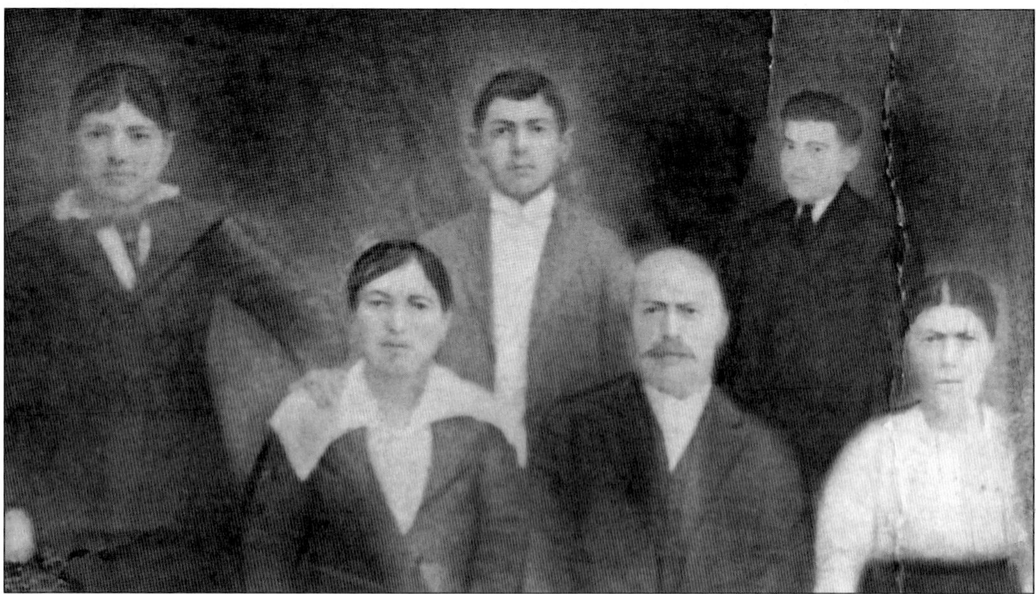

The Envia Ameer Family. From left to right are (first row) Shalem Ameer, Usta Envia, and Ludia Ameer; (second row) Esther Ameer, Samuel Ameer, and Luther Ameer. Luther moved to Turlock, California, and Samuel to Chicago and then later to California. Everyone in the Ameer family initially immigrated to the United States and resided in Yonkers. (Susanne Ameer Monasa.)

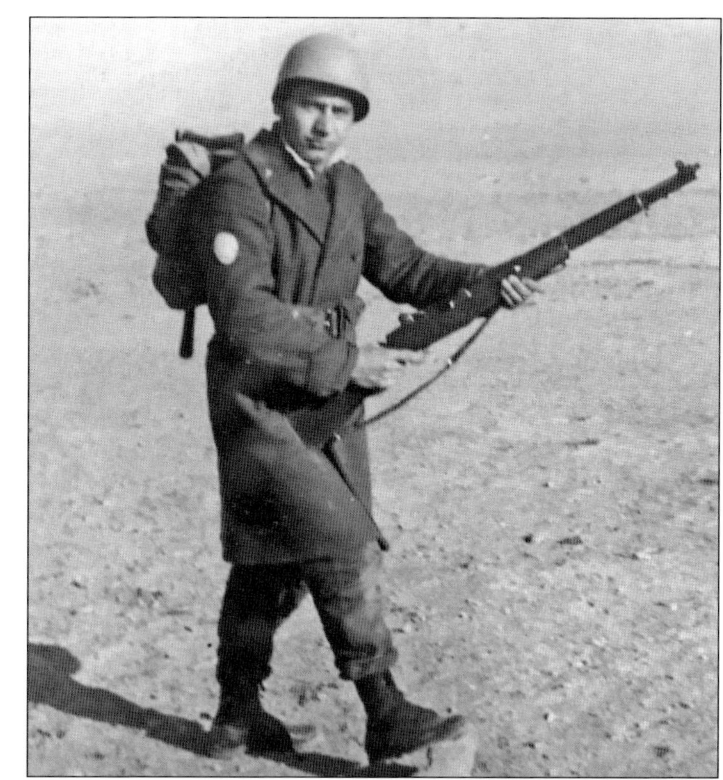

Yosib (Joseph) Gevargis. Joseph is pictured while in the army in Urmia in 1961. (Courtesy of Juliet Gevargis-Mizimakoski.)

The Jerjis Sisters. This photograph was taken at a church in Mar Givargis in the villages of Gorapah-Sheinabad, in the city of Urmi, in 1964. From left to right are (seated) Shushan and Sarah; (standing) Beatrice Gevargis and Shamiran. (Courtesy of Jacquie BabayiKunka.)

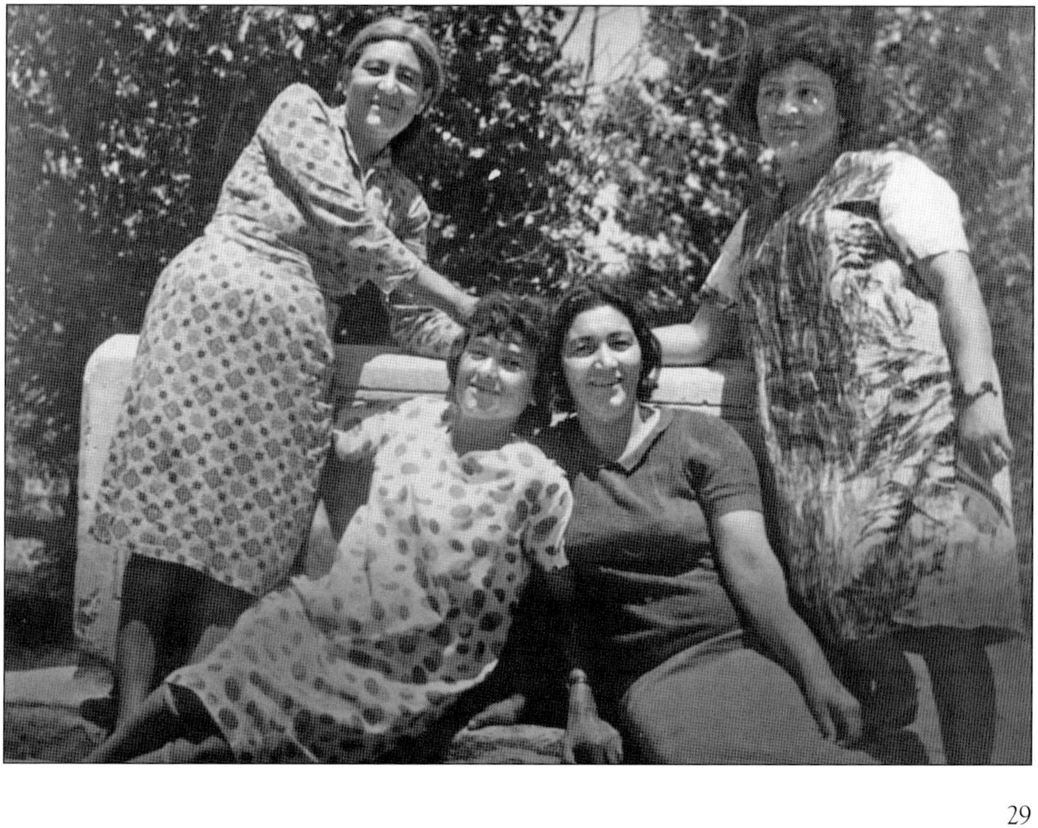

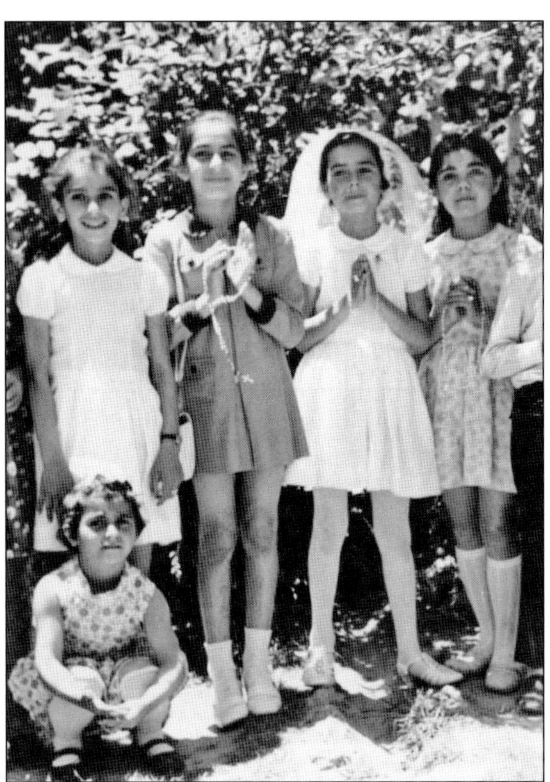

Jo Babayi's First Communion, 1968. At the Urmi Assyrian Catholic Church, Jo Babayi (second from right) is pictured with her sisters (standing from left to right) Jacquie, Claudette, and Jarmen. Cousin Betty Mirza is in the front of the girls. (Courtesy of Jacquie BabayiKunka.)

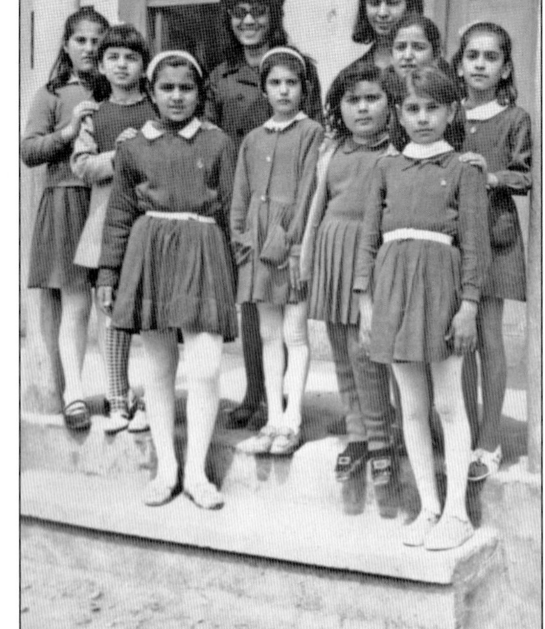

Fifth Grade. This is a 1966–1967 photograph of the Pishdad Assyrian School in Urmi with Jacquie Babayi, second row, far right, and her classmates. (Courtesy of Jacquie BabayiKunka.)

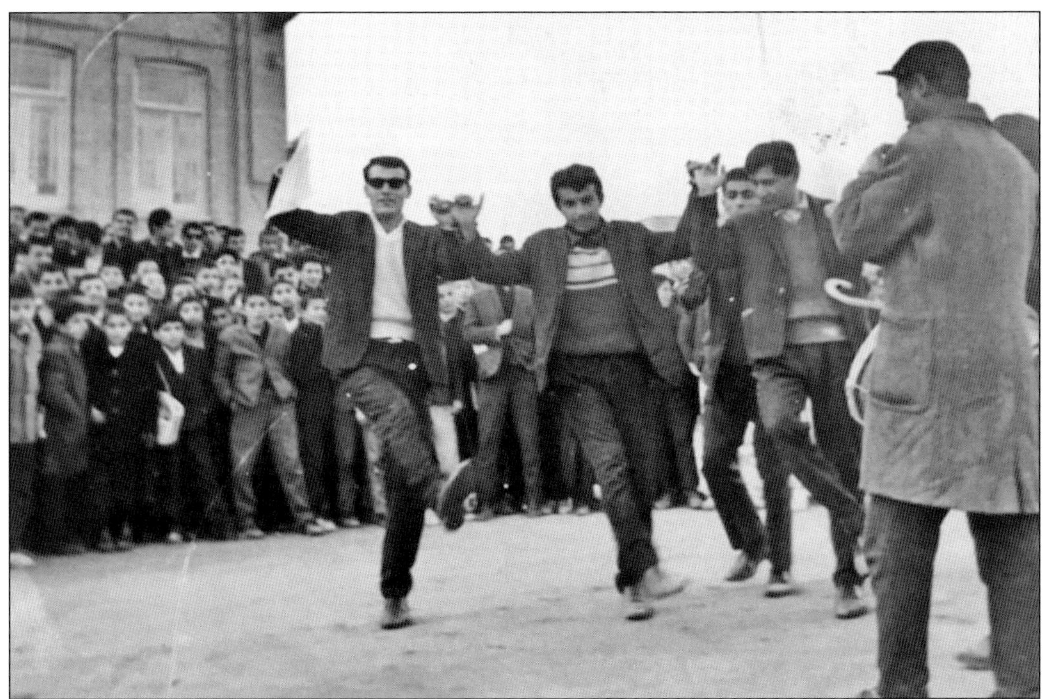

CELEBRATION AT THE FERDOWSI SCHOOL. This magnet high school, named after the Iranian poet and author of *Shahnameh*, was for students in Urmi with a passion and aptitude in mathematics. Pictured dancing in 1966 are, from left to right, Gurgen (an Armenian friend), unidentified, and Yosib Gevargis. Behind Yosib is Yonan Gevargis. (Courtesy of Juliet Gevargis-Mizimakoski.)

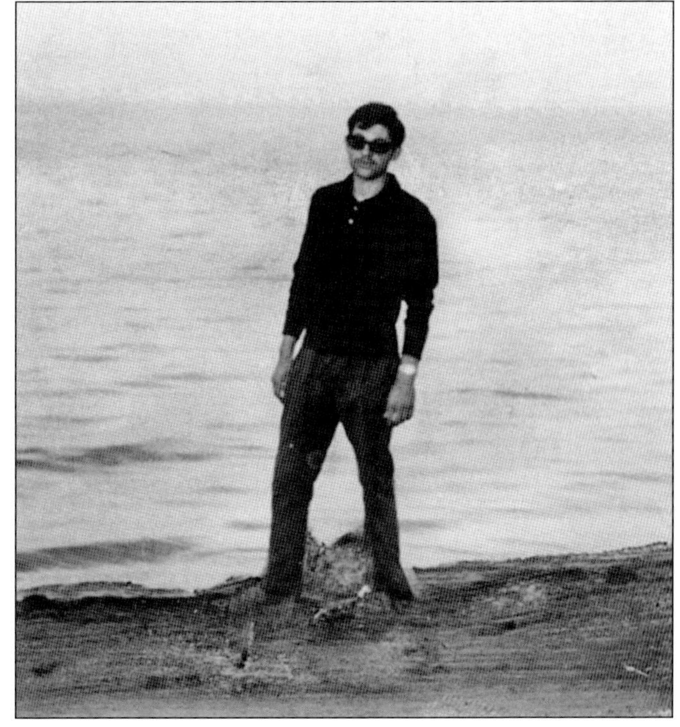

LAKE URMIA, 1968. Julian Gevargis is pictured on the shores of Lake Urmia, which was once the second largest saltwater lake in the world. The lake began to dry out because of human activity like dam building and over-usage of feeder rivers. During the early 20th century, residents in surrounding areas could scoop salt off the river waters. The deep-green river turned red from algae and then eventually dried out. Recent efforts to restore the lake have begun to produce results. The United Nations Development Program has effectively implemented water management. (Courtesy of Juliet Gevargis.)

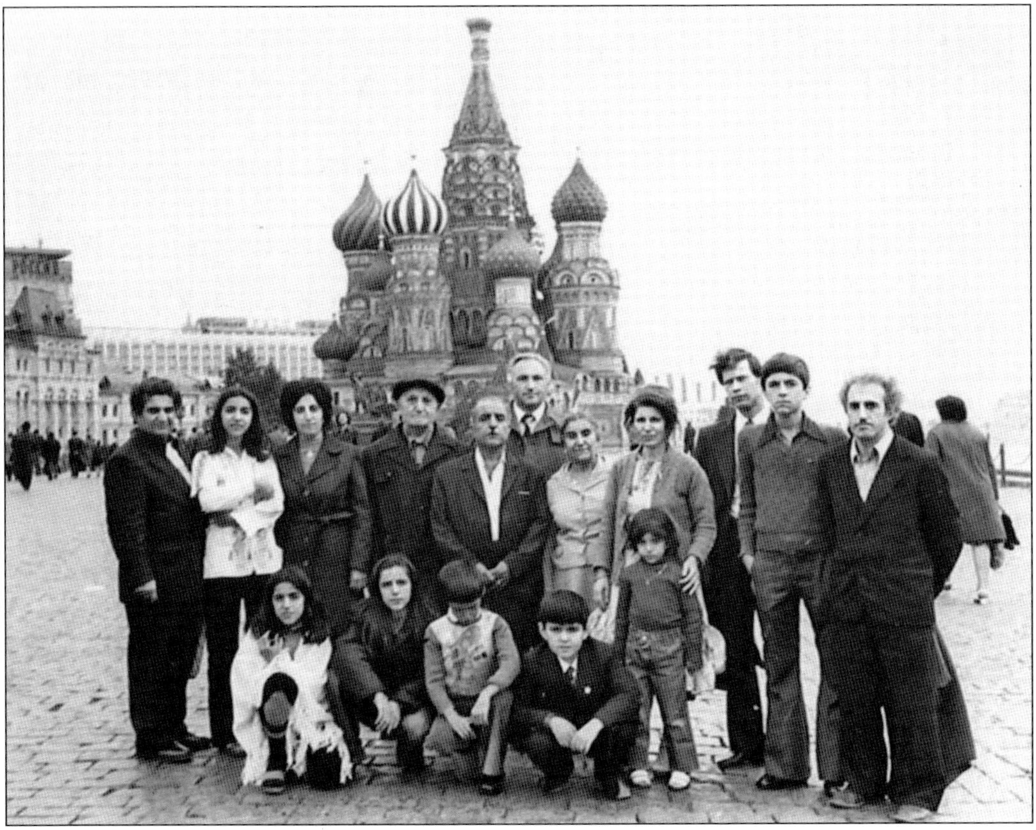

THE GEVARGIZ FAMILY. Nadia and Leva Gevargiz were born in Russia in the 1930s. Their parents had to return to Iran right before the Iron Curtain was drawn. Nadia's parents and siblings lived in Qazwin, the ancient capital of Iran, around the 1940s. (Courtesy of Angela Gevargiz.)

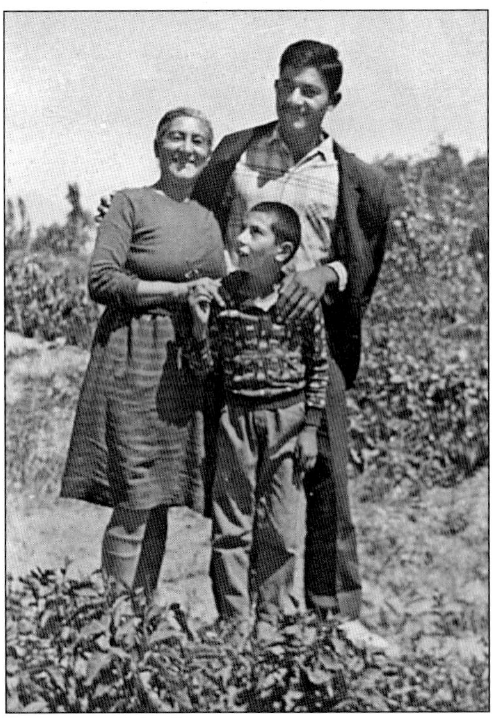

GRAPE FARM. Pictured here are Beatrice Gevargis with her younger son, John, and older son, Julian, on their grape farm in Geogtapa, Urmia, in 1970. (Courtesy of Juliet Gevargis.)

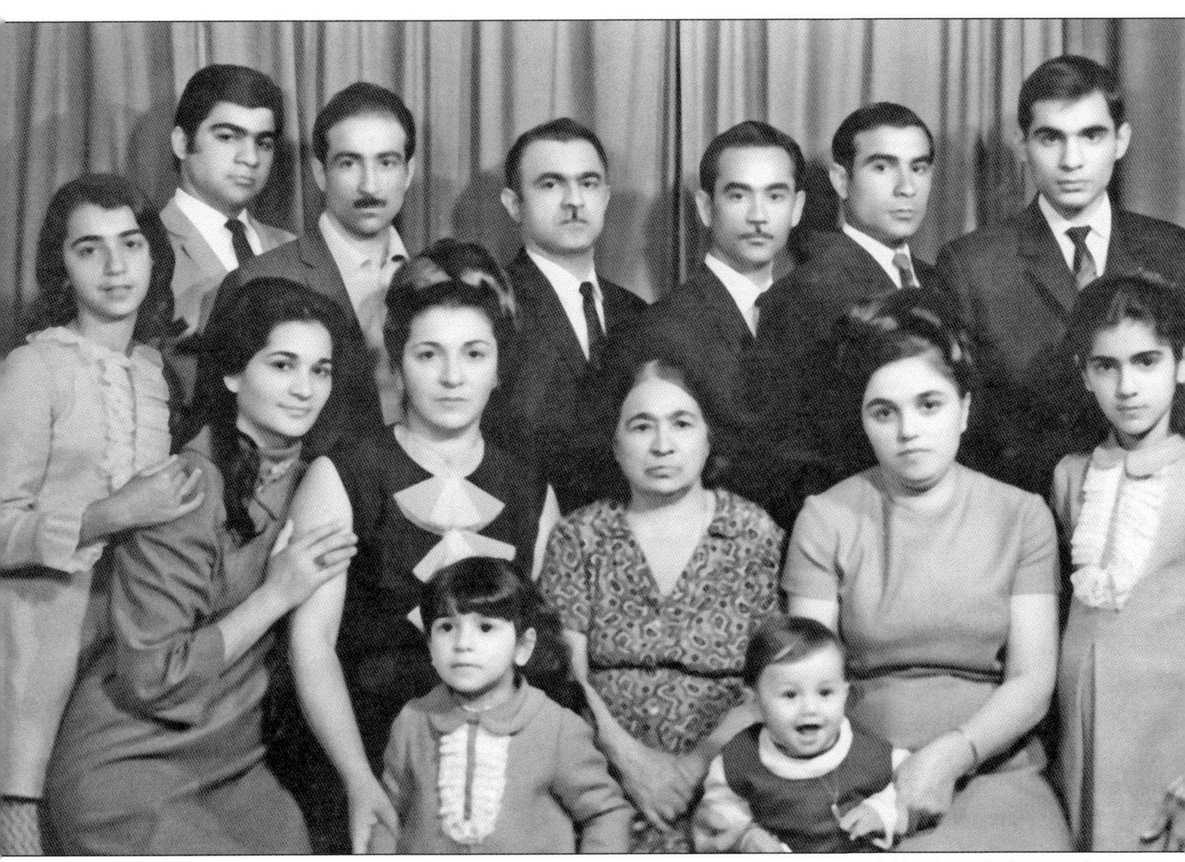

Ishoo-Mirza-Gevary Family. This photograph was taken in Tehran in 1969. From left to right are (first row) children Linda Eshoe and Susy Gevarguize; (second row) Nellie Tatevossian, Raya Yaldaloo, Luba Eshoe, Luba Eshoo Mirza Gevary, Svetlana Gevarguize, and Lili Eshoe Yoohana; (third row) David Gavary, Odishoo Mirzazadeh, Misha Eshoe, Sorishoo Gevarguize, Yohana Eshoe, and Daniel Ishoo. The family adopted different last names for various reasons. (Courtesy of Susy Gevarguize.)

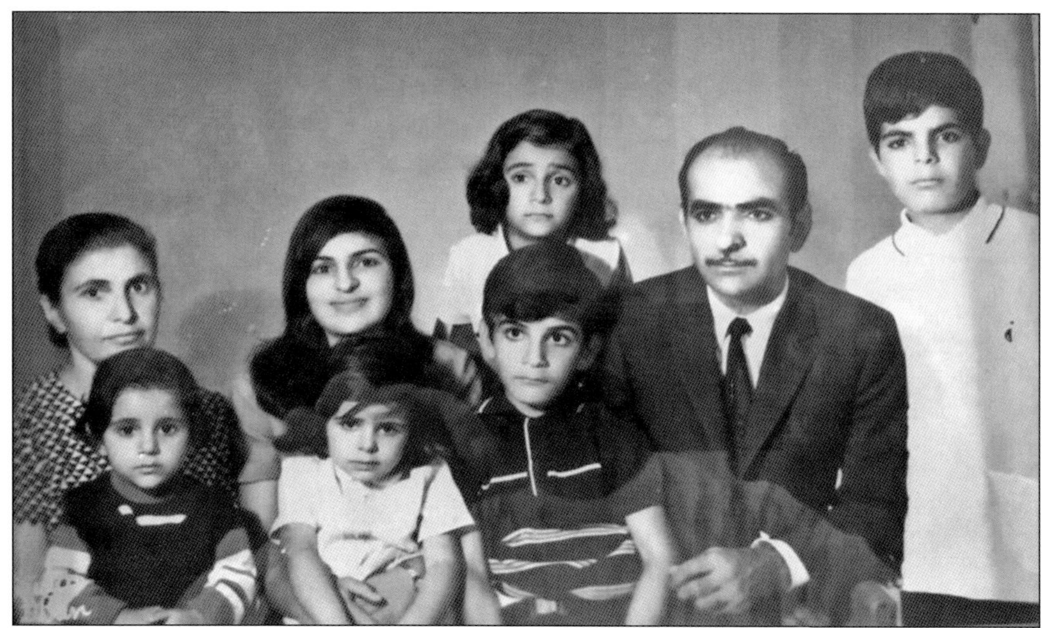

The Shlimoun Family. Pictured here are Youkhanna and Yulia Shlimoun with their children. From left to right in the first row are Olga, Sharon, and Koper. Next to Yulia are Rosa, Mimi, and Sam. This picture was taken just before they immigrated to the United States from Lebanon. (Courtesy of Olga Shlimoun Ferreira.)

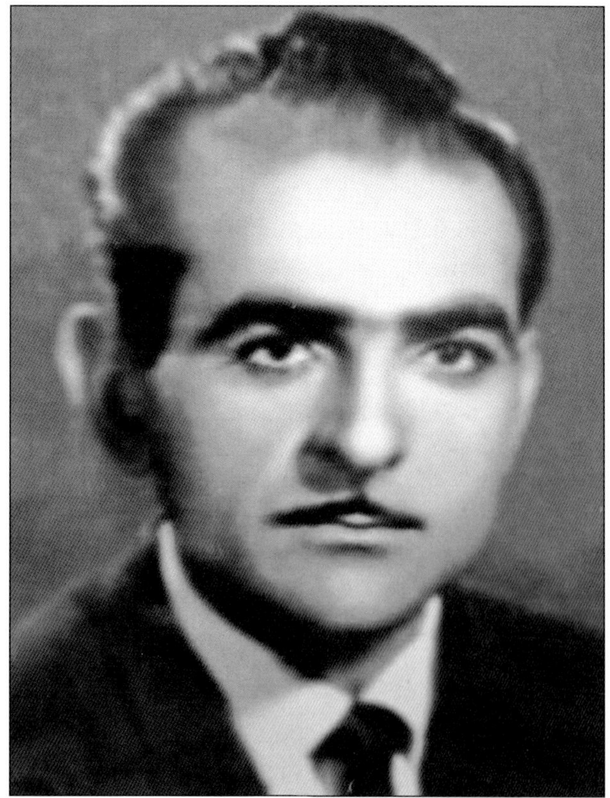

Youkhanna Shlimoun. This photograph was taken in Lebanon in 1972, before the Shlimoun family began its migration to Yonkers. (Courtesy of Olga Shlimoun Ferreira.)

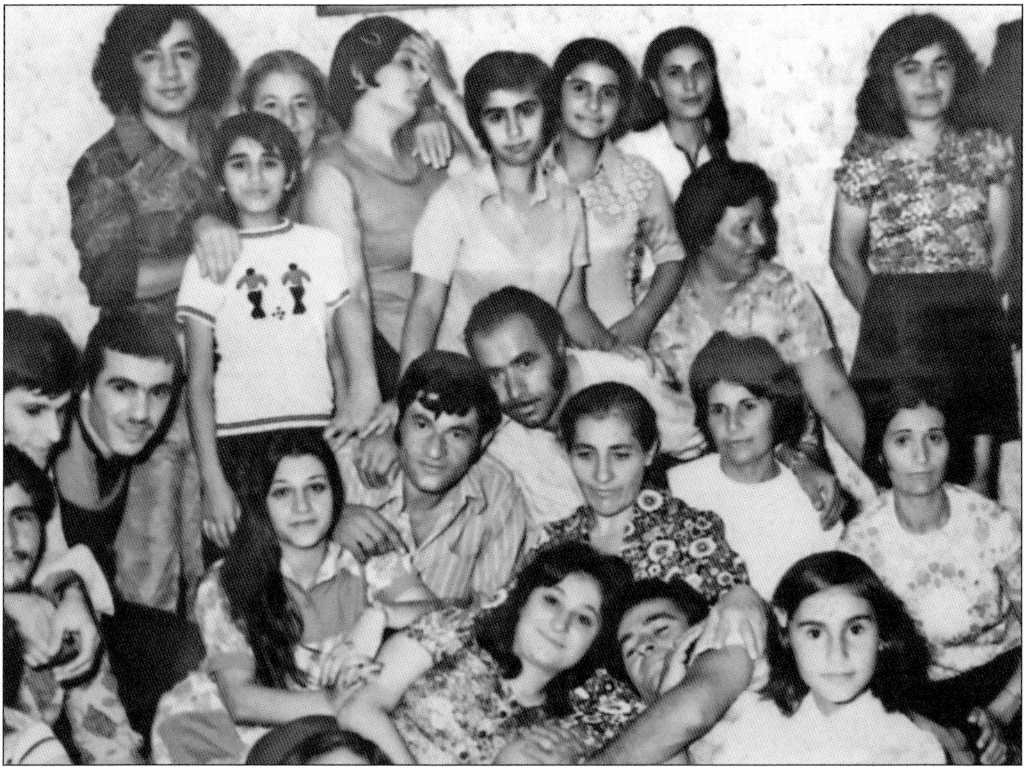

Going Away Party for Julian Gevargis, 1972. This photograph was taken at Sara Shabdin's house in Urmia (she is seated at right, looking off to the side). Sara's son Julian (center, in striped shirt), pictured next to his cousin George Gevargis, was leaving for the United States. Hano Digaleh is sitting in front of Julian with his cousin's husband, Yohanna (Ukana) Ivan. At far left, (from left to right) the man whose face is cropped is Sara's son, Isaac Shabdin, and family friends Fraydun Agassi and Sargon ?. (Courtesy of Juliet Gevargis-Mizimakoski.)

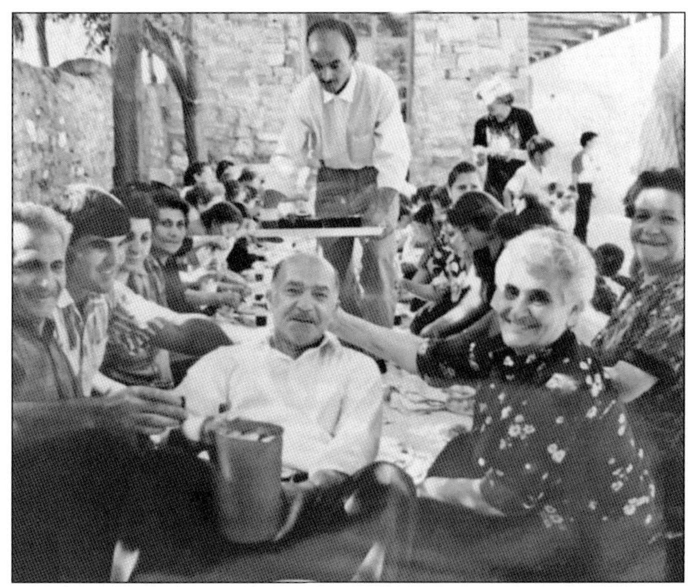

Dookhrana in Mar Sargis. On the outskirts of the city of Urmi in 1984, the Babaie family and friends celebrate Remembrance Day of Assyrian Saints and their respective churches. The man sitting at the front holding the pitcher is Dariavoosh Babaie; Bulbul Babaie is to the right. The woman behind her is Lido Younan, the sister of Dariavoosh. The man on the left of Dariavoosh is Bulbul's brother Armin. The rest are family and friends. (Courtesy of Jacquie BabayiKunka.)

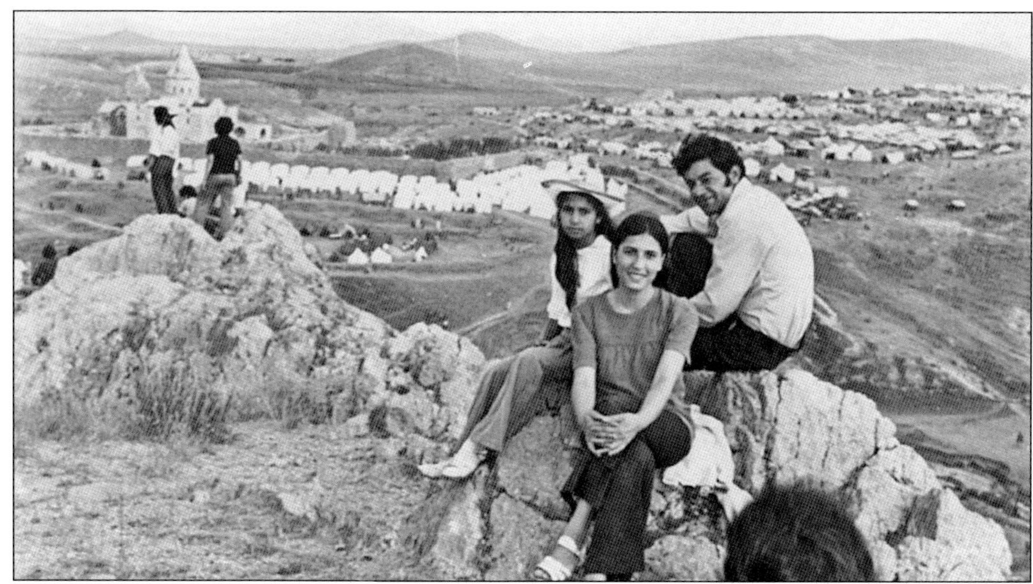

Cousins. Mimi (in foreground) and her younger sister Caroline Shabdin are pictured with their cousin Julian Gevargis in Urmi in 1970. (Courtesy of Juliet Gevargis-Mizimakoski.)

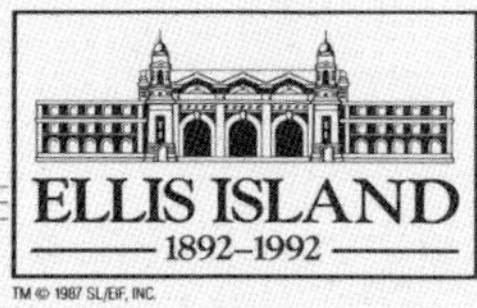

TM © 1987 SL/EIF, INC

The Statue of Liberty-Ellis Island Foundation, Inc.

proudly presents this

Official Certificate of Registration

in

THE AMERICAN IMMIGRANT WALL OF HONOR

to officially certify that

Yonan Kambar

came to the United States of America from

Gulpashon, Persia

joining those courageous men and women who came to this country in search of personal freedom, economic opportunity and a future of hope for their families.

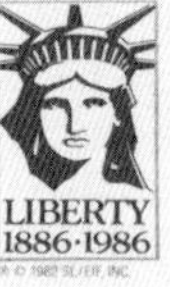

Lee A. Iacocca
The Statue of Liberty-Ellis Island Foundation, Inc.

Yonan Kambar's American Immigrant Certificate. The Statue of Liberty–Ellis Island Foundation issued this certificate celebrating the immigration of Yonan Kambar from Gulpashon, Persia, to the United States through Liberty Island. Yonan's name appears on the Wall of Honor at Ellis Island, the only national monument that acknowledges family heritage and the status of the United States as a nation of immigrants. (Author's collection.)

Three

Settling in Yonkers, New York

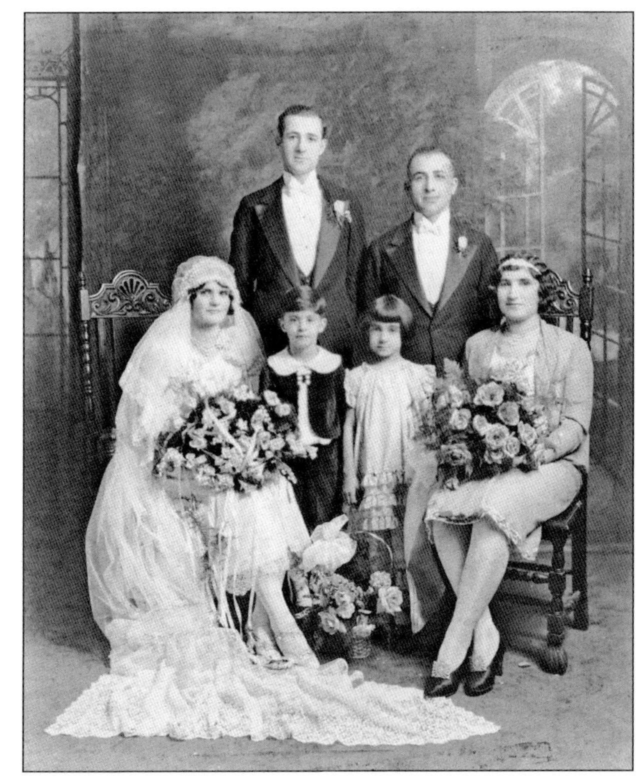

The Marriage of Blandina Paulus (Jacobs) and Nicholas Benjamin, January 28, 1928. From left to right are bride Blandina, who was known as Blandina Jacobs after she came to live with her cousin Dave Jacobs in Yonkers; Sam Jacobs; Betty Jacobs; Nanajan Yohannan; and Elisha Yohannan. The wedding took place at Fernbrook Hall on Lawrence Street in Yonkers. Even though the wedding took place during a snowstorm, the guests celebrated the nuptials for two days. (Courtesy of Shirley Benjamin.)

STATE OF NEW YORK

Affidavit for License to Marry

STATE OF NEW YORK
County of Westchester
City of Yonkers

Benjamin I David and Batishva David

applicants for a license for marriage, being severally sworn, depose and say, that to the best of their knowledge and belief the following statement respectively signed by them is true, and that no legal impediment exists as to the right of the applicants to enter into the marriage state.

FROM THE GROOM:		FROM THE BRIDE:	
Full name	Benjamin I David	Full name	Batishva David
Color	White	Color	White
Place of residence	43 Jefferson St Yonkers	Place of residence	44 Riverdale Av Yonkers NY
Age	25 yrs	Age	18 yrs
Occupation	Tailor	Occupation	Hat finder
Place of birth	Persia	Place of birth	Persia
Name of father	Isaac	Name of father	Joseph David
Country of birth	Persia	Country of birth	Persia
Maiden name of mother	Hannah Jacob	Maiden name of mother	May Baba
Country of birth	Persia	Country of birth	Persia
Number of marriage	first	Number of marriage	first
Former wife or wives living or dead	—	Former husband or husbands living or dead	none
Is applicant a divorced person	—	Is applicant a divorced person	—
If so, when and where divorce or divorces were granted		If so, when and where divorce or divorces were granted	

Benjamin I. David, GROOM — Batishva David, BRIDE

Subscribed and sworn to before me this 30. day of November 1910

Joseph F. O'Brien, Clerk

BENJAMIN ISAAC DAVID AND BATISHVA DAVID'S WEDDING LICENSE. Benjamin Isaac David (son of Isaac Benjamin and Hannah Jacob) and Batishva David (daughter of Joseph David and May Baba) filed with New York State to wed in Yonkers on November 30, 1910. Both resided at 44 Riverdale Avenue in Yonkers. They married on December 3, three weeks after Benjamin's arrival in the United States. (Courtesy of Joe David.)

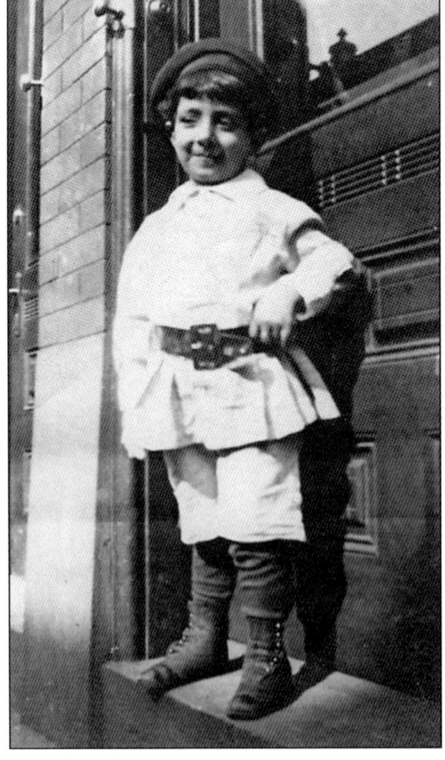

CLARENCE JACOBS. This picture was taken on May 8, 1918. Clarence was the son of Louise Benjamin Jacobs and Sam Eshmail Jacobs, from Urmia and Tiflis, Russia, respectively. Sam's father, Jacob Eshmail, had relocated the family from Persia to Russia while he worked on railroad construction. Clarence's father was the brother of David Eshmail Jacobs. In Bronxville, Clarence owned a liquor store called Lydon's Liquor Store. His father owned the Washington Café in Yonkers. (Author's collection.)

Avemelk Moorad, World War I. Abe Moorad, born in Gulpashan in Urmia, served in World War I at the age of 20. He received an honorable discharge on June 28, 1919, suffering from "shell shock." Upon his return to the United States, he was hospitalized in New York and eventually transferred to Hines Hospital in Chicago, where he later died on March 4, 1939. He was survived by his mother, Bathsheba, and father, Yonon, and his siblings Emma, John, and Jennie. (Courtesy of Michele Yohanna.)

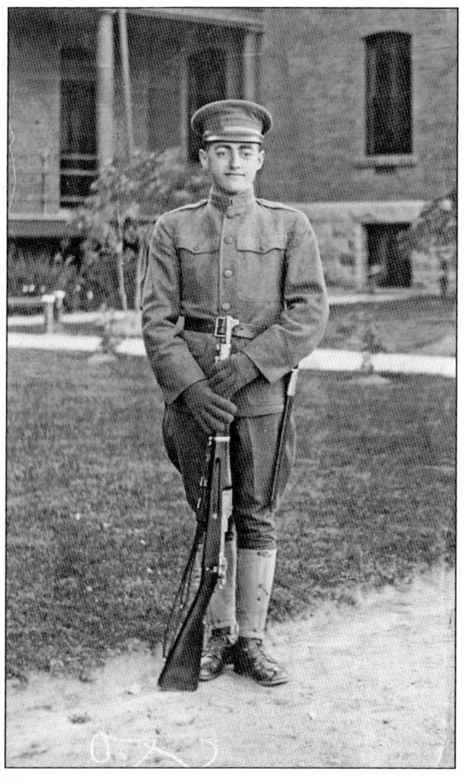

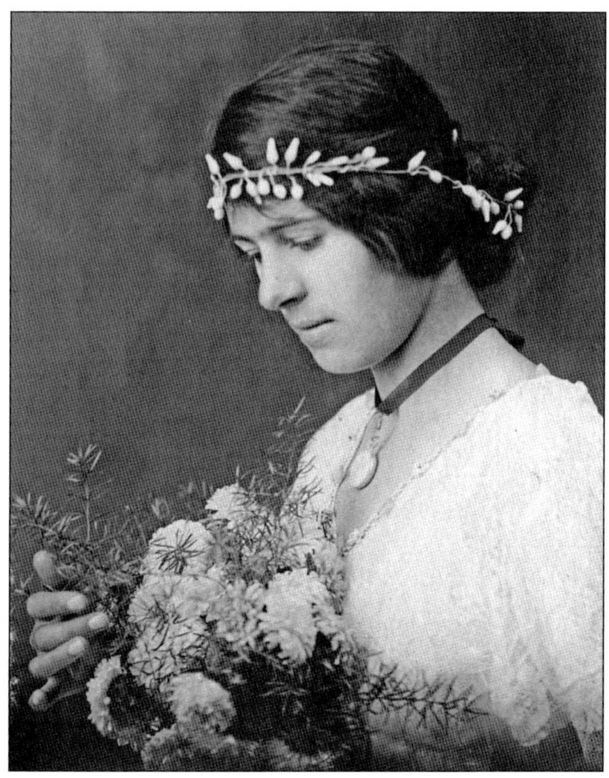

Emma Benjamin Jacobs. This photograph may be of Emma's wedding day on October 3, 1913. (Author's collection.)

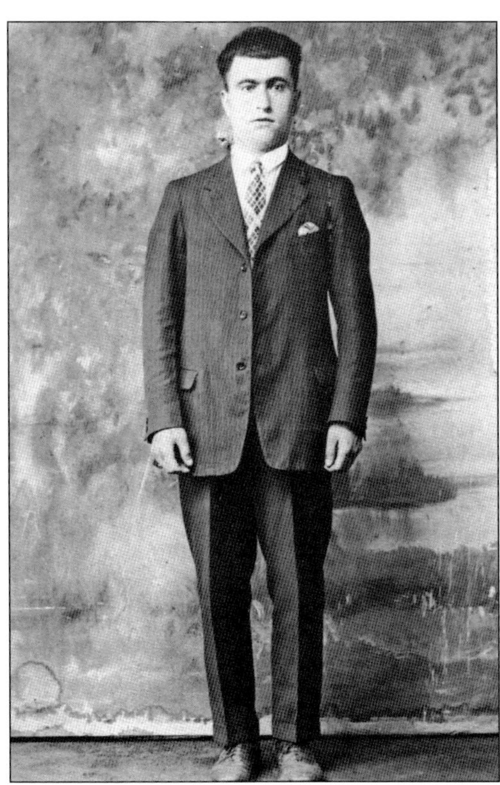

PAULUS AZIZ. This picture of Paulus Aziz was taken in a studio in Yonkers in 1925. (Courtesy of Alice Aziz David.)

In the Name of the Father, and of the Son, and of the Holy Ghost. Amen.
This is to certify that, on Saturday,
the Twenty eighth day of January, in the year of Our Lord One Thousand Nine hundred and Twenty eight, in St. John's Church, Yonkers, N.Y. Diocese of New York, I joined together in
Holy Matrimony
Nicholas Benjamin
and Blandina Jacobs
according to the form prescribed by the Book of Common Prayer, and in conformity with the Laws of the State of New York in the United States of America.
In witness whereof I have hereunto affixed my signature this Twenty eighth day of January One Thousand Nine Hundred and Twenty eight
Witnesses:
Elisha Yohannan
Nanajan Yohannan
Isaac Yohannan

GEORGE W. JACOBS AND CO. PHILADELPHIA.

WEDDING CERTIFICATE, JANUARY 28, 1928. Blandina Paulus Jacobs wed Nicholas Benjamin at St. John's Episcopal Church on Getty Square in Yonkers. In spite of a massive snowstorm, the two-day wedding reception was held at Fernbrook Hall at 26 Lawrence Street. Assyrian food was served. (Author's collection.)

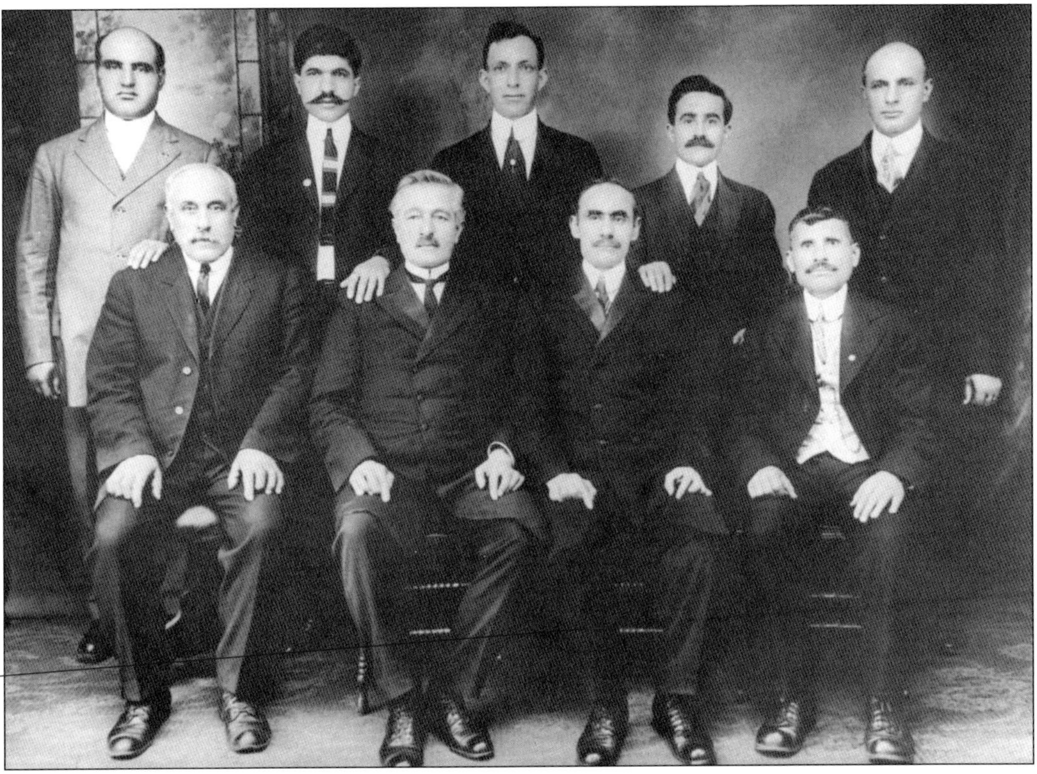

ASSYRIAN MEN. Rev. David Benjamin Jacob is second from left in the first row. Mooshi Sulliman is on the far left in the second row. (Author's collection.)

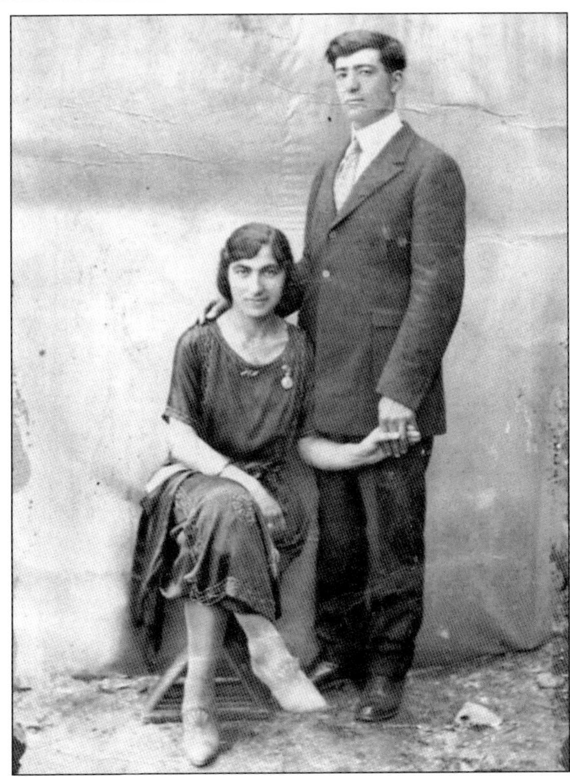

THE BENJAMINS. Almas Joseph and Teddy Benjamin are pictured in the 1920s. (Author's collection.)

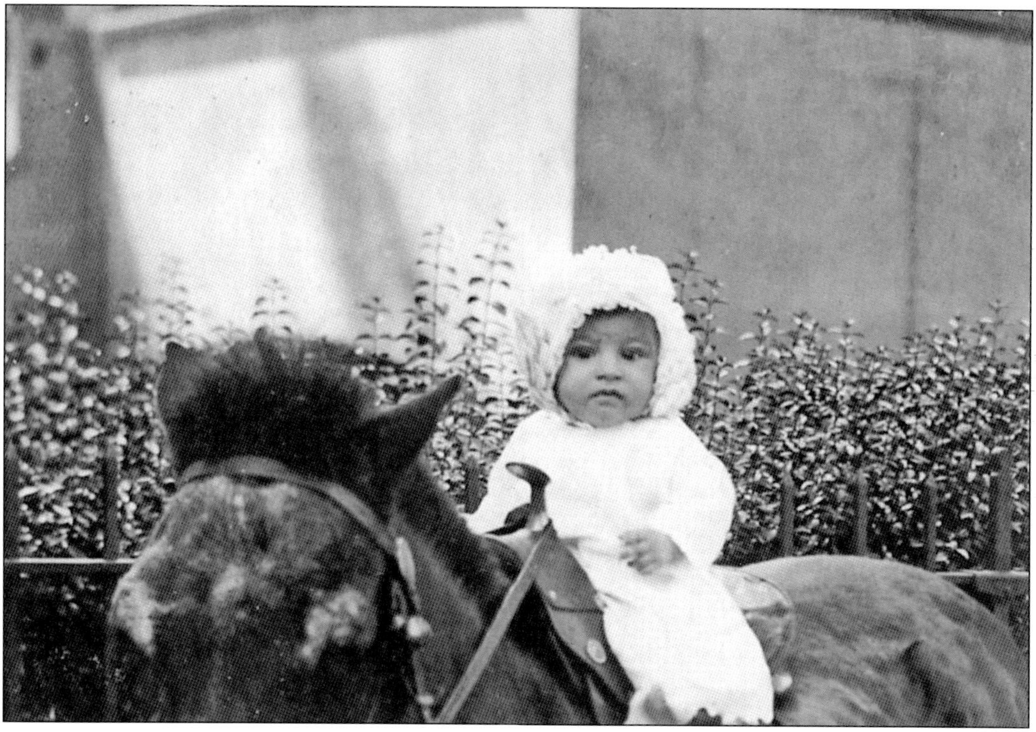

PONY SITTING. William Kambar was only four months old when this picture was taken in April 1925 in Yonkers. A salesman walked the streets selling pony rides. (Author's collection.)

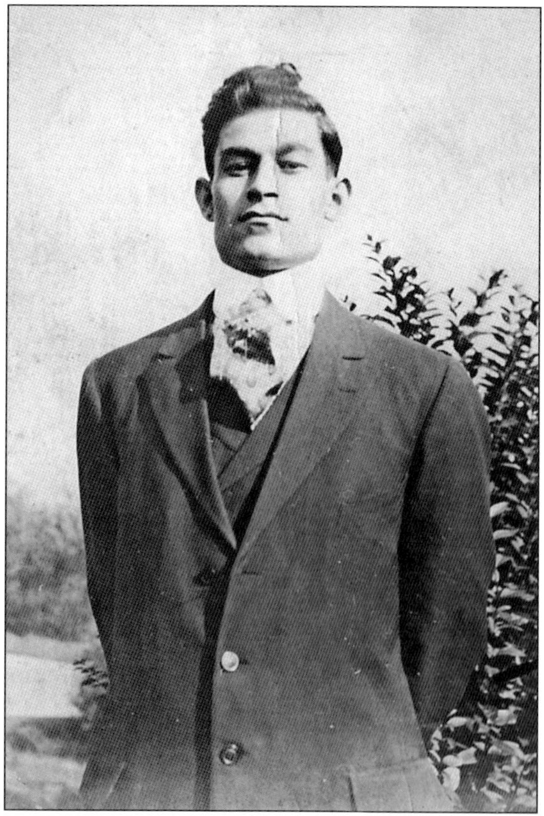

YONAN KAMBAR. Yonan Kambar poses at 43 Jefferson Street in Yonkers in the late 1910s or early 1920s, possibly at the David family home. He worked as a hatter at the Campbell hat factory in Yonkers. (Author's collection.)

Emma Moorad Kambar and Son William Kambar, 1928–1929. Emma Kambar is pictured with her eldest son, William (Bill). (Author's collection.)

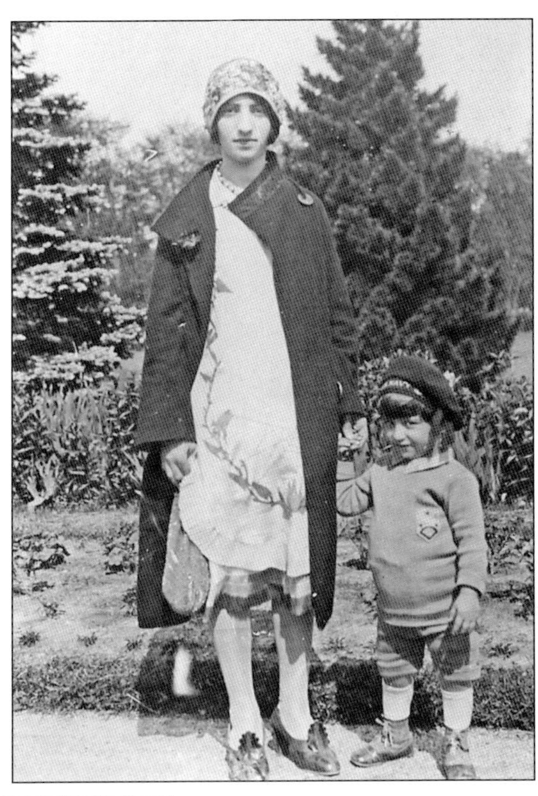

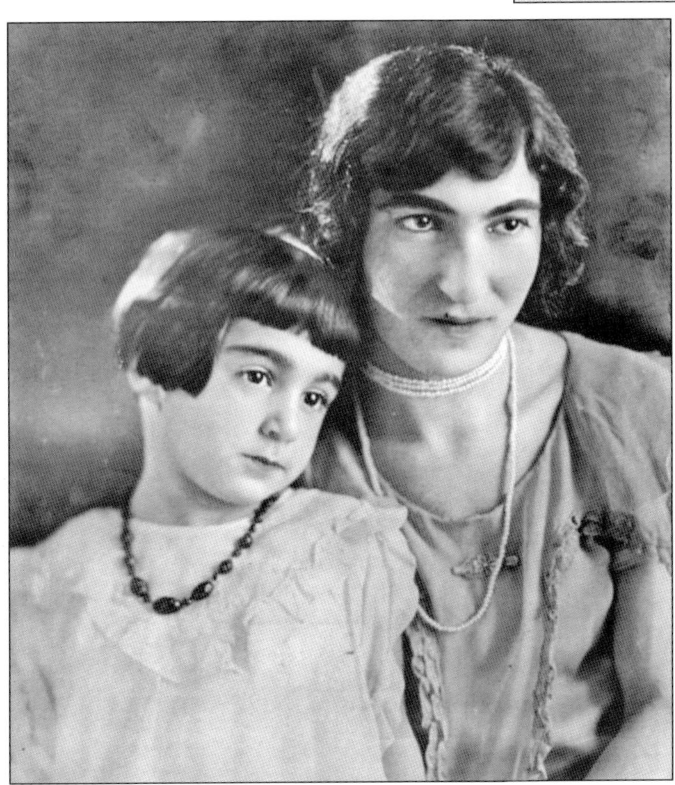

Mother and Daughter. Almas Joseph Benjamin is pictured with her daughter Betty Benjamin in the 1920s. (Courtesy of David Muldoon.)

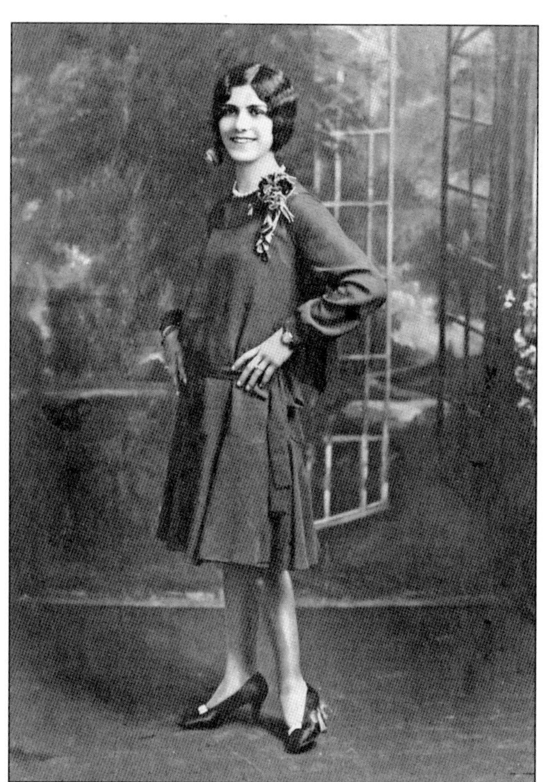

NANCY EDDY, 1920S. Pictured here is Nancy Eddy, cousin to the Benjamins. (Courtesy of Lydia Kambar.)

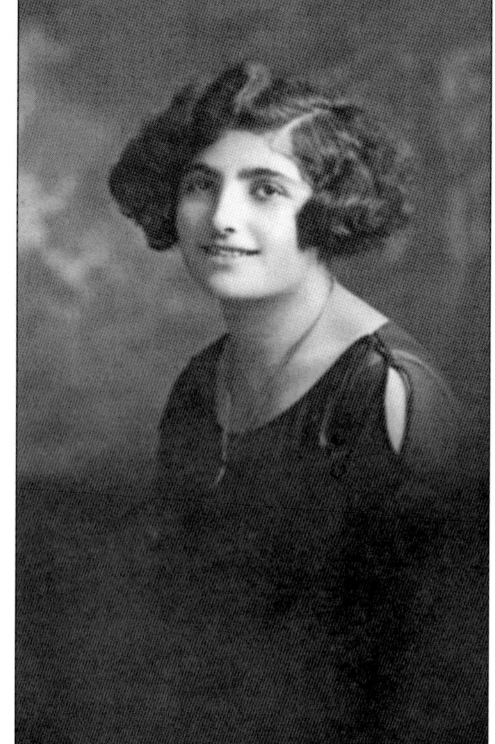

MARUSA JACOBS ASLAN. "Musha" lived on Post Street in Yonkers and was the daughter of Nazlu and Jonathan Jacobs. She, her parents, and siblings James and Florence emigrated from Russia in 1921. Her father and mother opened a restaurant called Jacobs Lunch at 72 Riverdale Avenue in Yonkers. (Author's collection.)

Brothers-in-Law. From left to right are Dave Jacobs, Theodore Benjamin, and Jacob Benjamin. The Jacobs and Benjamin families became friends in Russia when Jacob Benjamin went there to work and met Dave. When Jacob arrived in Yonkers, he coincidentally met up again with Dave. Benjamin sisters married two Jacobs brothers; Louise married Sam Jacobs and Emma married David Jacobs. Additionally, the sister's youngest brother, Nicolai, married David Jacobs's first cousin, Blandina Paulus Jacobs. (Courtesy of Shirley Benjamin.)

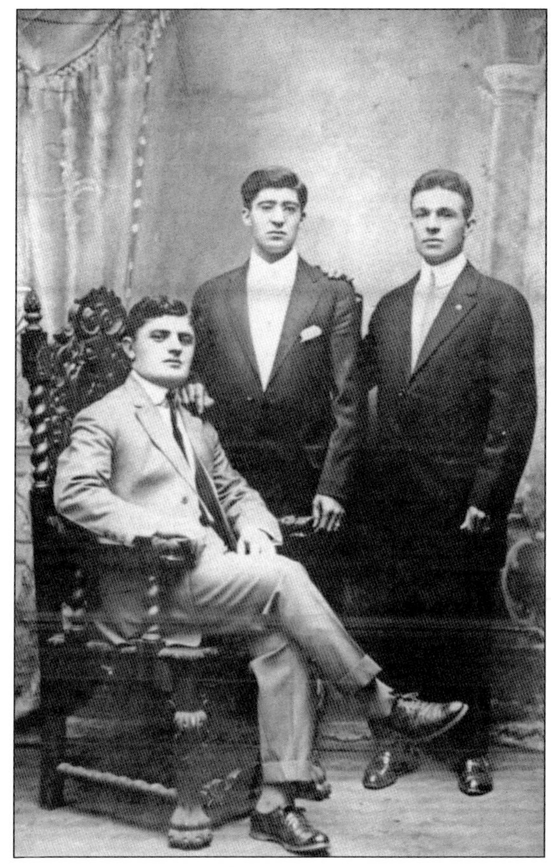

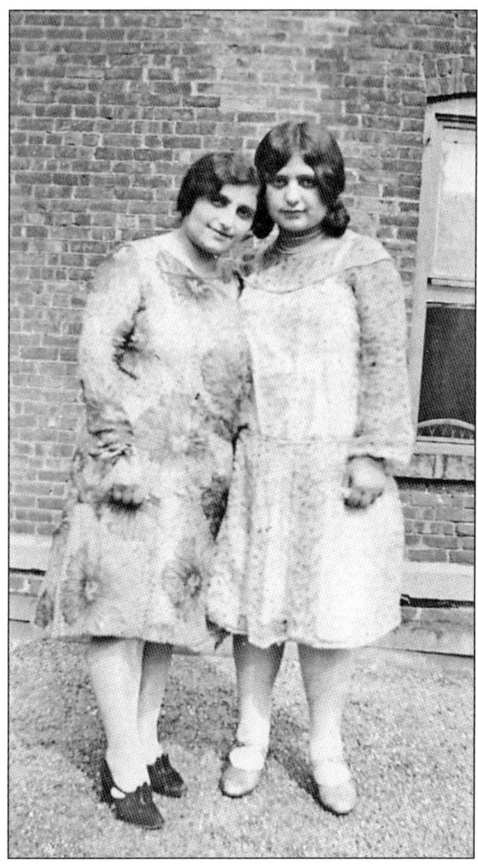

The Jacobs Sisters. Marusa "Musha" (left) and Florence Jacobs pose on their rooftop in Yonkers in the late 1920s. (Courtesy of Shirley Benjamin.)

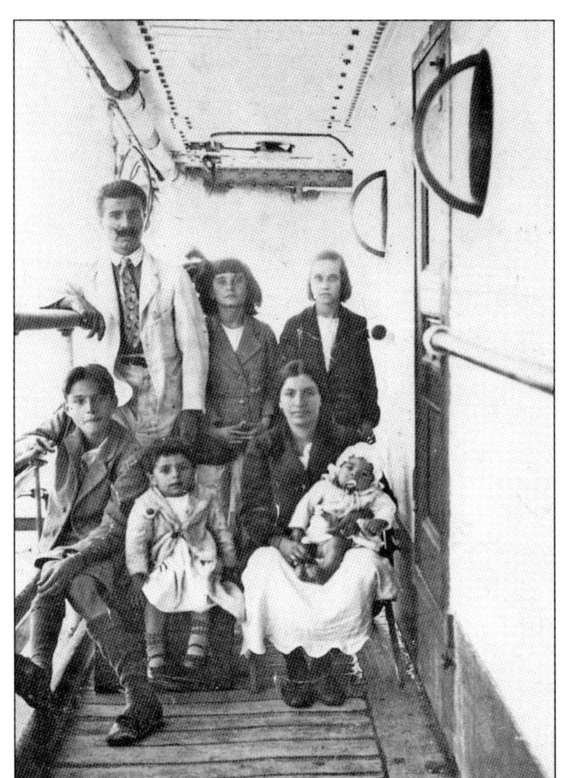

Boat Trip. From left to right are (first row) Michael Aivaz, Jonathan Aivaz, and Veronique Aivaz with her infant son Benjamin; (second row) Joseph Aivaz (father), unidentified, and Lucy Aivaz in the early 1920s. Joseph is Lucy and Mike's stepfather who brought his five elder children to the United States in 1926. In 1930, Isaac Bob was born, and in 1931, Josephine Mary was born in the United States. (Author's collection.)

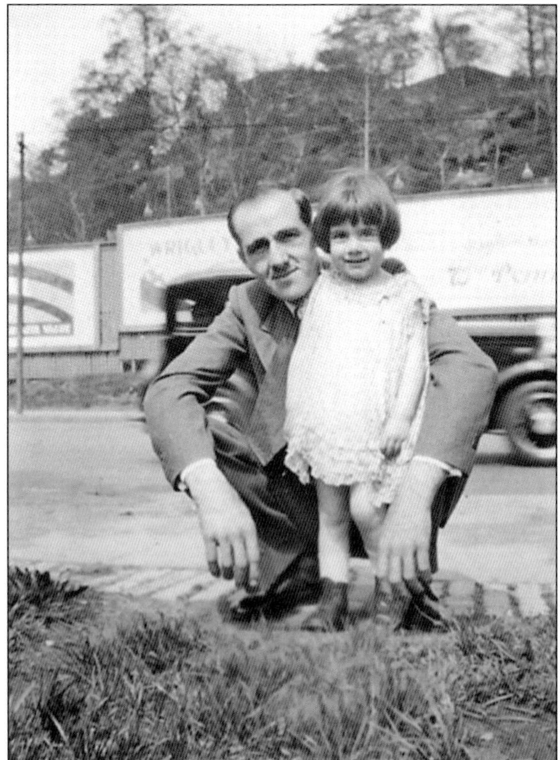

Lincoln Park. Nick and Lydia Benjamin are pictured on McLean Avenue and South Broadway in 1931. Lydia is wearing a dress her mother, Blandina, made. (Author's collection.)

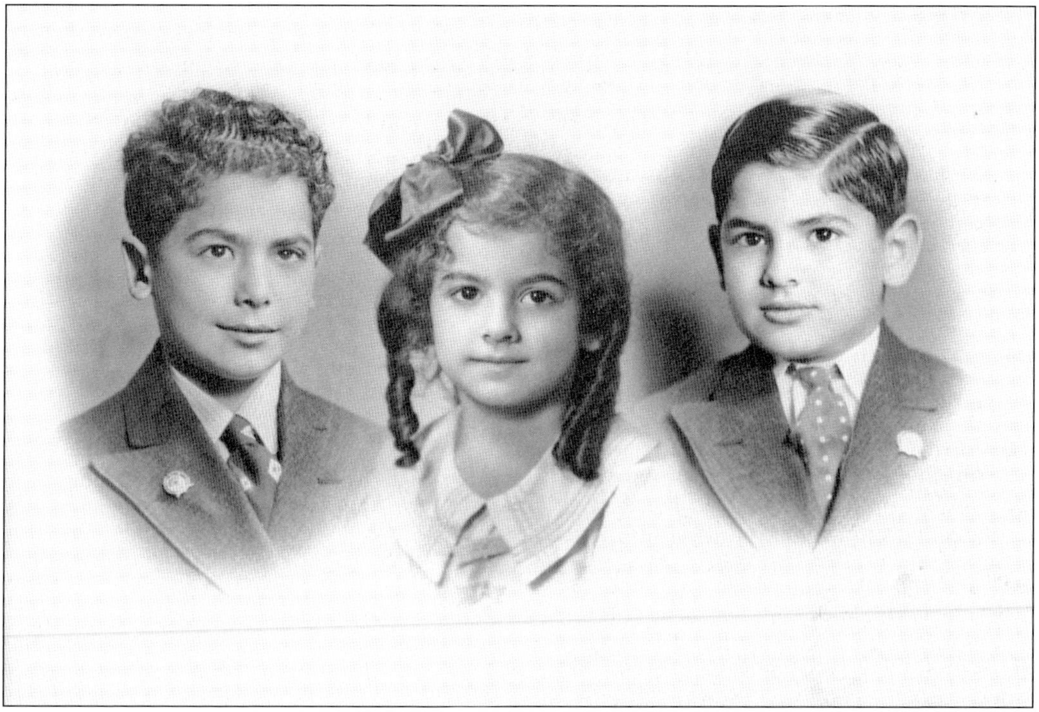

THE ASLAN CHILDREN. Pictured here from left to right are Vicky, Emmy, and Wilfred Aslan, the children of Sam and Marusa Aslan, in 1938. (Courtesy of Shirley Benjamin.)

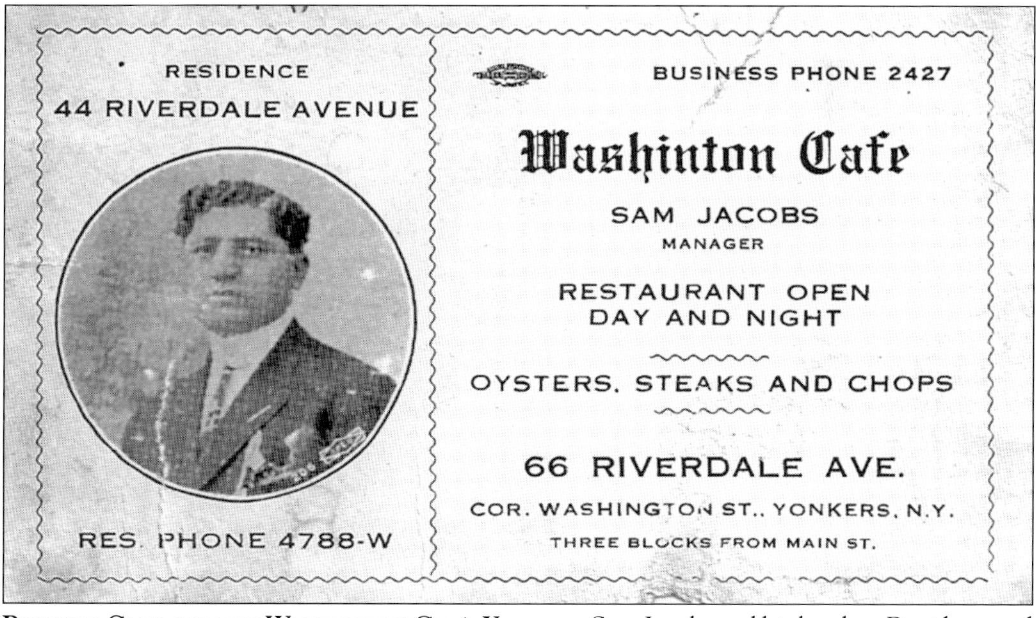

BUSINESS CARD FOR THE WASHINGTON CAFÉ, YONKERS. Sam Jacobs and his brother, David, started this business on Riverdale Avenue and Washington Street. This corner became the Assyrian gathering place. (Courtesy of Shirley Benjamin.)

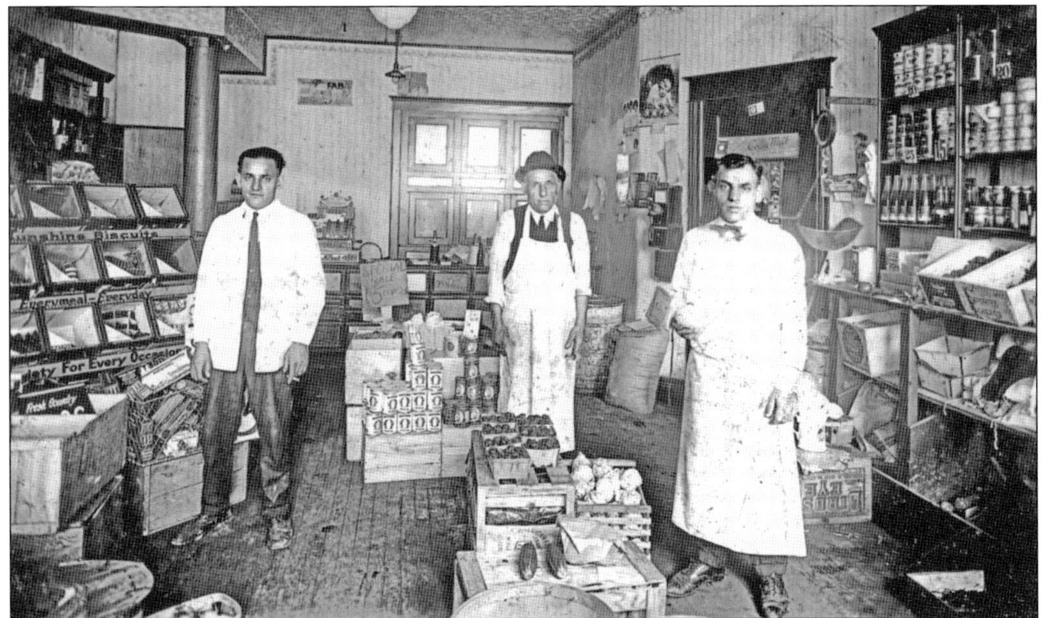

The Schliman Store, Yonkers. In 1905, George Schliman's father and brother came to the United States and settled in Yonkers. In 1909, they applied for George to come to America. His mother was not well enough to make the journey, so her daughter stayed with her. George arrived in 1909. His father was sent a telegram announcing his arrival, but when they went to Ellis Island to fetch him, 19-year-old George had been sent to Russia. The family was told that no one came for him. George stayed in Russia for four years to raise enough money to return. In 1913, George came to the United States and settled with his family in Yonkers, where they opened a little restaurant and a fruit and vegetable delivery business (pictured). (Courtesy of Georgina Kerr George.)

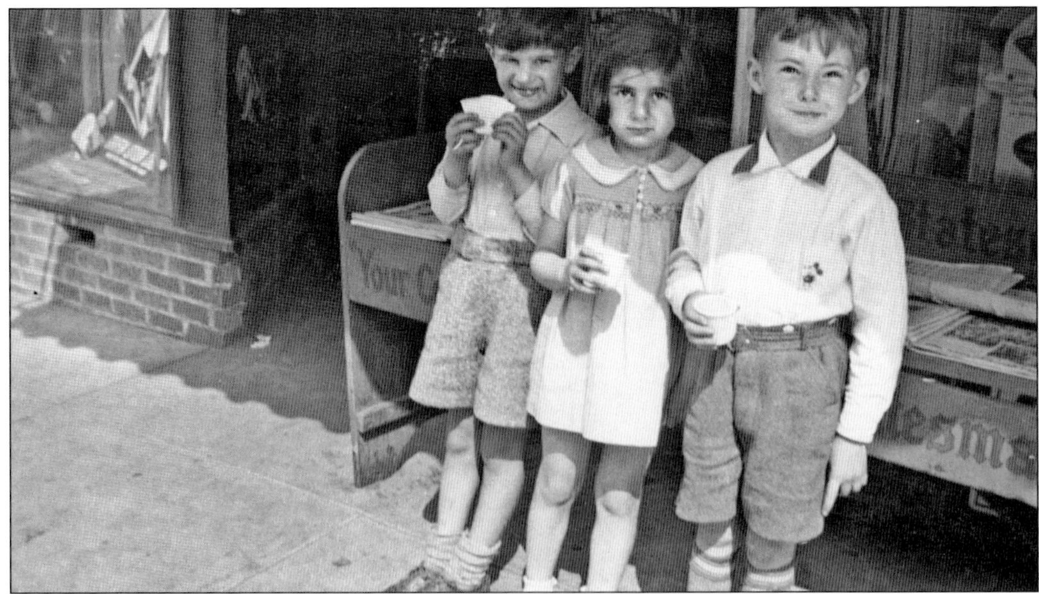

Cousins. From left to right are Johnny Jacobs, Lydia Benjamin, and David Benjamin posing in front David's father Nathan's store at 462 Riverdale Avenue, near the corner of Valentine Lane in Yonkers in 1934. (Author's collection.)

Cousins Benjamin. David Benjamin and Lydia Benjamin pose in front of Nathan Benjamin's store at 462 Riverdale Avenue in 1932–1933. (Author's collection.)

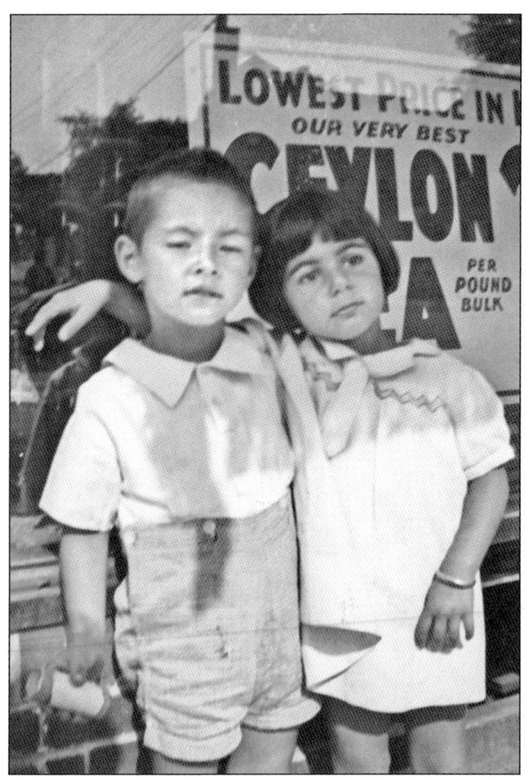

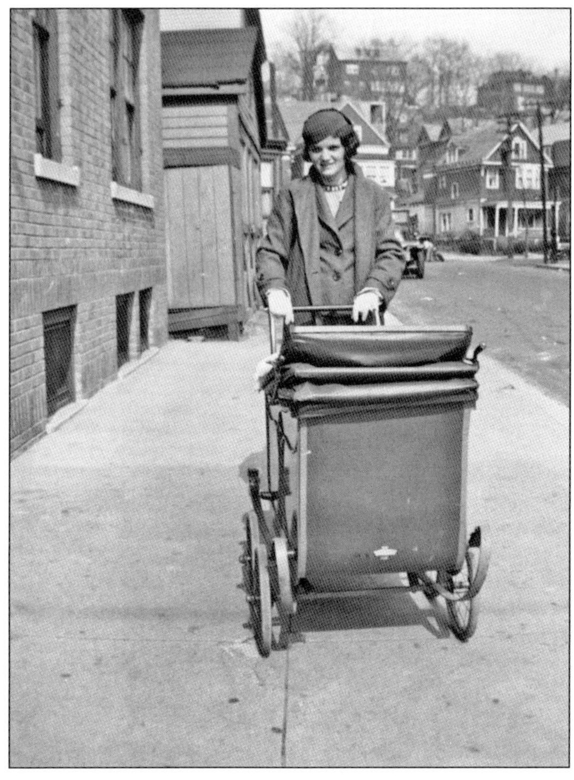

Blandina and the Pram, 1933. Blandina Benjamin and baby Shirley Benjamin are pictured in front of 15 Radford Street at the corner of McLean Avenue in Yonkers. (Author's collection.)

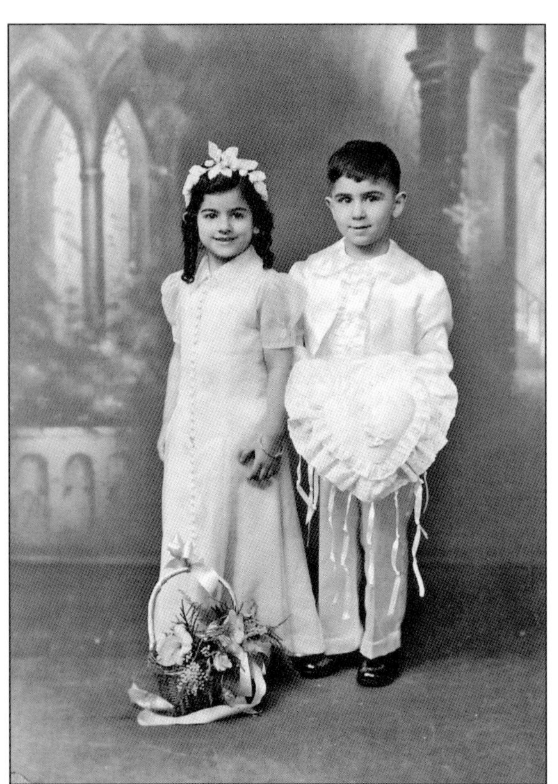

Emmy Aslan and Dicky Nadder. Marusa Jacobs Aslan made the wedding party gowns, including Emmy's flower girl dress and Dick's ring bearer outfit for the wedding of Florence Jacobs to Joseph Gabriel in 1938. (Courtesy of Shirley Benjamin.)

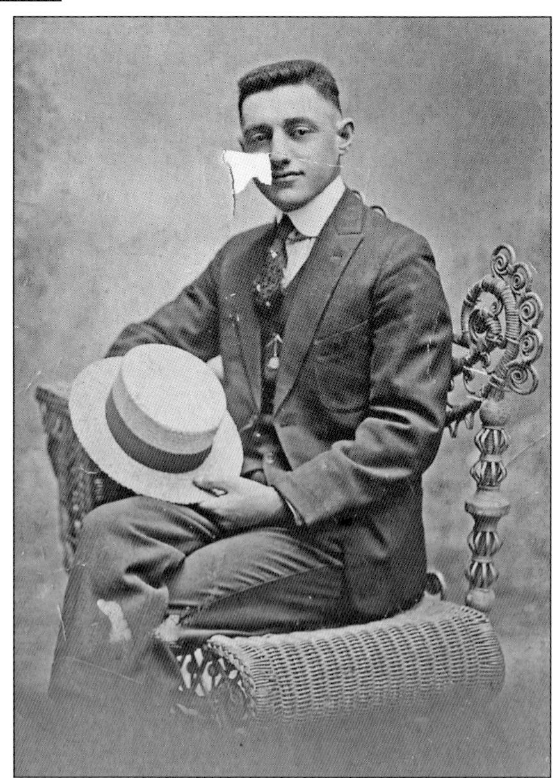

Avemelk Moorad with Hat. Abe Moorad is pictured in the 1920s. He was the brother of Jennie (Jan), John, and Emma. (Author's collection.)

THE MOORADS. Pictured in the 1930s on Groshon Avenue are, from left to right, Emma, Bathsheba (mother to Emma and Jan), and Jan with Nanaka, Bathsheba's mother-in-law, who lived with them. (Author's collection.)

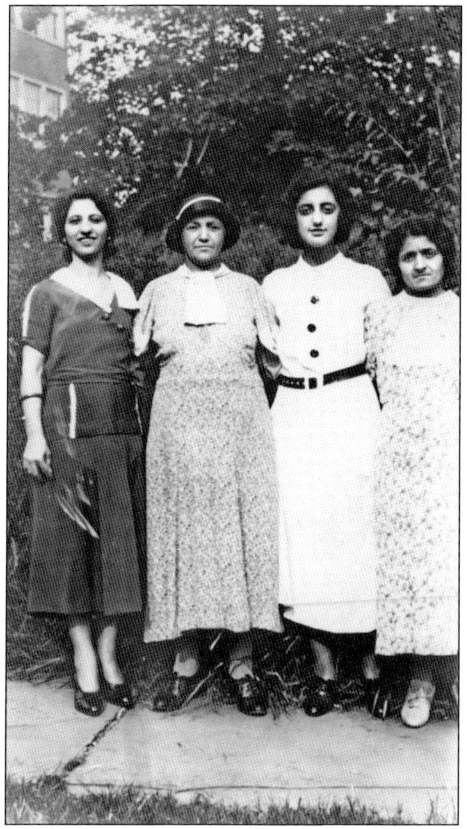

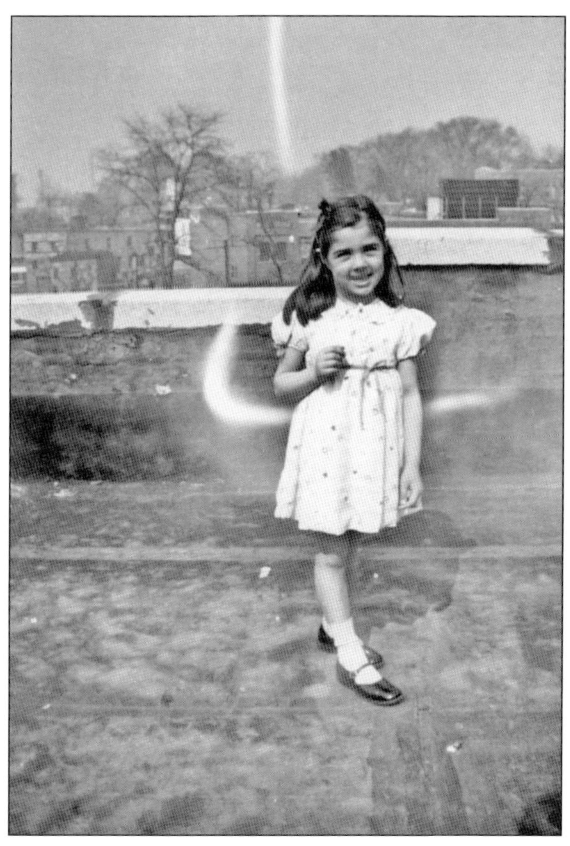

SUNNY DAY. Shirley Benjamin is pictured on the rooftop of 34 Pier Street in Yonkers in 1937. (Courtesy of Shirley Benjamin.)

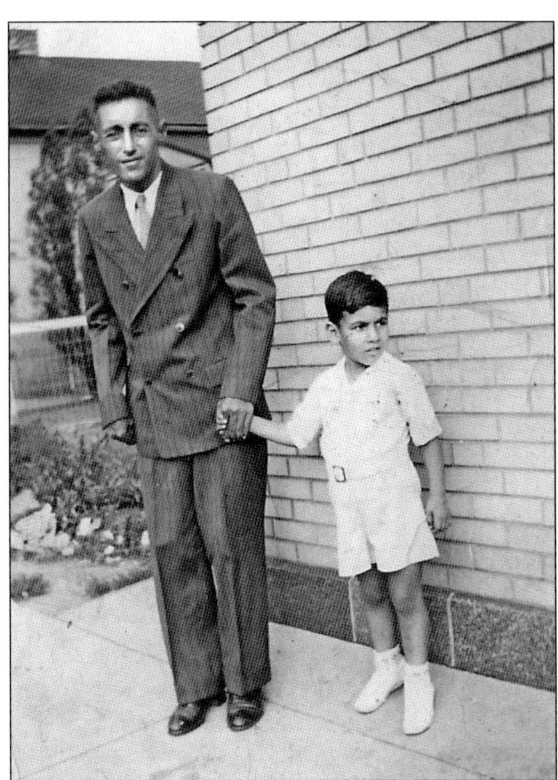

Avemelk (Abe or Abi) Moorad and Robert Kambar. Abi is with his nephew, Robert, in October 1936. (Author's collection.)

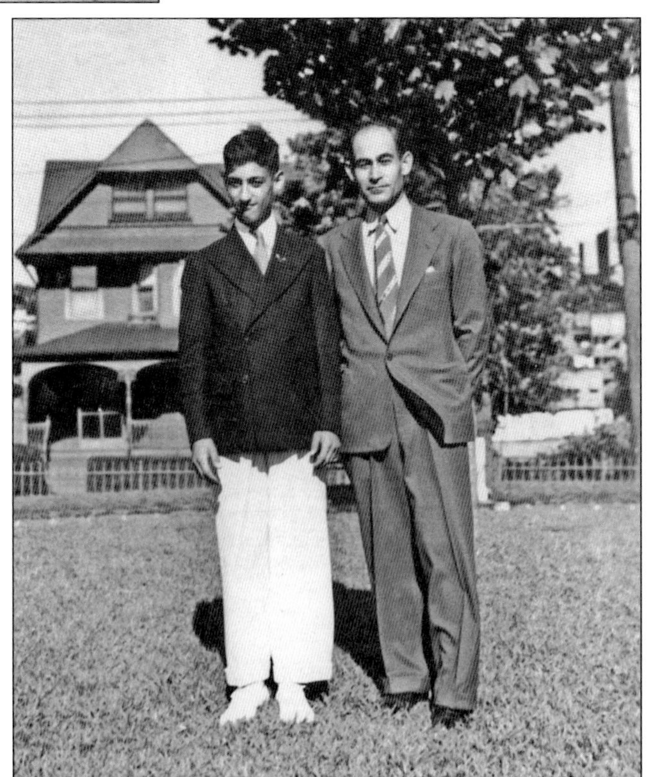

Father and Eldest Son. William (left) is pictured with his father, Yonan Kambar, in July 1939. (Author's collection.)

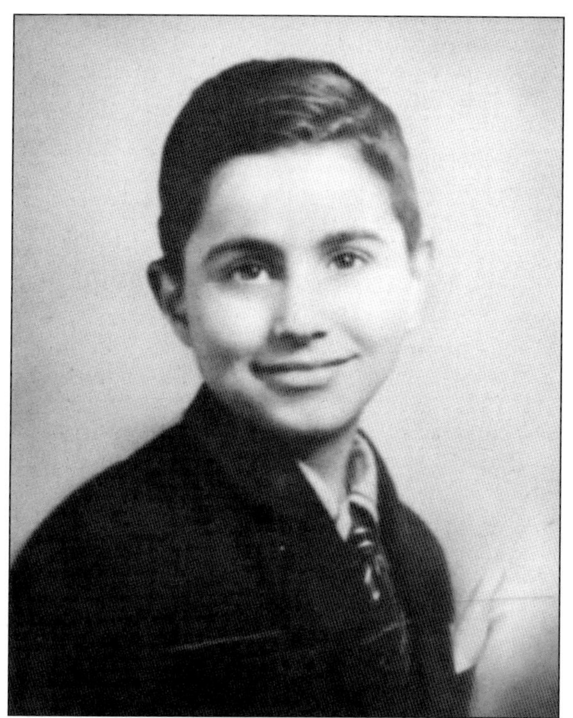

William Sargis. Billy is pictured at 10 years of age in 1937. (Courtesy of the Lilly and William Sargis family.)

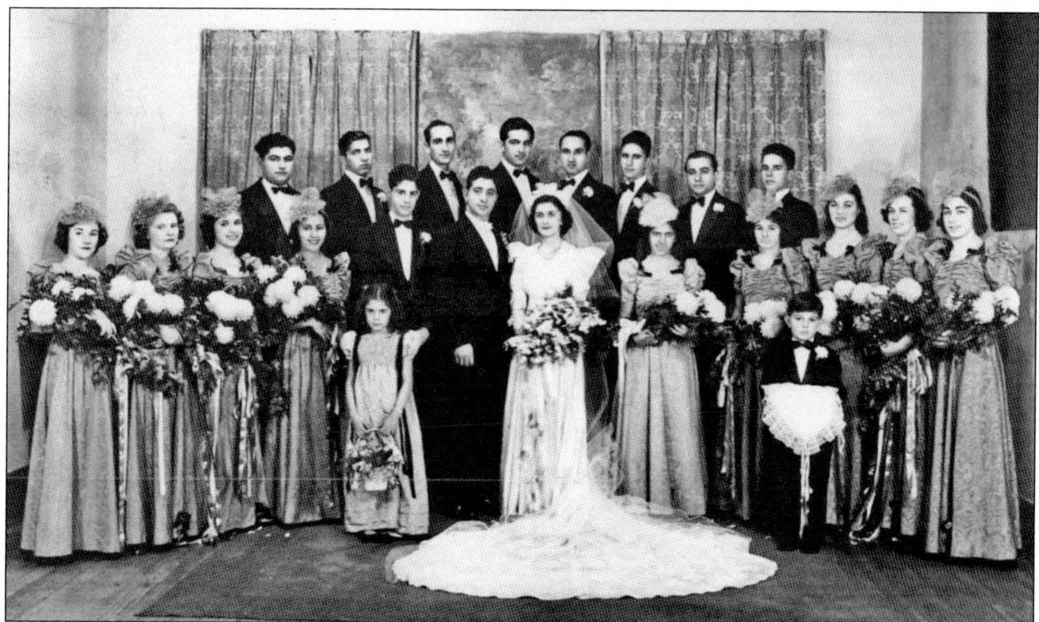

Margaret M. Yonan Jacobs and Clarence Jacobs's Wedding. Pictured on November 11, 1939, are flower girl Shirley Benjamin (front left) and ring bearer Eugene Jacobs (front right). The Bridesmaids are, from left to right, unidentified, Darlene and Charlene Yonan, Regina Baba, unidentified, Jennie Yonan Mercier (maid of honor and bride's sister), Elizabeth Jacobs, unidentified, and Betty Benjamin. The groomsmen are (left to right) Sam Jacobs (next to the groom), Jimmy Jacobs, William Yonan (the bride's brother), Arthur David, Frank Yonan (bride's brother), Bob Sulliman, unidentified, Izzy Yonan, and unidentified. (Courtesy of Jean Jacobs Correa.)

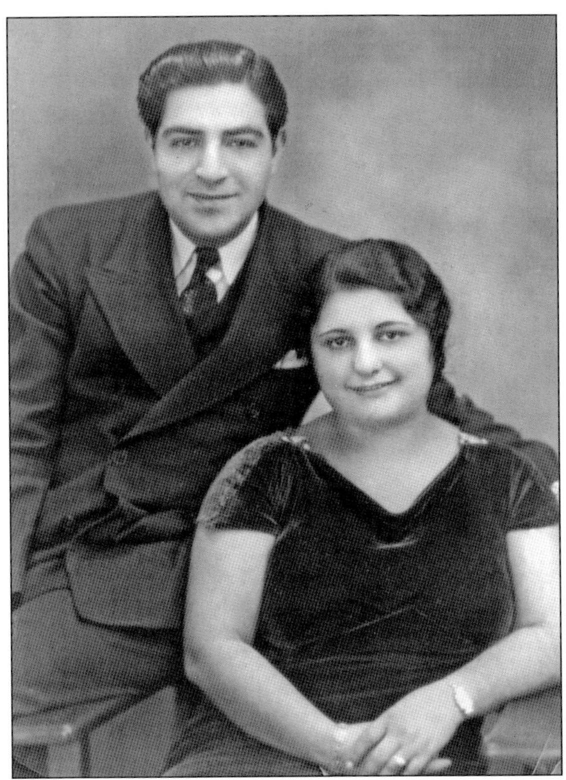

The Gabriels. Florence Jacobs Gabriel and her husband, Joseph, are pictured in the late 1930s. (Courtesy of Nancy Lee Jacobs.)

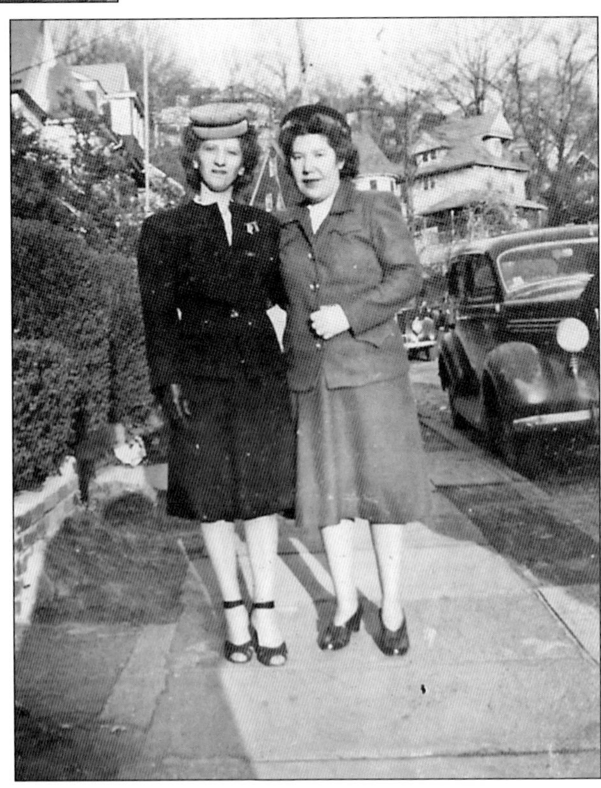

Good Friends. Emma Moorad Kambar (left) and Miriam Hasrato are pictured on Easter Sunday, April 21, 1946, at 39 Caroline Avenue in Yonkers. (Author's collection.)

Jan Moorad with Grandmother Bathsheba and Great-Aunt Nanajan. The three women posing are (from left to right) Nanajan, Jan, and Bathsheba on Monday, June 22, 1936, in Yonkers. (Author's collection.)

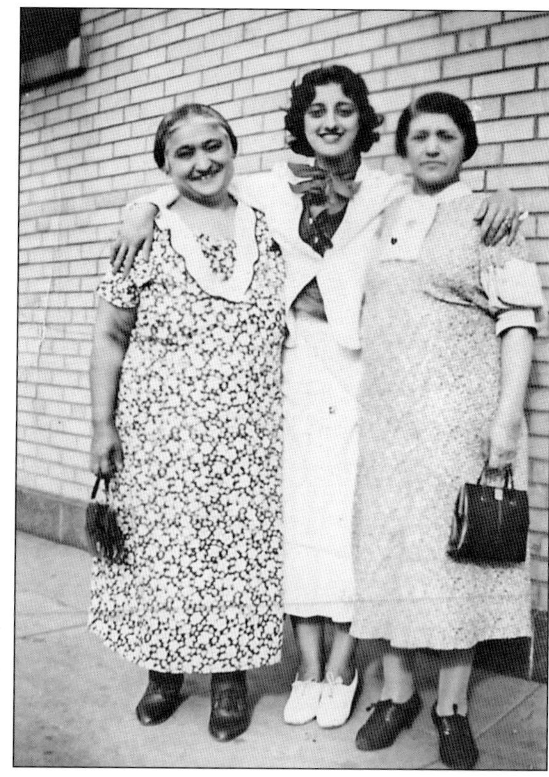

Summer of 1942. Robert Kambar, 10 years old, is pictured at 39 Caroline Avenue in Yonkers. (Author's collection.)

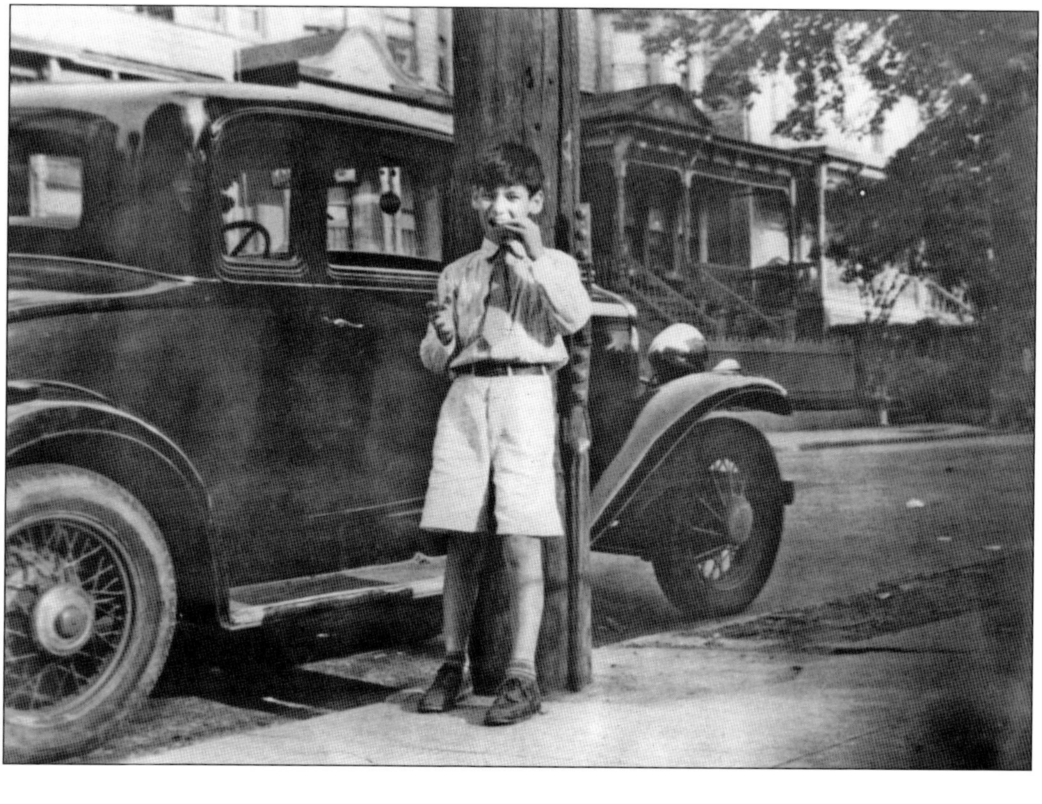

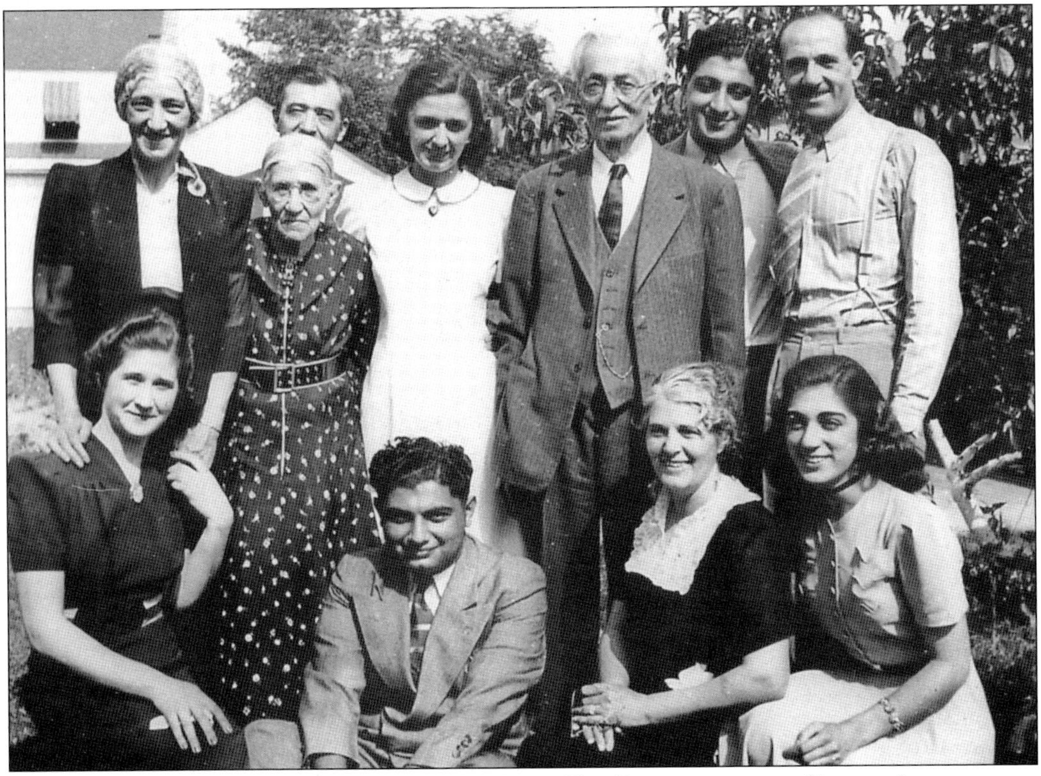

THE BENJAMINS WITH COUSIN JIMMY JACOBS AND MARGARET AND CLARENCE JACOBS. The Benjamins resided at David Jacobs's Kensington, New Britain, Connecticut, farmhouse before moving to Yonkers after the Great Depression. (Courtesy of Shirley Benjamin.)

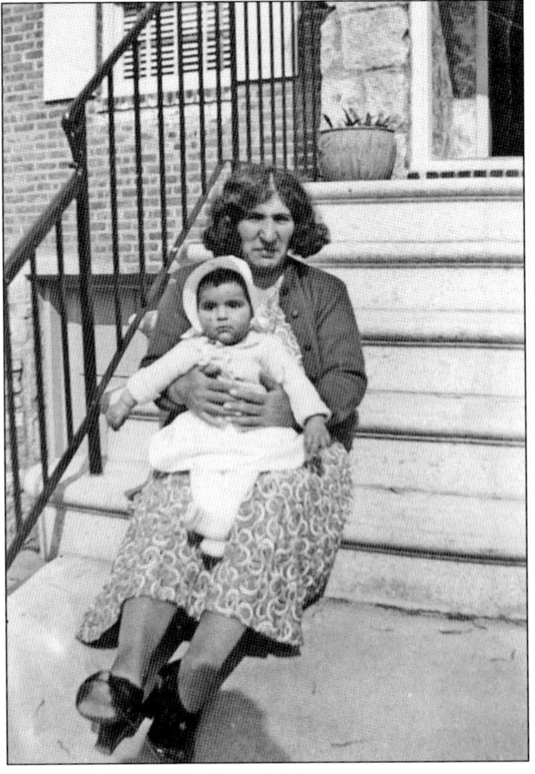

BABY ESTELLE WITH MOTHER'S FRIEND. Pictured here are Estelle Vitti and Nanasi (Nancy) Shimon, her grandmother's close friend, in front of Estelle's grandmother's house at 58 Clifton Avenue in Yonkers in 1941. (Courtesy of Estelle Vitti.)

The Kambar Brothers with Jan Moorad Yohanna, 1941. William, the eldest, is holding his baby brother, Kenneth. Robert "Bobby" is standing on Jan's left. (Author's collection.)

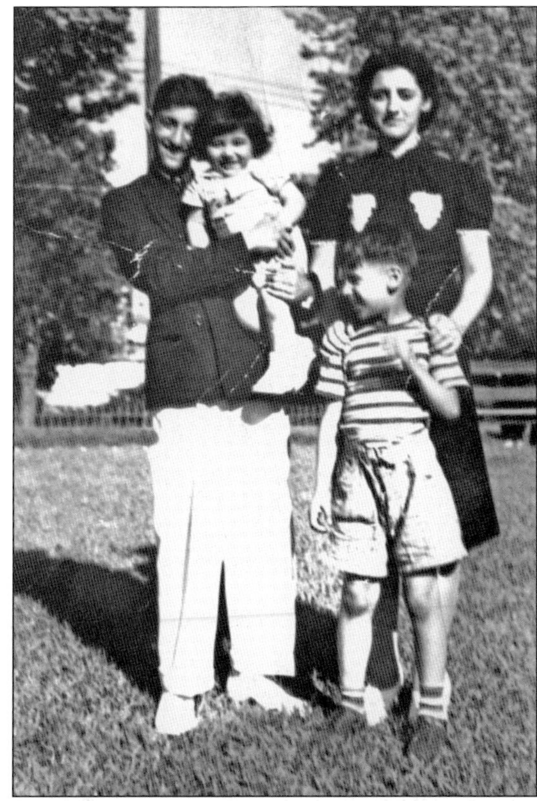

Cousins and Neighbor. Pictured from left to right in a yard on Caroline Avenue in Yonkers in 1943 are unidentified, Shaaron Yohanna, and Kenneth Kambar. (Author's collection.)

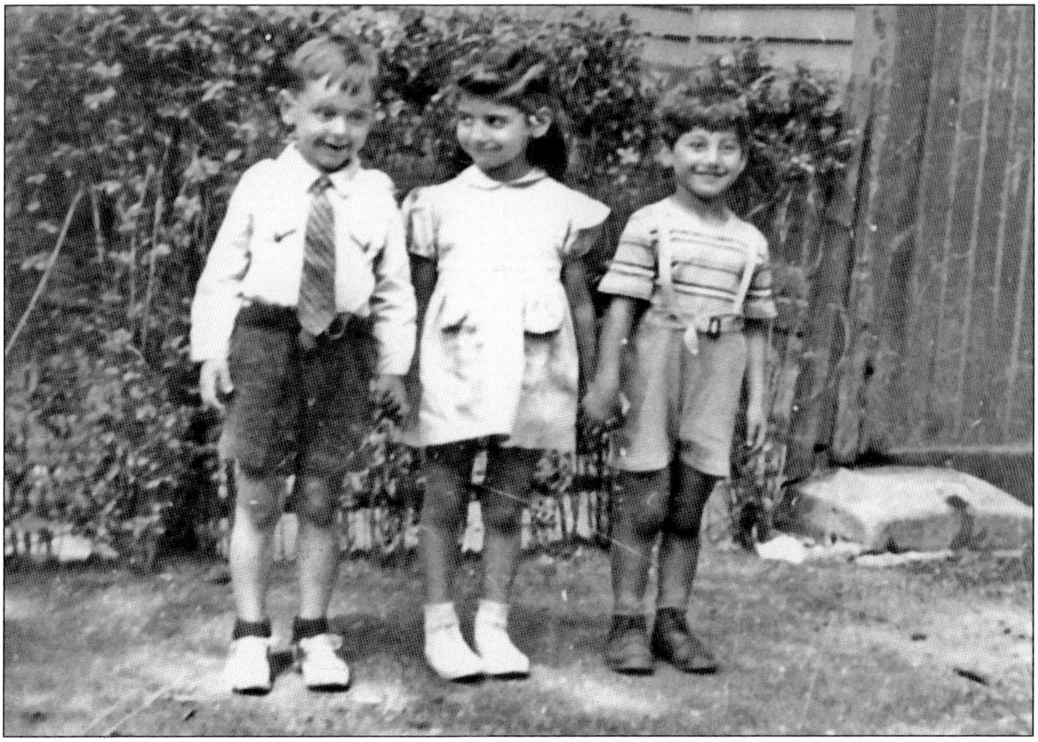

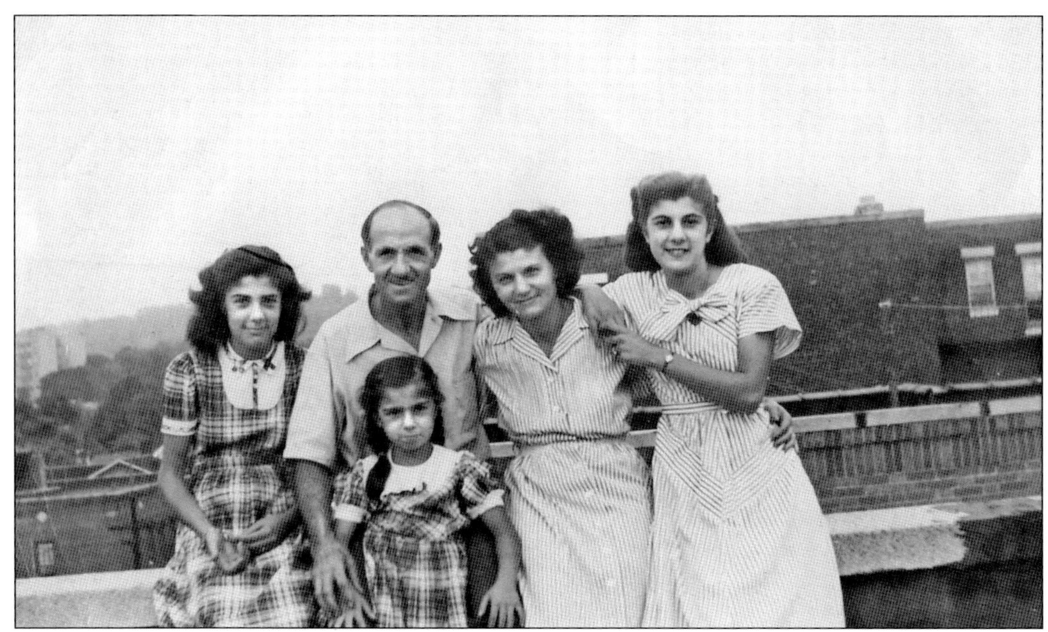

The Benjamin Family on Pier Street Roof. Nick and Blandina pose for a photograph with their girls, from left to right, Shirley, Joanne, and Lydia, on the rood of 34 Pier Street in Yonkers in 1945. (Author's collection.)

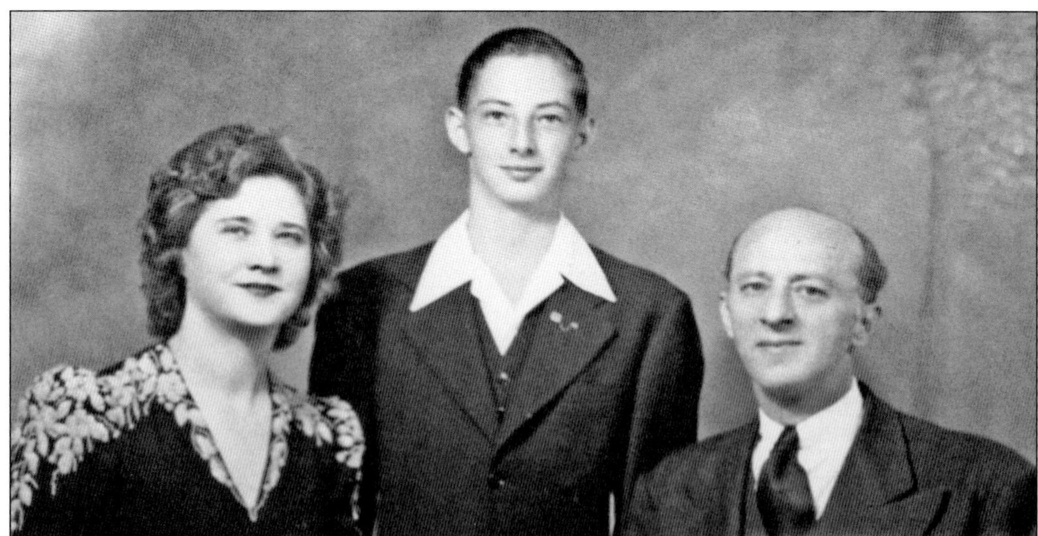

The Benjamins. Pictured here are Lucy and David Benjamin with their son Nelson (or Nathan). Lucy was the owner of the popular shop Lucy's Knitting Studio on South Broadway in Yonkers. After serving in the Navy, Nathan became the owner of a candy store on the corner of Riverdale Avenue and Valentine Lane in Yonkers. David served in the Army and eventually relocated his family to New Jersey. (Courtesy of Shirley Benjamin.)

The Gabriel Women. From left to right are Nanajan Gabriel, Nansara "Sara" Gabriel (mother of Alexander and Joseph Gabriel, the husbands of Nanajan and Florence), and Florence Gabriel (daughter of Nazlu Jacobs). The photograph was taken in Philadelphia. (Courtesy of Nancy Lee Jacobs.)

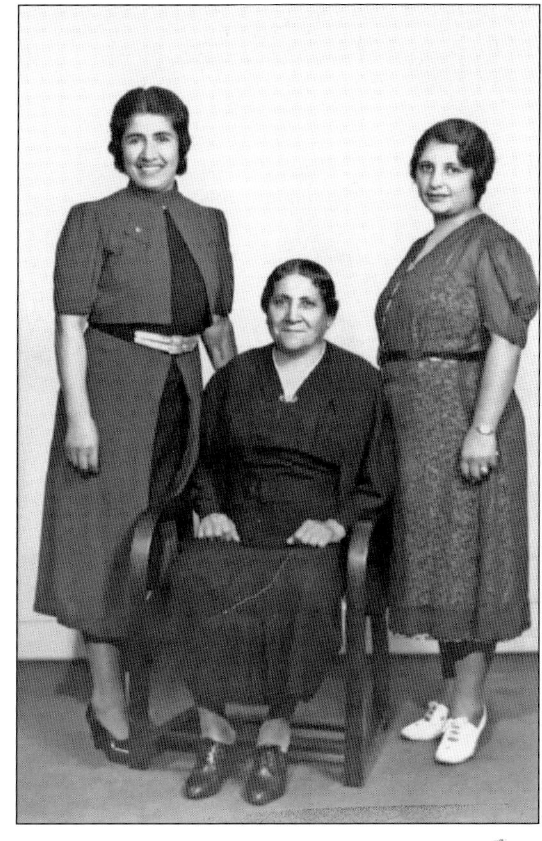

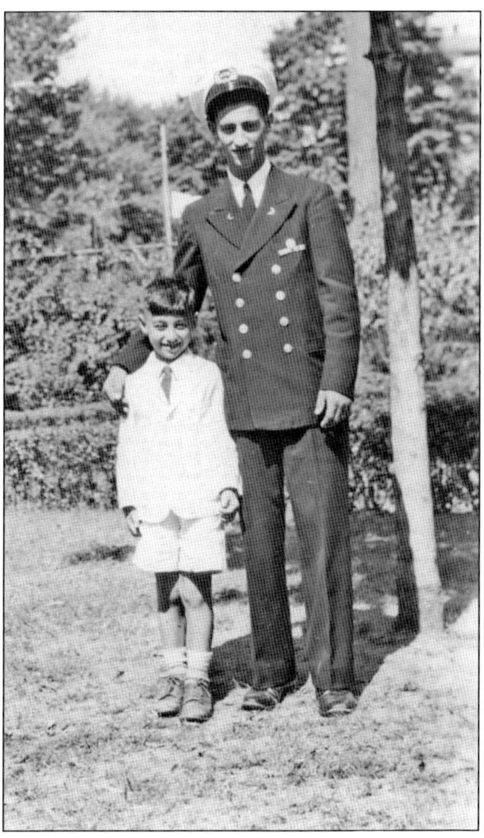

Kambar Sons. William Kambar is pictured in his Merchant Marine uniform with brother Kenneth in 1945–1946 in Yonkers. (Author's collection.)

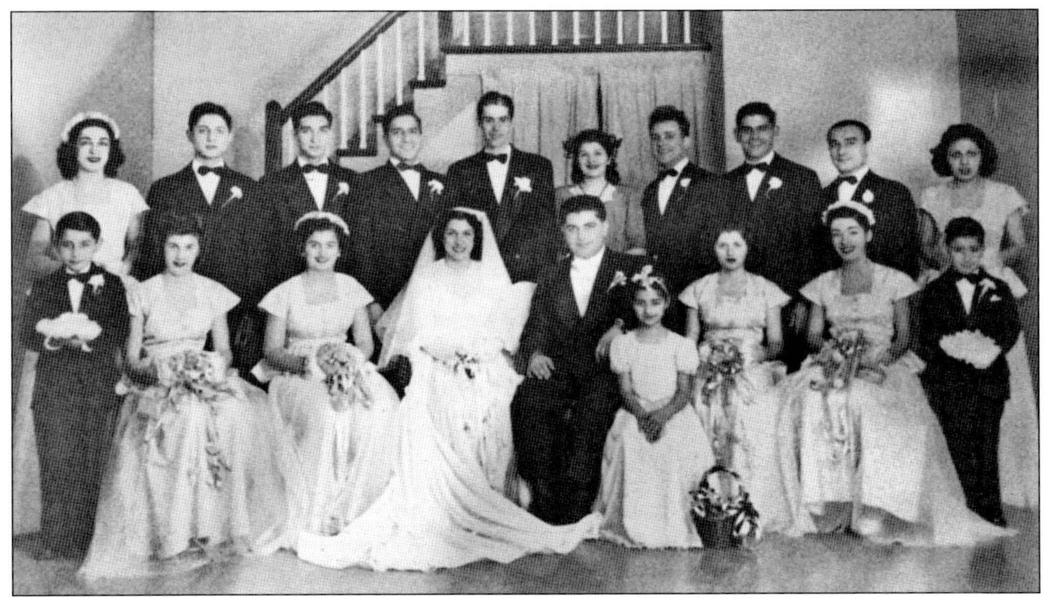

Florence and Jimmy Jacobs's Wedding. Pictured on November 16, 1946, are, from left to right, (first row) unidentified, Lydia Benjamin, Emmy Aslan, Florence Jacobs (bride), Jimmy Jacobs (groom), unidentified flower girl, unidentified, Nancy Sarmast, and Roger Jacobs; (second row) Betty Benjamin, Alfred Caram, two unidentified, Sam Jacobs, Elizabeth Jacobs, unidentified, Victor Aslan, one of the Shlemon brothers, and Katherine Sargis. (Author's collection.)

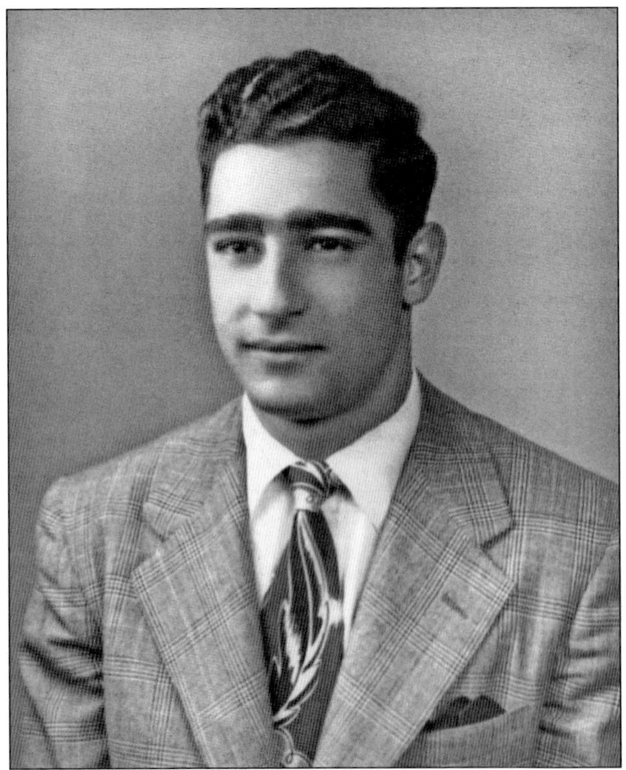

Fred Benjamin. Fred poses for his Gorton High School graduation in 1948 in Yonkers. (Courtesy of David Muldoon.)

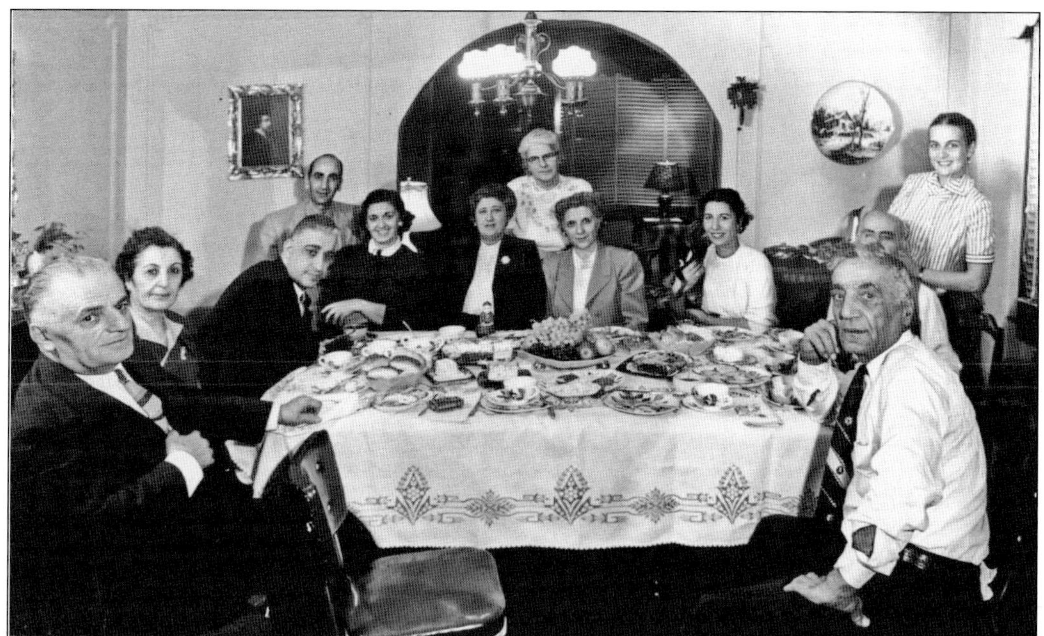

Family and Friends. From left to right are Dave Jacobs; Batishua David; Clarence Jacobs; Joseph David; Margaret Jacobs; Alice Yohannan; Nancy Eddy; Emma Jacobs (standing); unidentified; Helen David (standing); her husband, Theodore David; Joseph Benjamin David; and Saul David, Batishua's brother, who was living in Michigan. They have gathered for dinner at Emma and Dave Jacobs's home on Belvedere Drive in Yonkers in the late 1940s. (Courtesy of Jean Jacobs Correa.)

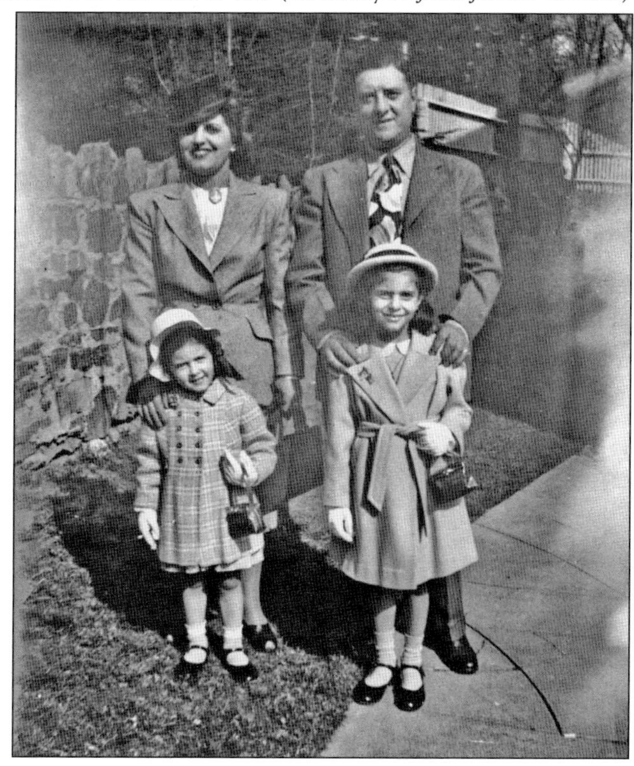

Vitti Family, Easter Sunday, April 6, 1947. Pictured are Zenhela, Jimmy, Nancy, and Estelle Vitti. The photograph was taken on Clifton Avenue in Yonkers. (Courtesy of Estelle Vitti.)

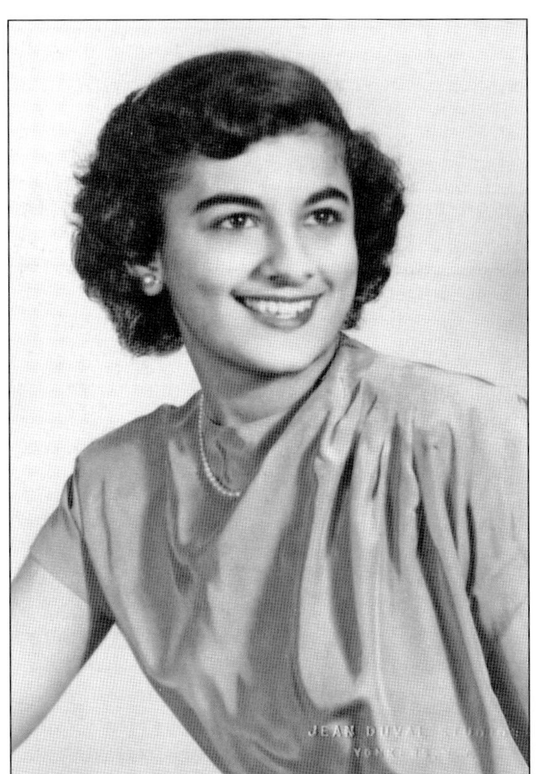

EMMY ASLAN. This picture of Emmy was taken when she was working at Ohrbach's in the 1950s. (Author's collection.)

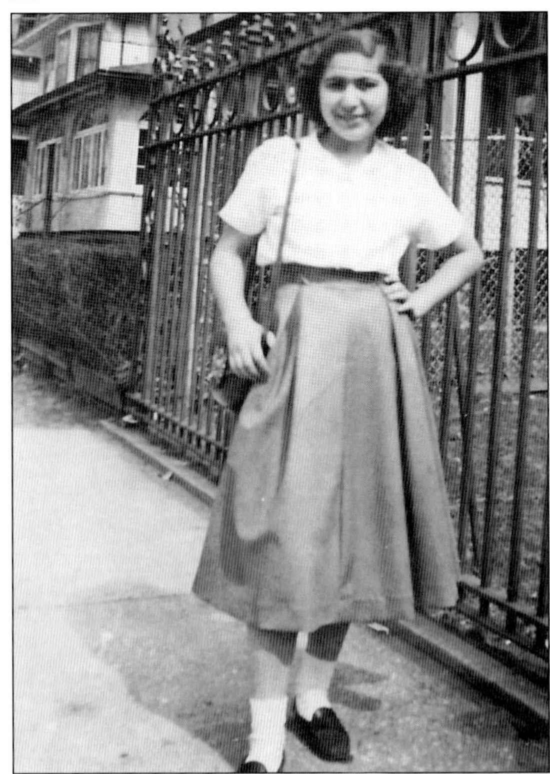

HAWTHORNE JUNIOR HIGH SCHOOL GRADUATION, 1952. Alice Aziz David is pictured at Sunset Park, now Anthony O'Boyle Memorial Park, at Downing Street and Hawthorne Avenue. (Courtesy of Alice Aziz David.)

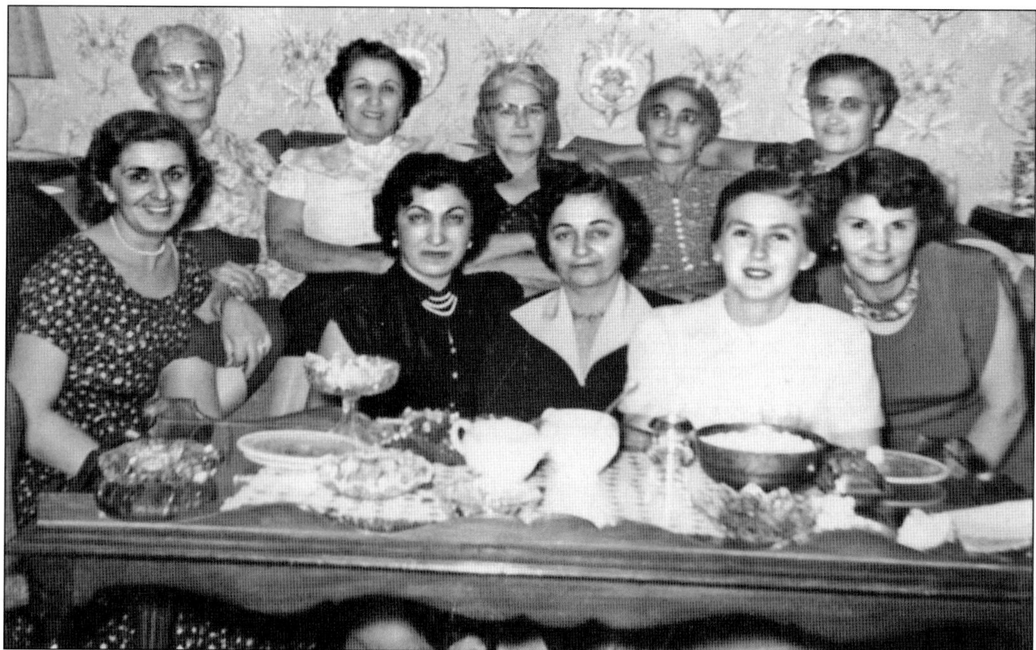

Women Gathering. From left to right are (first row) Margaret Jacobs; Almas Benjamin (Alice); Judith Caram; Jean Jacobs; and Blandina Benjamin; (second row) Nancy Eddy's mother, Nancy Eddy, (possibly Batishua David); Emma Jacobs; unidentified; and Julia Ameer on Belvedere Drive, Yonkers, on May 29, 1953. (Courtesy of the Benjamin family.)

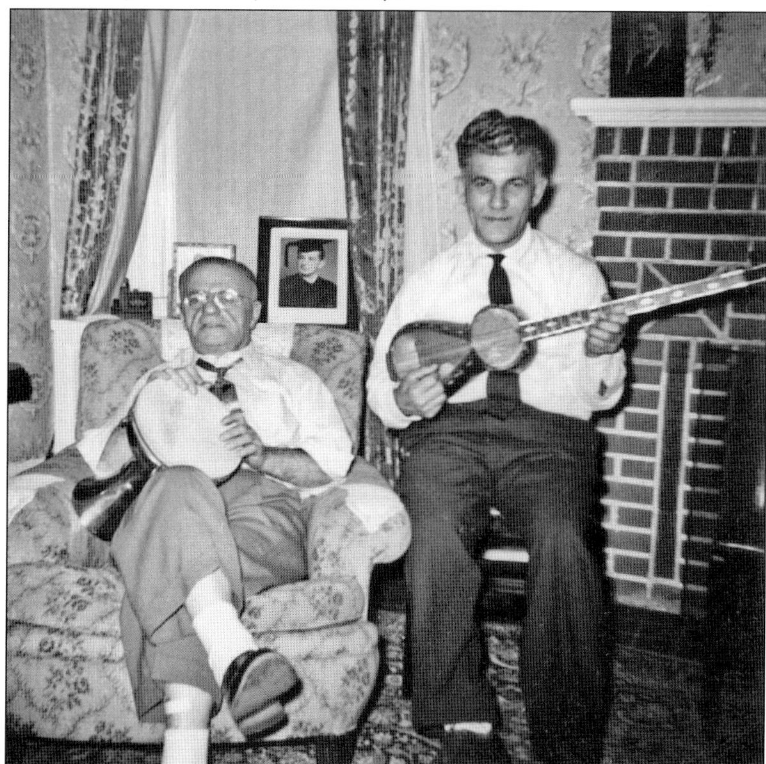

Music on Belvedere Drive. David Jacobs and Jerry Caram (or Karam) entertain family in Yonkers on May 29, 1953. (Courtesy of Shirley Benjamin.)

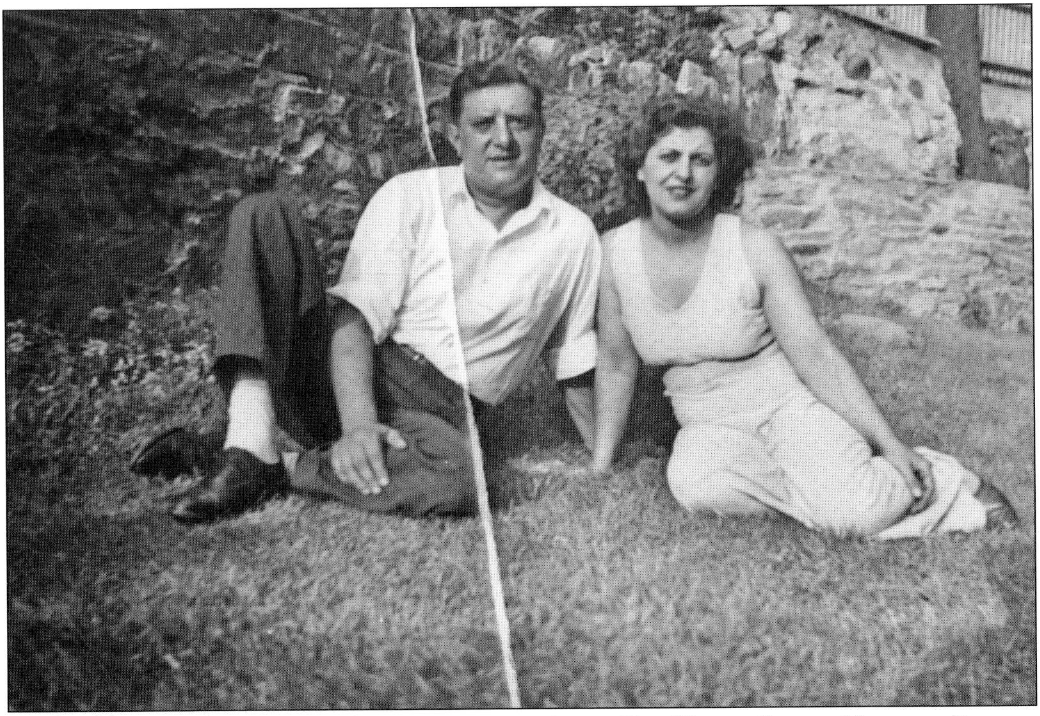

The Vittis. Pictured here are Jimmy and Zenhela Vitti on Clifton Avenue in 1941. (Courtesy of Estelle Vitti.)

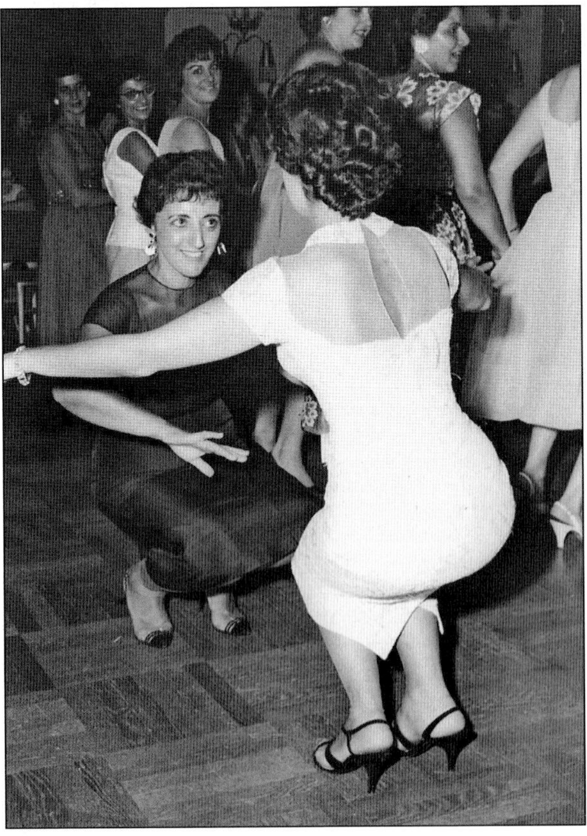

Assyrian Convention, Traditional Dancing. Jan Darcy is pictured dancing with Beatrice Ameer in 1958 or 1959. (Courtesy of Ruth Kambar.)

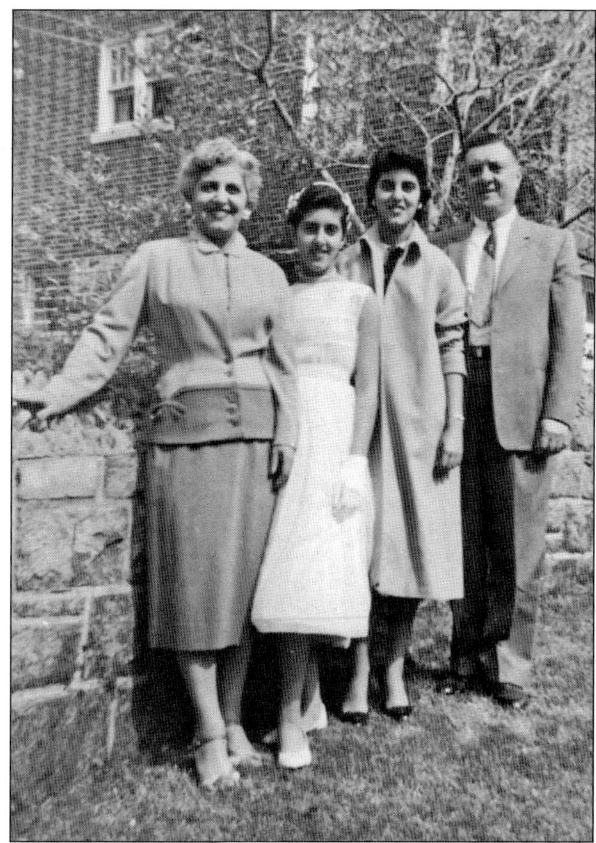

Nancy Vitti's Confirmation. Nancy Vitti was confirmed at Christ Church in Riverdale, New York, in 1954. Posing on Clifton Avenue in Yonkers are, from left to right, Zenhela, Nancy, Estelle, and Jimmy Vitti. (Courtesy of Estelle Vitti.)

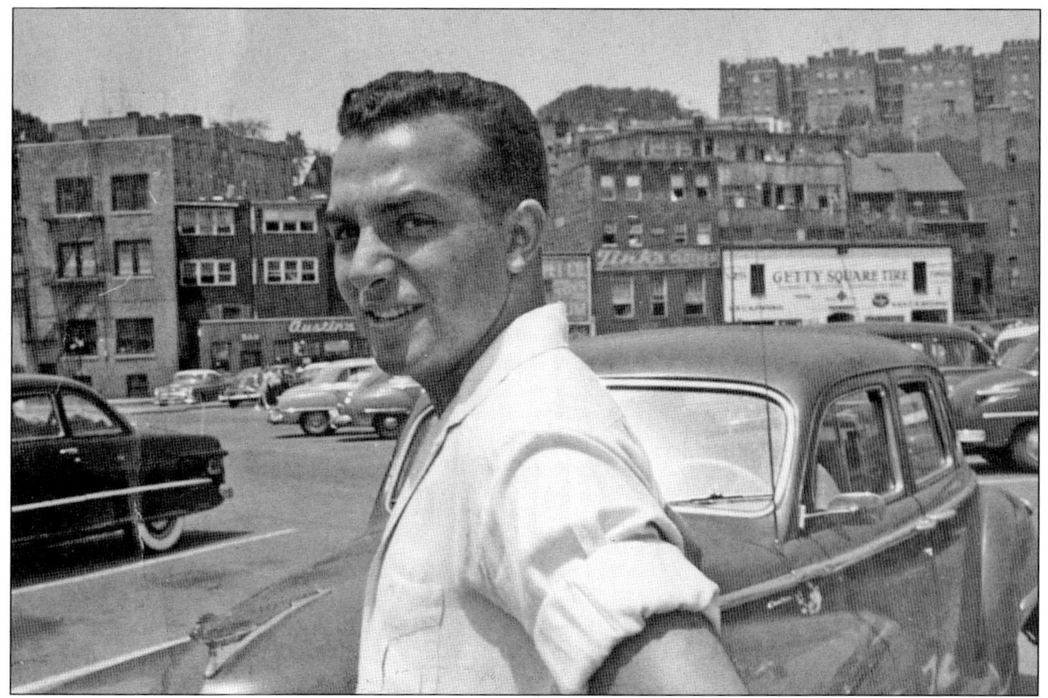

Darius Baba. Darius Baba is pictured in Getty Square, the hub of Yonkers, in July 1955. (Courtesy of the Baba family.)

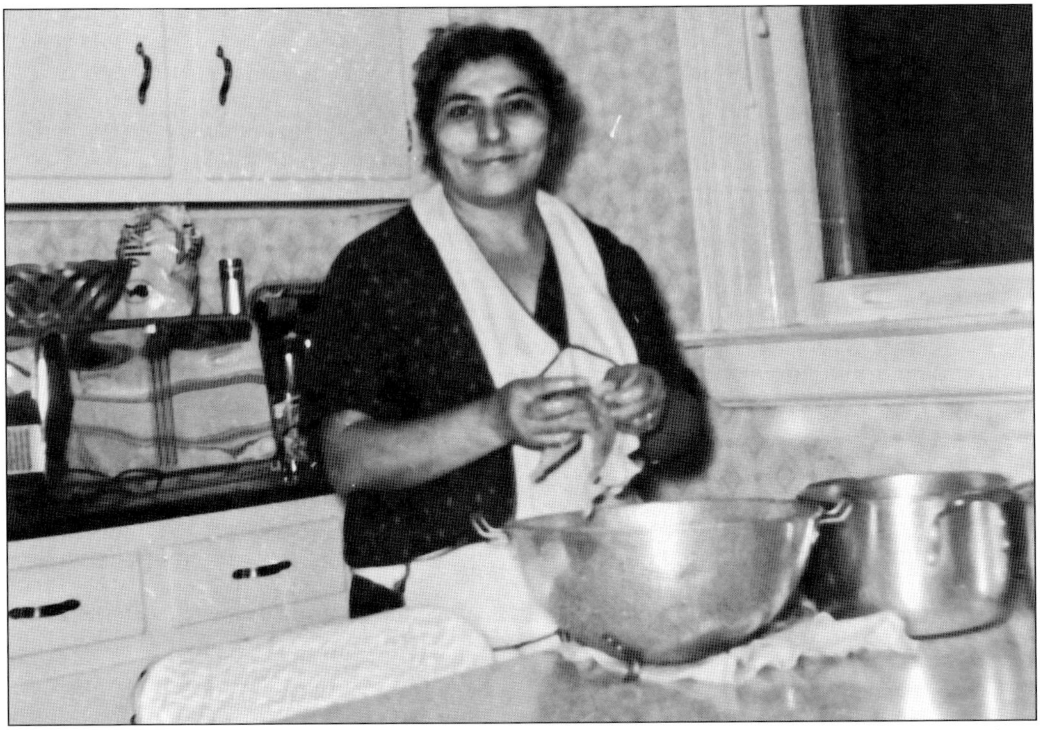

MAKING DOLMA DURPEE. Ketro Aziz is pictured in her kitchen at 131 Saratoga Avenue in Yonkers in 1963. (Courtesy of Alice Aziz David.)

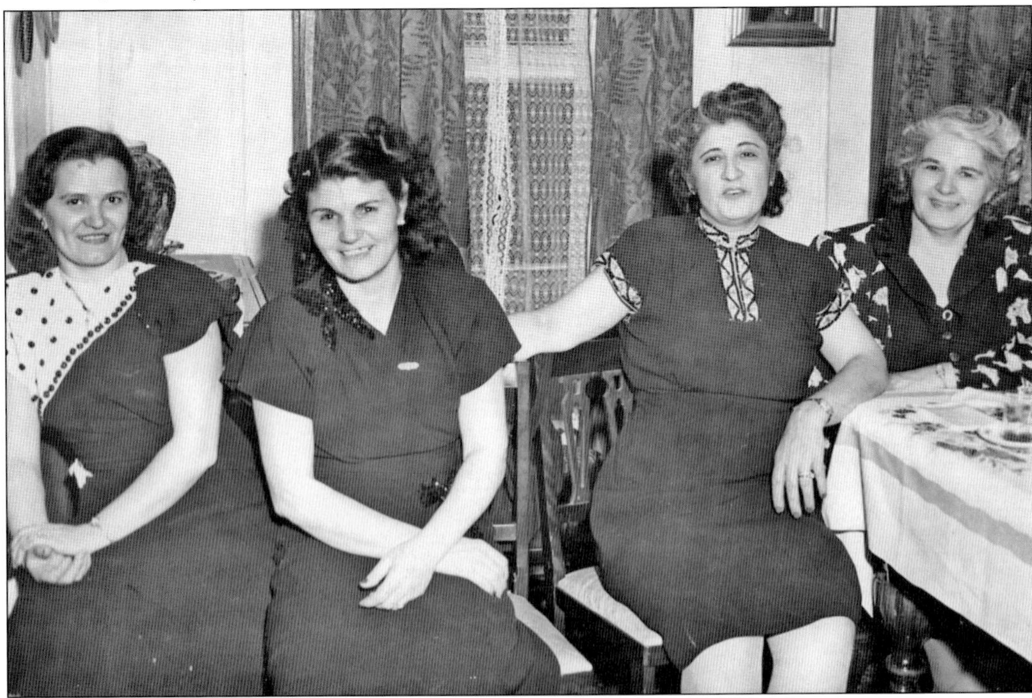

FOUR WOMEN. Pictured here are Margaret Eshoo, Blandina Benjamin, Alice Yohannan, and Emma Jacobs in the 1940s. (Courtesy of Shirley Benjamin.)

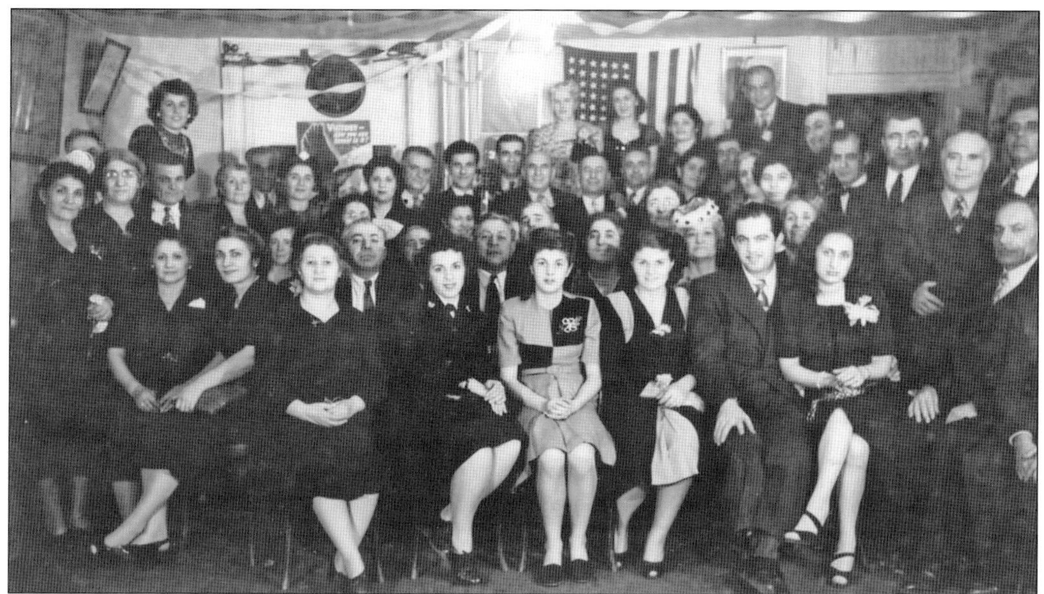

The Assyrian American Association. This picture sits in the office of the Assyrian American Association. It features Lydia Benjamin (front row, center, with the lighter colored dress), with her mother, Blandina Benjamin on her left. Behind Blandina, to her immediate left, is Louise Jacobs wearing a hat. Directly in front of the American flag, standing from left to right, in the lighter colored dress is Emma Jacobs with Margaret Jacobs, Marusa, and Sam Aslan. The third person to Emma's left is her husband, Dave Jacobs. (Courtesy of Shirley Benjamin.)

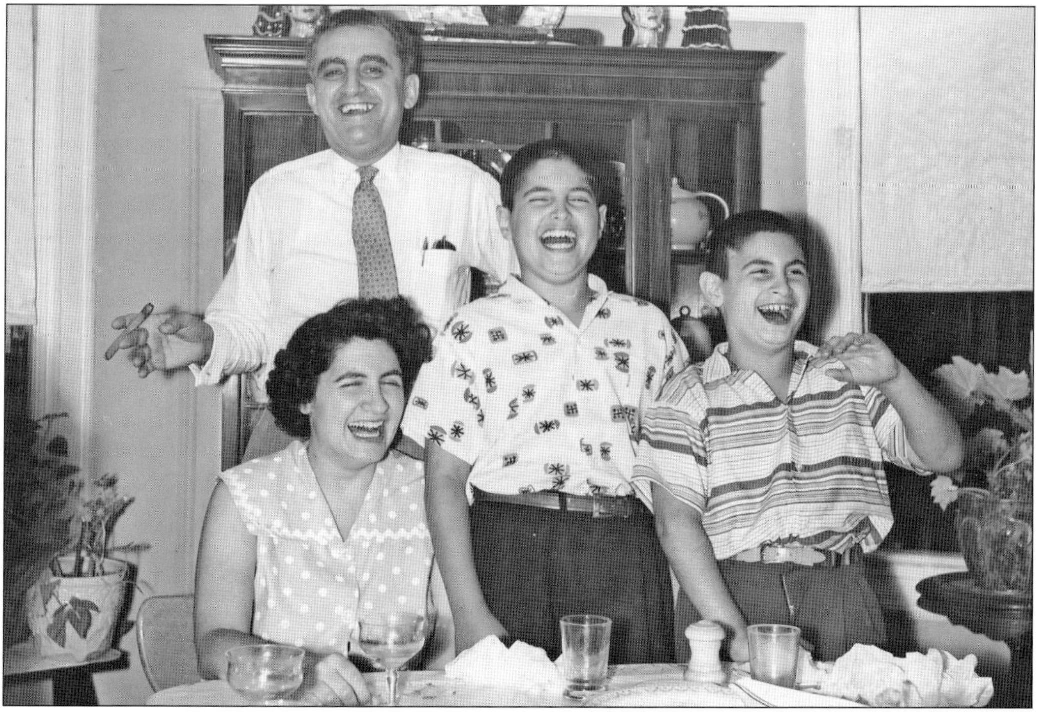

The John Moorad Family. Pictured here is the Moorad family (from left to right): John Sr., Elizabeth, John, and James, in 1960s Yonkers. (Author's collection.)

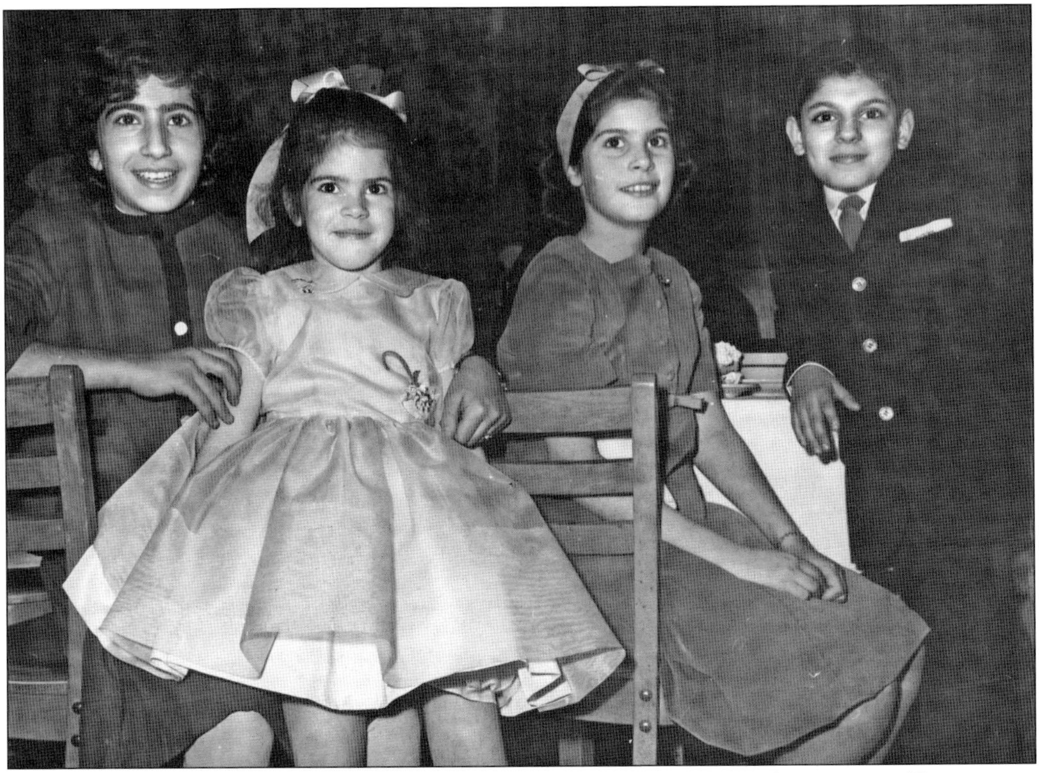

Cousins at Gloria and Eugene Jacobs's Wedding. From left to right are Liz Jacobs, Jean Jacobs, Louise Jacobs, and Karl Jacobs in January 1963. (Author's collection.)

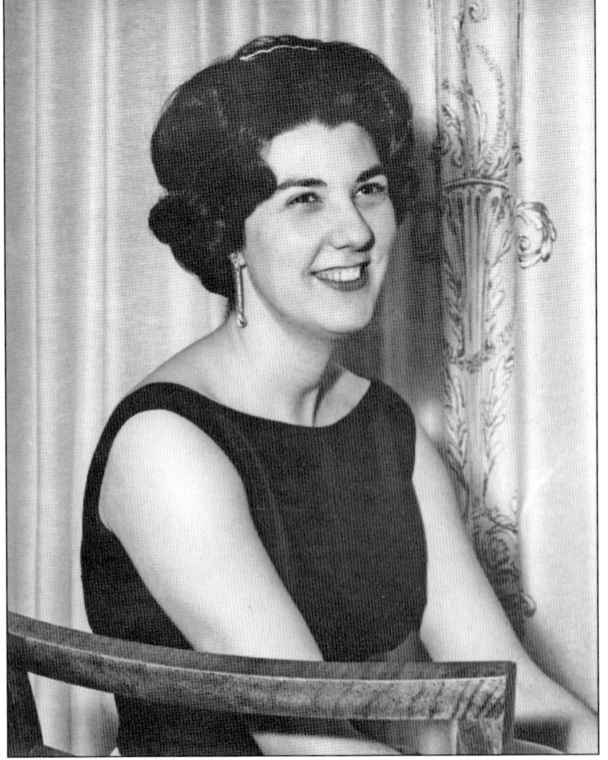

Wedding Ready. Shirley Benjamin poses before the wedding of her cousin Eugene Jacobs to Gloria Greco in January 1963. (Author's collection.)

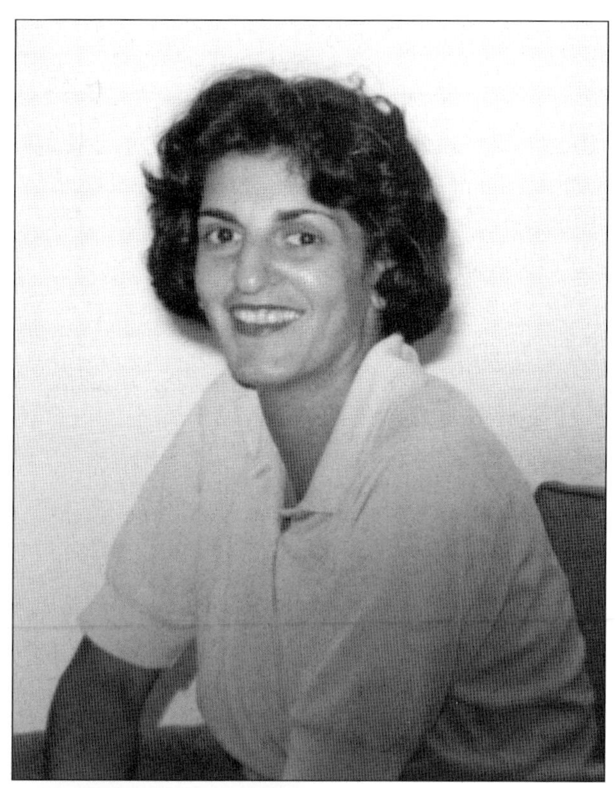

Sue Ameer Jacobs, 1964. Sue Ameer Jacobs poses for the camera at her cousins' home on North Broadway in Yonkers. (Author's collection.)

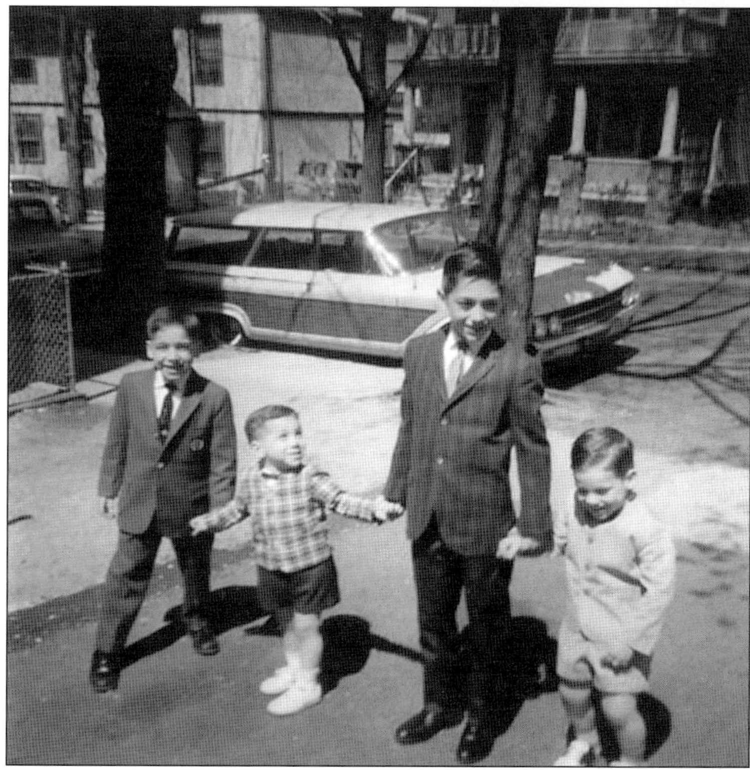

The Muldoon Brothers. Pictured here are, from left to right, Robbie, David, John, and Tommy Muldoon in 1964. (Courtesy of David Muldoon.)

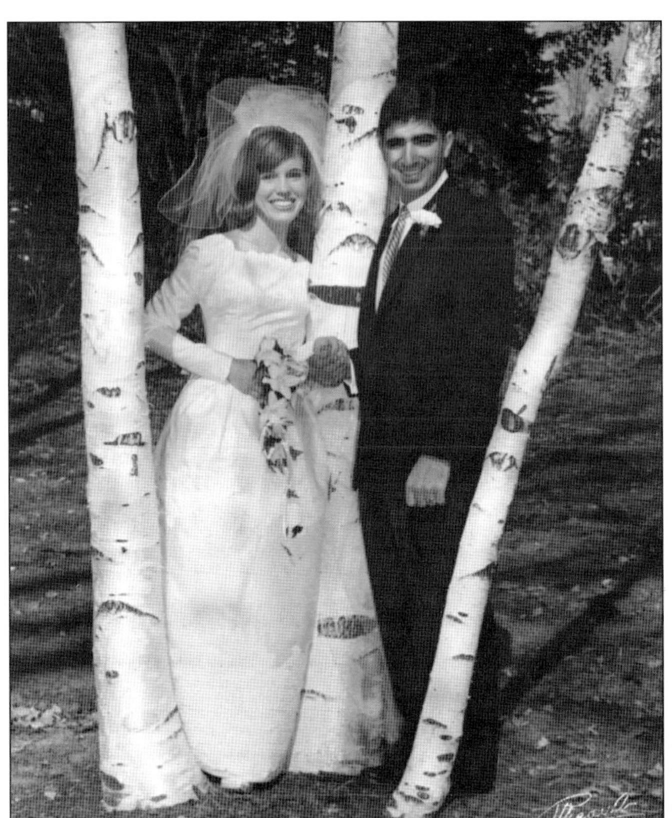

NANCY AND ROGER JACOBS. Pictured on October 24, 1964, in Epsom, New Hampshire, Nancy and Roger (son of Clarence and Margaret Jacobs) wed. (Courtesy of Jean Jacobs Correa.)

BENDER CHILDREN, 1969. From left to right are Te-See, Charly, and Beth, siblings raised in Yonkers on Franklin Avenue several blocks from their grandparents Emma and David Jacobs's home on Belvedere Drive until they moved to Chappaqua in 1973. (Courtesy of Te-See Bender.)

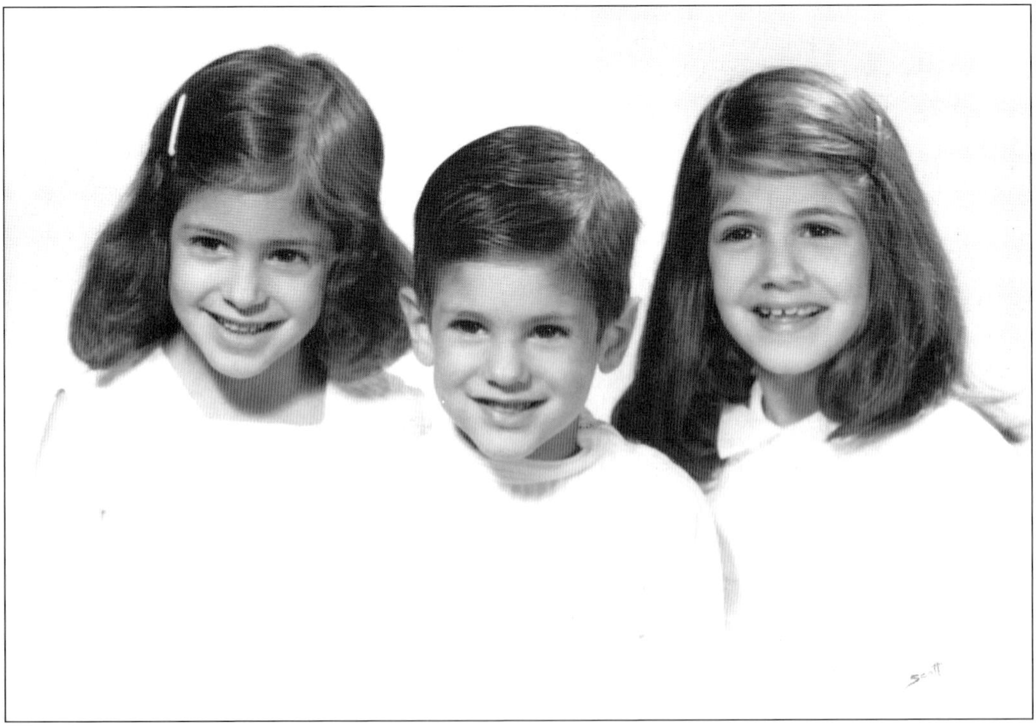

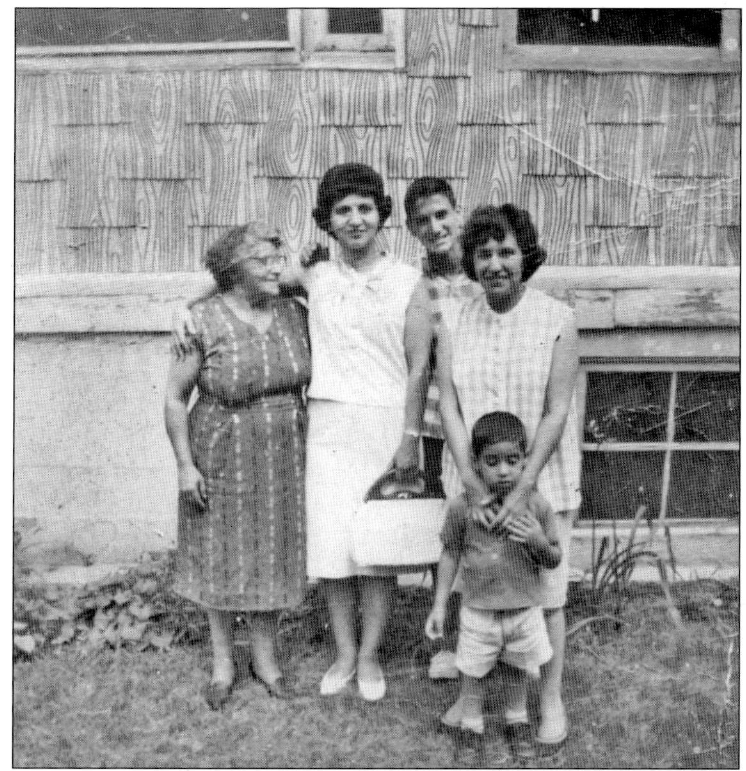

The Nweeia Family. Pictured here are (from left to right) Sophie Nweeia, Nellie Nweeia (Alexander's wife and Sophie's daughter-in-law), unidentified, Lucylle Elias (Sophie's daughter), and Lucylle's son Lance in front of their home at 55 Caroline Avenue in Yonkers in August 1965. (Courtesy of the William and Lilly Sargis family.)

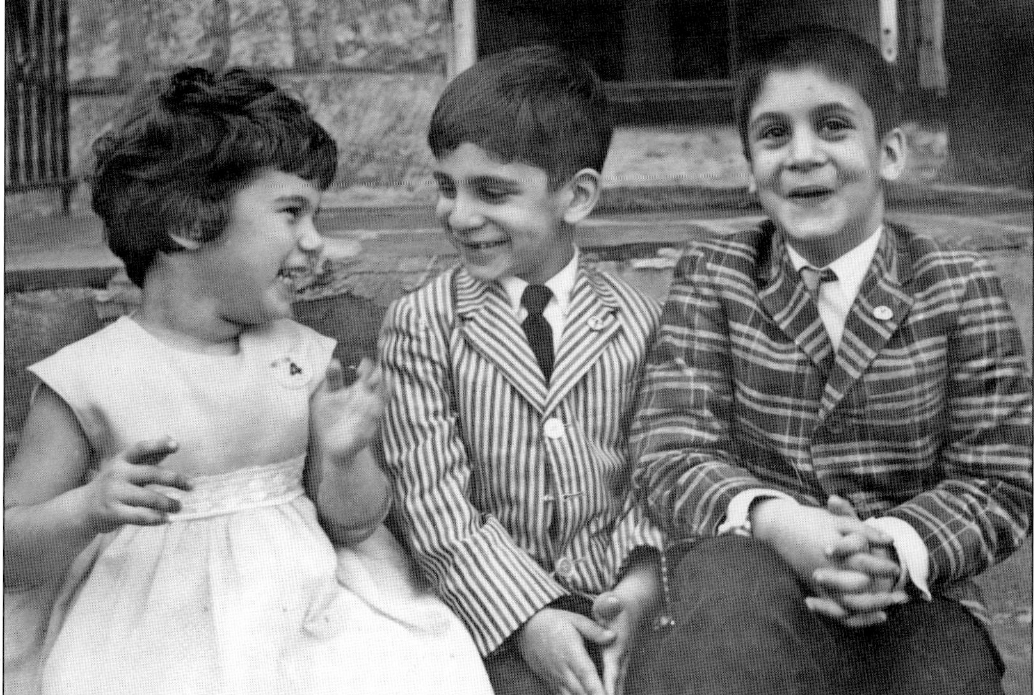

Ruth Kambar's Fourth Birthday. From left to right are cousins Ruth Kambar, John Jacobs, and Mark Jacobs at 89 Travers Avenue in Yonkers in 1967. (Author's collection.)

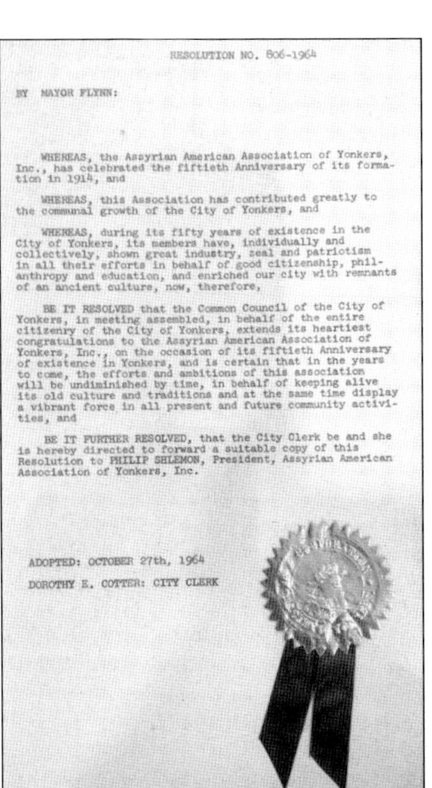

RESOLUTION NO. 806-1964

BY MAYOR FLYNN:

WHEREAS, the Assyrian American Association of Yonkers, Inc., has celebrated the fiftieth Anniversary of its formation in 1914, and

WHEREAS, this Association has contributed greatly to the communal growth of the City of Yonkers, and

WHEREAS, during its fifty years of existence in the City of Yonkers, its members have, individually and collectively, shown great industry, zeal and patriotism in all their efforts in behalf of good citizenship, philanthropy and education, and enriched our city with remnants of an ancient culture, now, therefore,

BE IT RESOLVED that the Common Council of the City of Yonkers, in meeting assembled, in behalf of the entire citizenry of the City of Yonkers, extends its heartiest congratulations to the Assyrian American Association of Yonkers, Inc., on the occasion of its fiftieth Anniversary of existence in Yonkers, and is certain that in the years to come, the efforts and ambitions of this association will be undiminished by time, in behalf of keeping alive its old culture and traditions and at the same time display a vibrant force in all present and future community activities, and

BE IT FURTHER RESOLVED, that the City Clerk be and she is hereby directed to forward a suitable copy of this Resolution to PHILIP SHLEMON, President, Assyrian American Association of Yonkers, Inc.

ADOPTED: OCTOBER 27th, 1964

DOROTHY E. COTTER: CITY CLERK

City of Yonkers Resolution No. 806-1964. Mayor Flynn of Yonkers presented a proclamation by David Jacobs celebrating the 50th anniversary of the Assyrian American Association's formation in 1914 to Philip Shlemon, president of the Assyrian American Association of Yonkers. (Courtesy of Fred Sarkiso.)

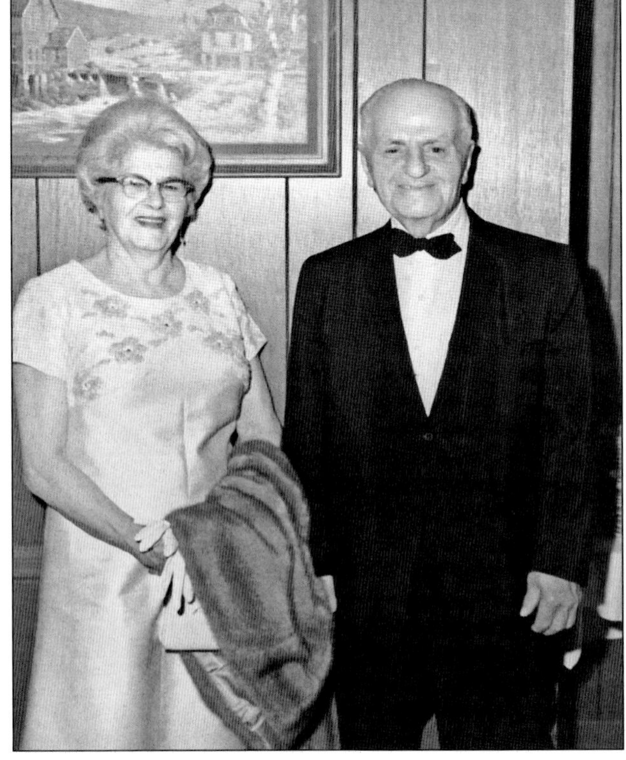

Assyrian Man of the Year David Jacobs, 1969. Pictured here are Emma and Dave Jacobs, known as "Mr. Information" to the Assyrians. He found employment for them, helped them become US citizens, and aided families in setting up homes and bringing family from Iran to Yonkers. Dave was instrumental in founding the first Assyrian National Association of America, organized in Yonkers in 1914. He worked with Rev. Joel E. Warda, Charles Dartley, the Hon. David Perley, Darius Benjamin (of Connecticut), Alex Gabriel (of Pennsylvania), Joseph Durna, and Samuel Aslan (of Yonkers) raising money to send representatives to the League of Nations in France to fight for the Assyrian cause. He was also one of the founders of the Assyrian Federation, an organization that responded to the 1933 massacre of Assyrians in Iraq. (Courtesy of Shirley Benjamin.)

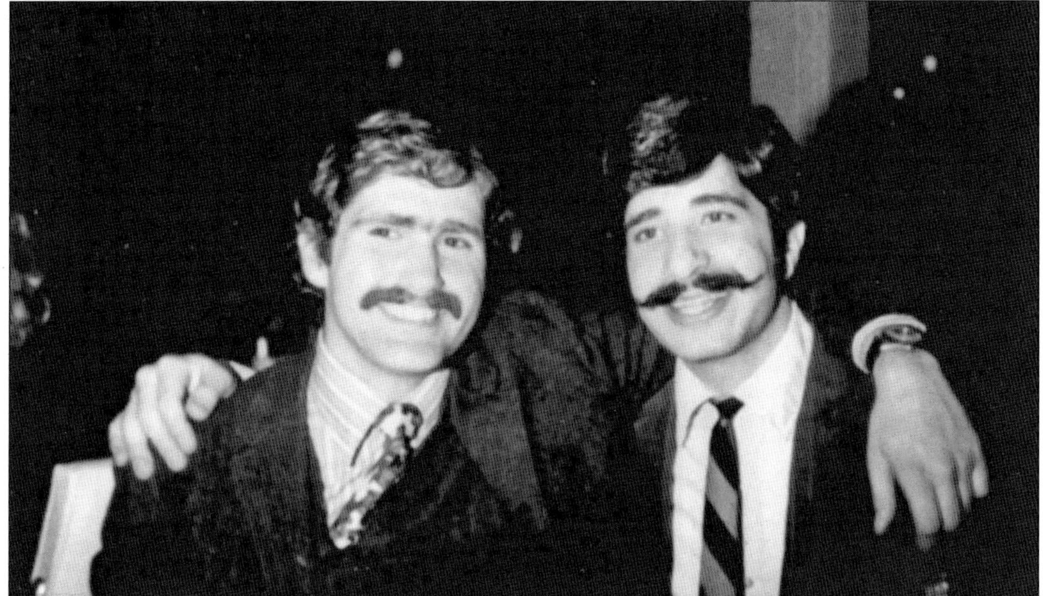

Jacobs Cousins at the Assyrian Man of the Year Celebration. In this photograph (are Billy Jacobs (left) and Kenneth Jacobs at the Assyrian Man of the Year celebration honoring the Assyrian American Association founder, David Jacobs, at the Assyrian American Association (the Assyrian Club) on Ludlow Street in 1969. (Courtesy of Jean Jacobs Correa.)

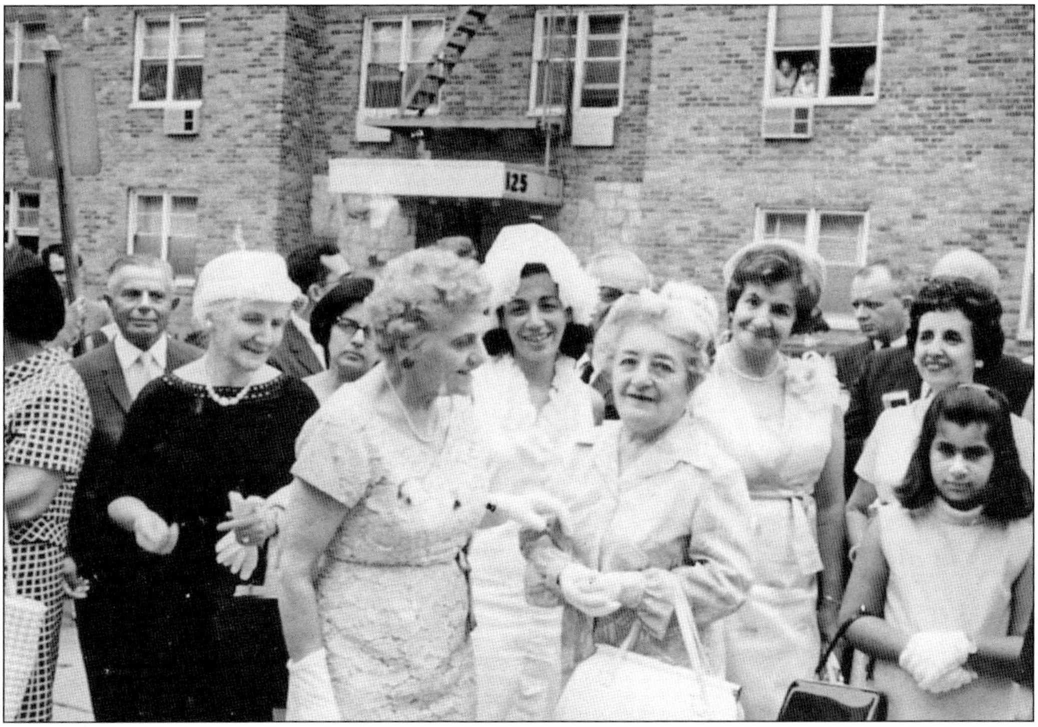

Eleanor Ameer's Wedding, 1968. From left to right outside of the South Presbyterian Church on Radford Street in Yonkers are Rabbi Lucy Shlimoun; unidentified; Nancy Sarmast; Agnes Ameer, mother of the bride; Lucy Sarmast; and Mabel Sayat. (Courtesy of Shirley Benjamin.)

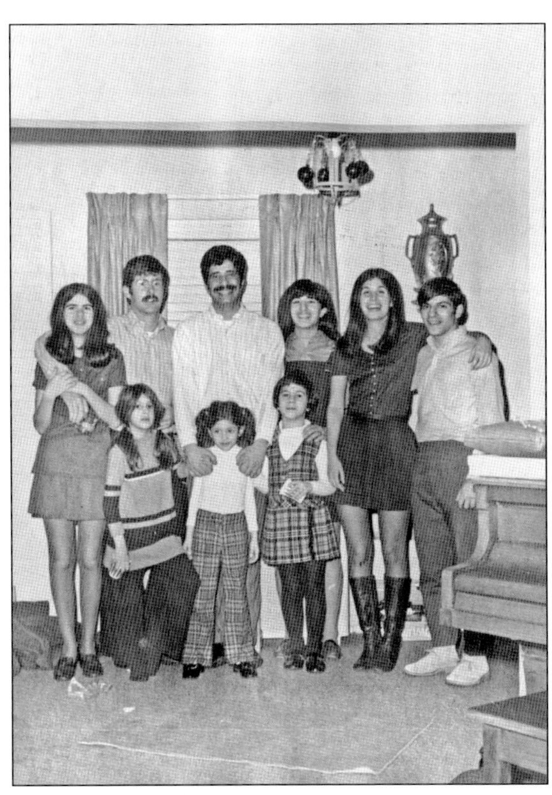

Cousins. From left to right are (first row) Beth Ann Bender, Theresa Bender, and Ruth Kambar; (second row) Jean Jacobs, Billy Jacobs, Kenneth Jacobs, Liz Jacobs, Louise Jacobs, and Karl Jacobs. They are pictured in 1970–1971 at 120 Franklin Avenue in Yonkers. (Author's collection.)

Sophie Alkas Nweeia. She owned a three-family house at 55 Caroline Avenue. She is pictured celebrating her 80th birthday. (Courtesy of the William and Lilly Sargis family.)

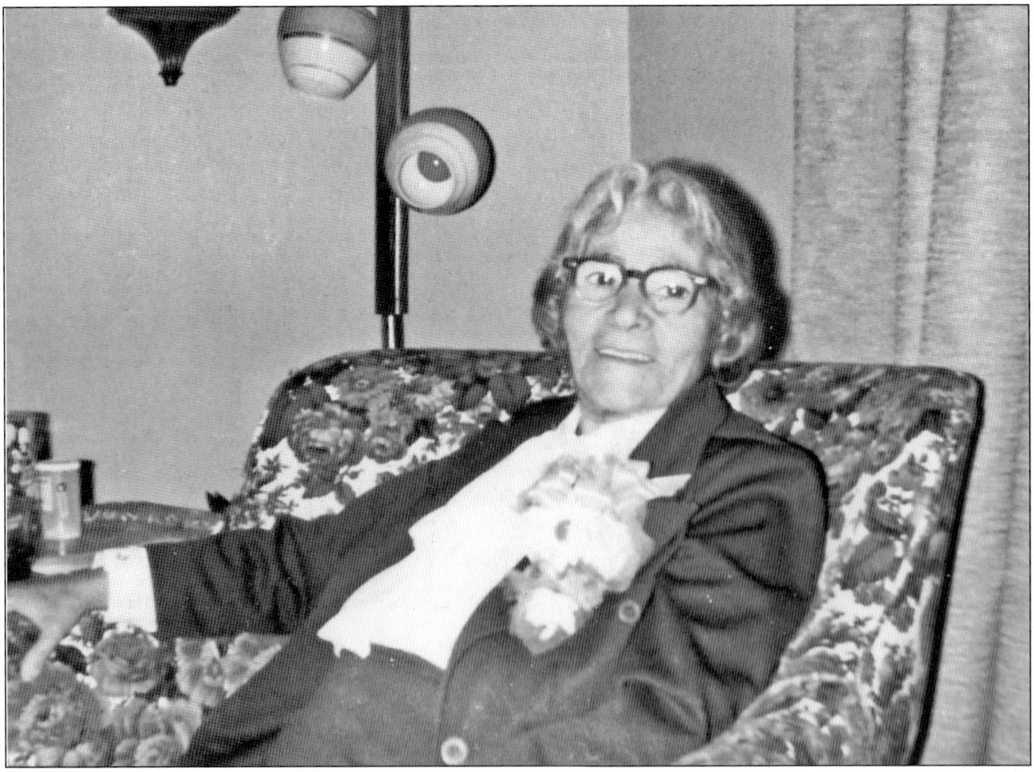

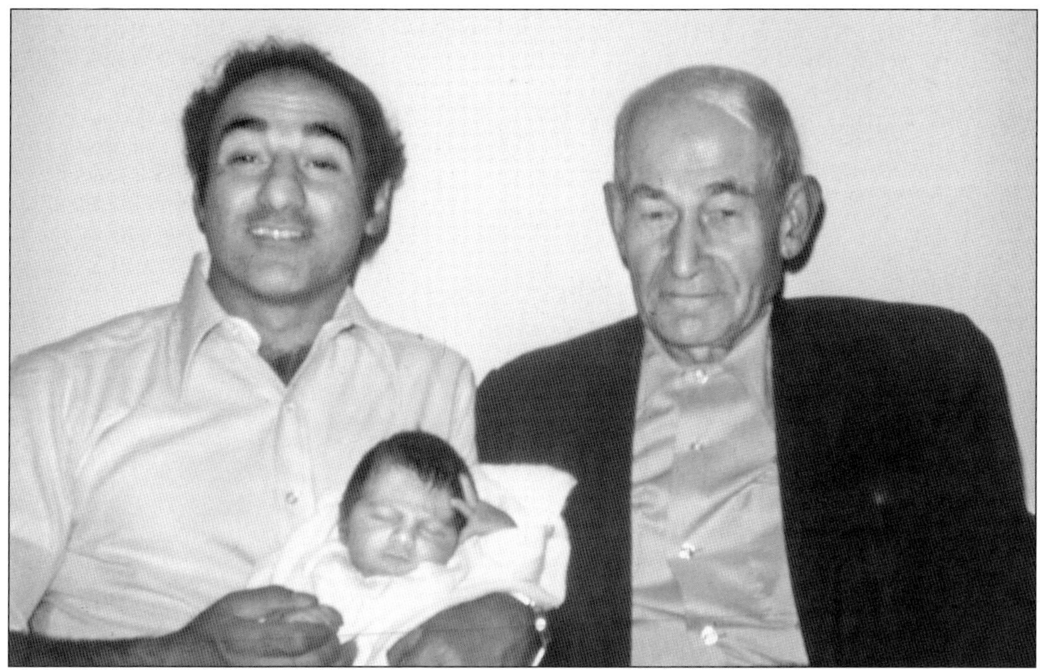

Three Generations. In 1970, Kenneth Kambar holds his baby girl, Kelly Anne, while sitting next to his father, Yonan Kambar. (Author's collection.)

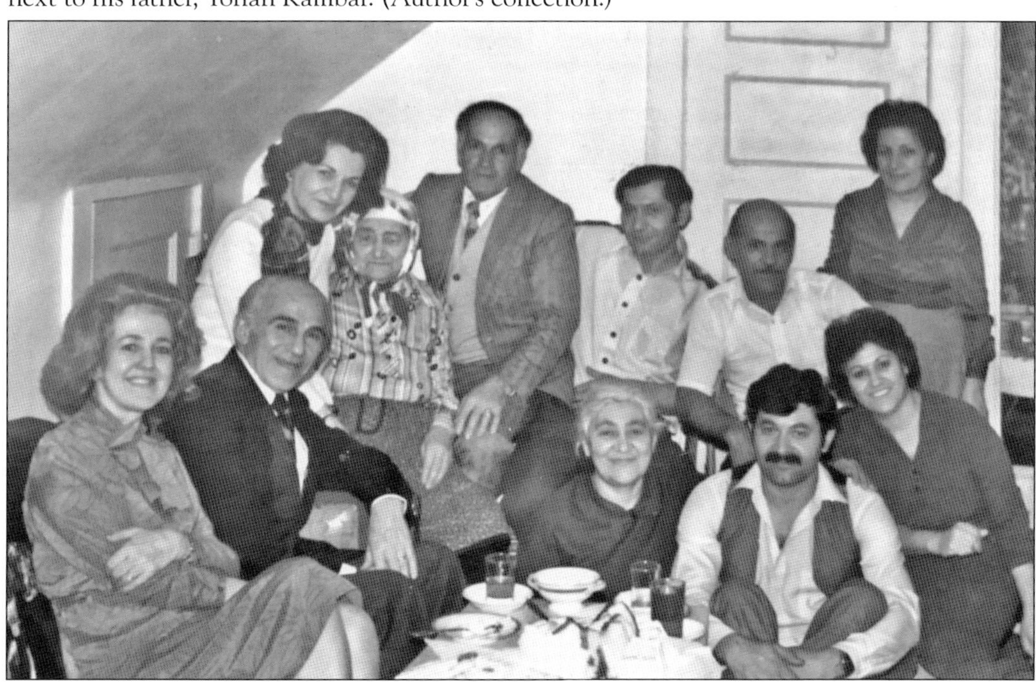

The Gevargis Family. Pictured on Highland Avenue in Yonkers in 1973 are, from left to right, Emma; her husband, Harold; Dorothy and Lilly (friends of the family); Nanajan; William Babayi (Jacquie and Josephine's father); Yosib Gevargis; Gevarges Mirza (Betty and Sarge's father); Shamo (kneeling in front of him); Julian Gevargis (wearing vest); and Beatrice Georges-Gevargis (white hair). (Courtesy of Juliet Gevargis-Mizimakoski.)

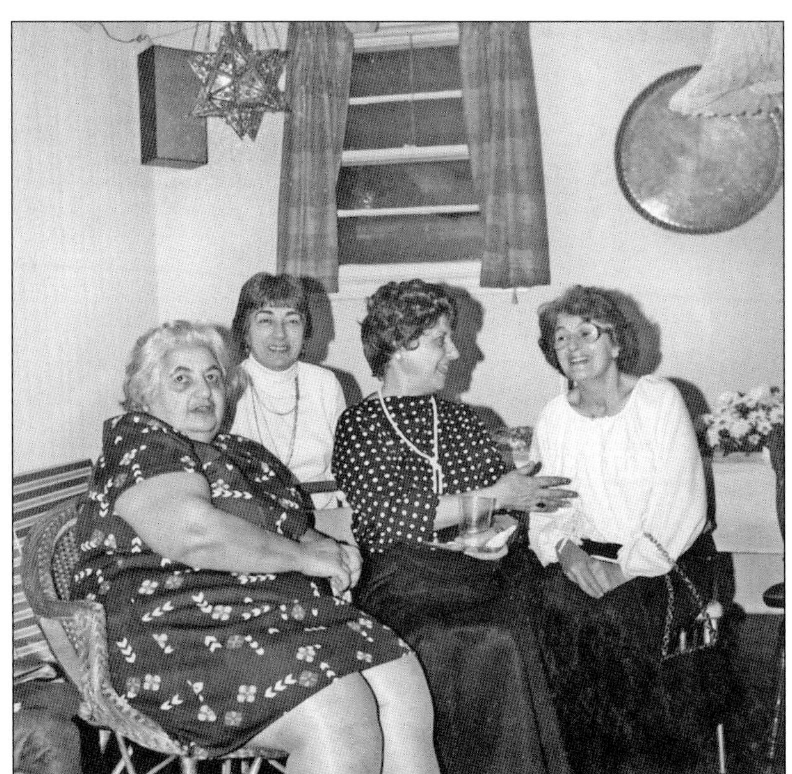

THE BENJAMINS' 50TH WEDDING ANNIVERSARY. Pictured are (from left to right) Florence Jacobs Gabriel, Betty Benjamin Muldoon, Elaine Sulliman Koelsch (from New Britain, Connecticut), and Elizabeth Jacobs Bender in 1978 at 89 Travers Avenue in Yonkers. (Author's collection.)

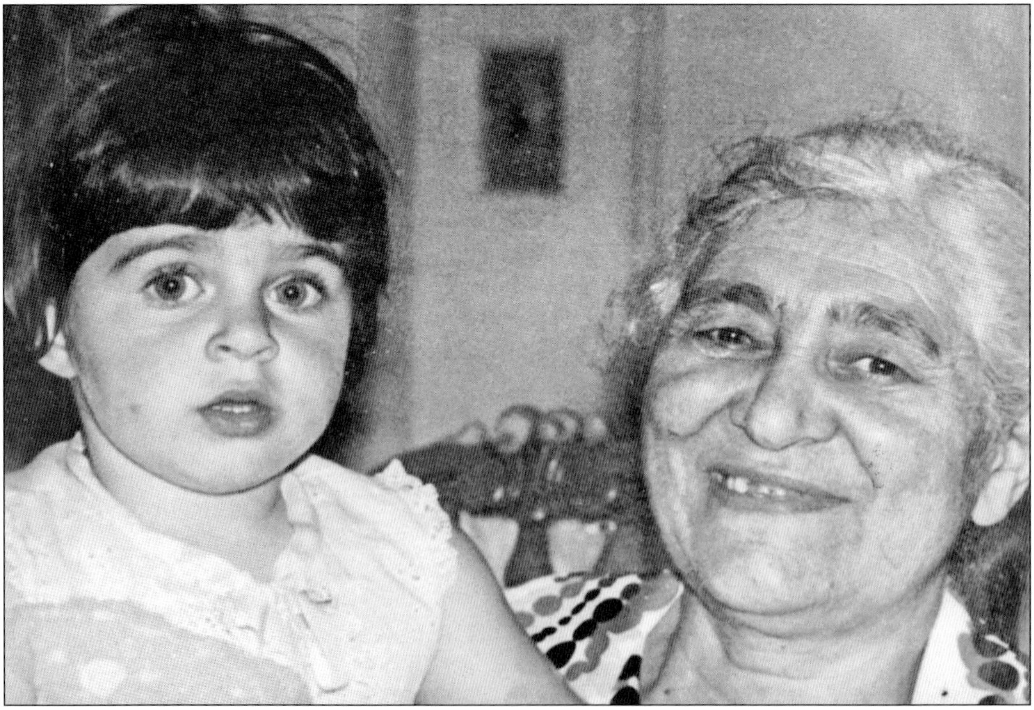

GRANDMOTHER AND GRANDDAUGHTER. Beatrice Gevargis holds her granddaughter Juliet Gevargis in Yonkers in 1982. (Courtesy of Juliet Gevargis.)

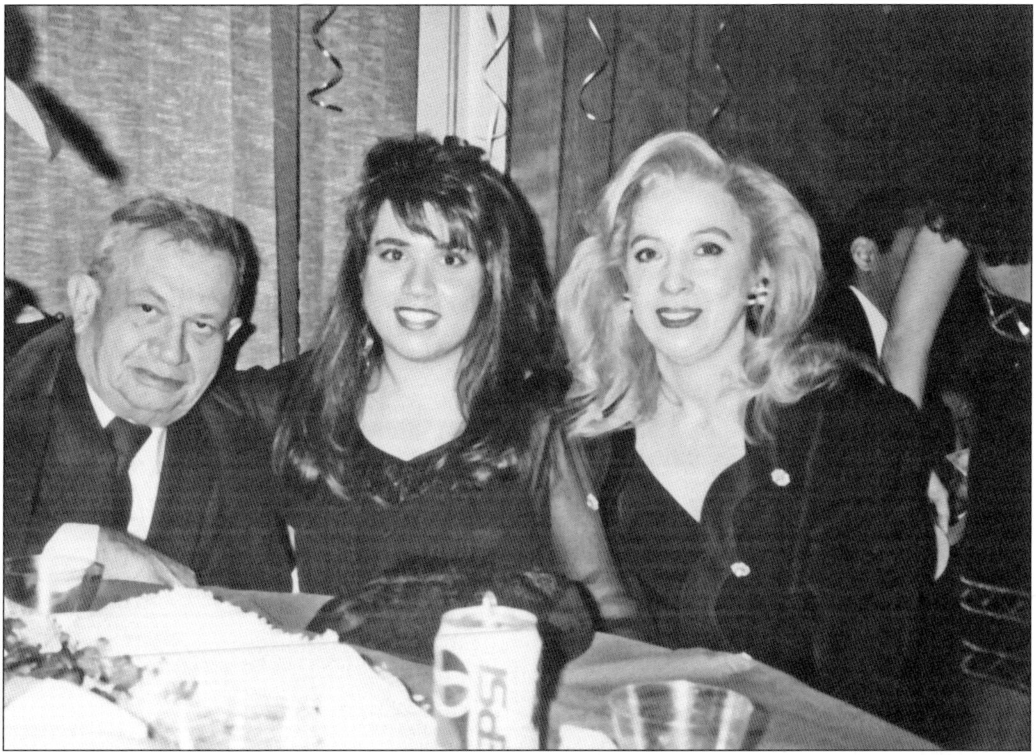

THE SARGISS FAMILY. Pictured are (from left to right) Ike, Alina, and Drieda at the Assyrian American Association at 82 Ludlow Street on December 31, 1995. (Courtesy of Susy Gevarguize.)

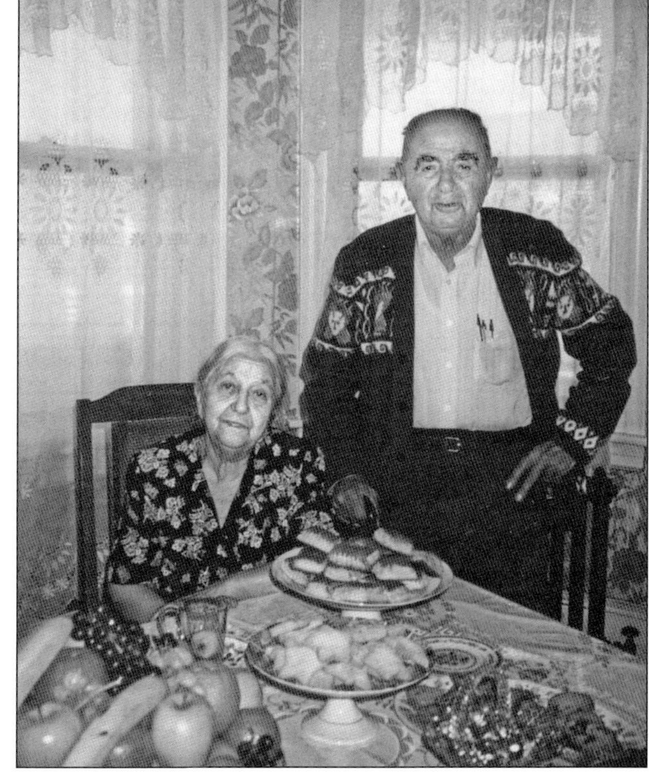

NANA AND SAVOO. Pictured at 27 Radford Street in Yonkers on Easter Sunday, April 11, 1993, are Noosha Zaya (keeping her maiden name) and her husband, Goriel Essapour. (Courtesy of Susy Gevarguize.)

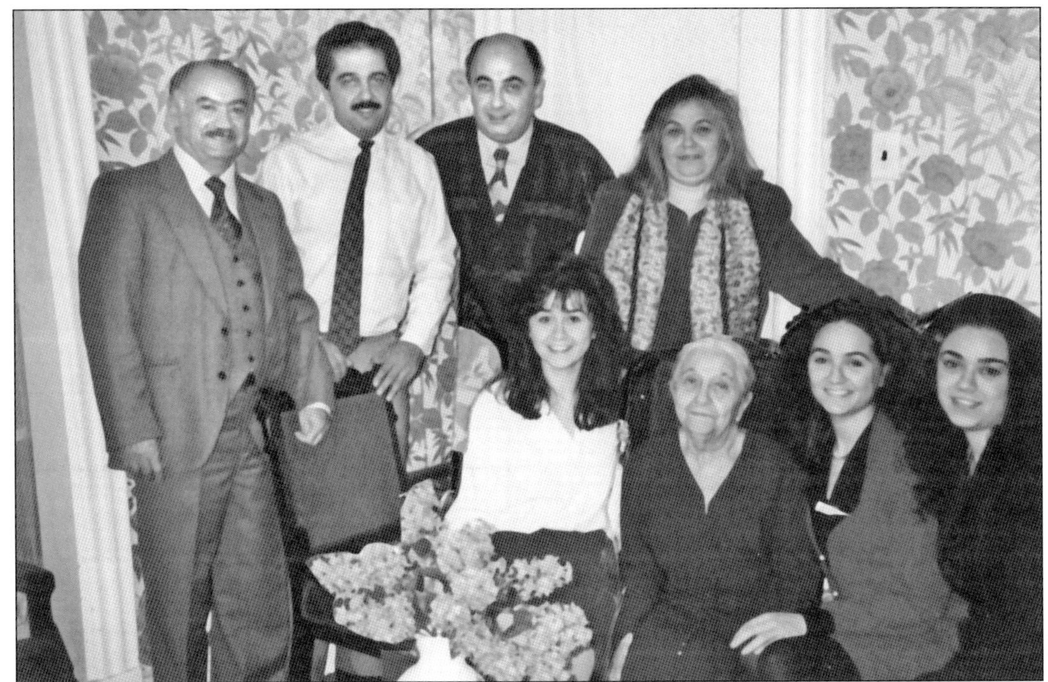

FAMILY PHOTOGRAPH. From left to right are (seated) Susy Gevarguize, Noosha Zaya, Sandra Gevarguize, and Stella Gevarguize; (standing) Sorishoo Gevarguize, Edmond Essapour, William Essapour, and Svetlana Gevarguize in 1995. (Courtesy of Susy Gevarguize.)

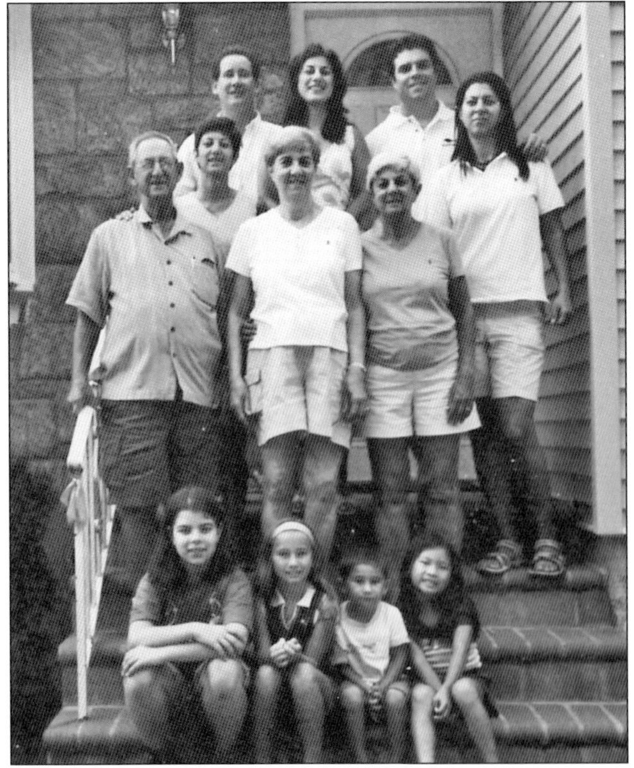

THE KAMBAR FAMILY. From left to right are (first row) cousins Emily Silvestri, Nicole Lydia Carpenter, Nicole's brother Maxwell Carpenter, and Emily's sister Teresa Silvestri; (second row) William Kambar, Shirley Benjamin, and Lydia Benjamin Kambar; (third row) William's daughter Kim Kambar Carpenter and Lydia's daughter Carol Kambar Silvestri; (fourth row) Bruce Carpenter, Ruth Kambar, and Todd Silvestri. This photograph was taken at 89 Travers Avenue in Yonkers in the summer of 2006. (Author's collection.)

Four

The Assyrian Churches

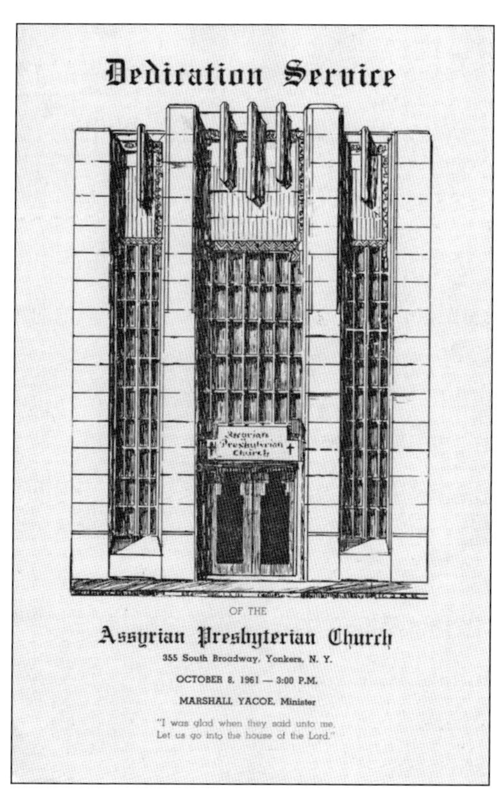

Assyrian Presbyterian Church Dedication. This pamphlet is from the October 8, 1961, dedication of the Assyrian Presbyterian Church at 355 South Broadway in Yonkers. The congregation purchased its first church building, a former County Trust Bank, for $25,000 in cash. This edifice was the first church the 40-year-old congregation had owned. Before the South Broadway address, the congregation shared a church space with the Hungarian Presbyterian Church on Jackson Street in Yonkers. Rev. Marshall Yacoe spoke to the congregation and guests from the Presbytery of Hudson River, Yonkers, and relatives of the Yacoe family, including his sister Shalem Badel, his nephew Rev. G. Pera from Baltimore, and relatives from Chicago. (Courtesy of Shirley Benjamin.)

A Brief Sketch of Some of the Work Accomplished in Persia

by the

Rev. David J. Benjamin

My parents were Assyrians and were taken by good missionaries out of the Kurdistan Mountains to be educated in the very deep doctrine of the Holy Scriptures and to teach and preach the sweet name of Jesus as the only Saviour and Mediator, among the Assyrians and Kurds.

I was ten years old when suddenly our house was surrounded by a large group of Kurds, who, in the name of their prophet, wanted to kill my father, because he was preaching the religion of Jesus Christ. One of these Kurds went to the roof, made a hole in it, and shot my father and mother. I screamed when I saw my father fall, and my aunt, hearing me, took me in her arms, got me out of the house, and hid me in a hole dug in the ground in which we baked our bread and cooked our meals. They had come to kill me also, but could not find me. After the Kurds had shot my parents, they broke into our home and hit my father and mother with many daggers.

My two sisters, fifteen and four years old, together with myself had no one to look to, but my oldest sister, with tears streaming down her face, was telling us we must trust in God, for He would be our father and would gather us together and take care of us. We had no earthly father or mother, no bread to eat, no bed to sleep in, and no voice to speak to us. It was hard for little children like us to understand it all. For one year, our uncles looked after us and then Dr. Stocking, a friend of father, took us to Urmia City and saved our lives from the cruel Kurds. Although we were safe now, we had further trouble, that of being separated. I was sent to the town school. In the summer I worked for one of the missionaries and in Winter, I went to school. I was in High School for four years; then I went to college to prepare for the ministry, which was my aim. I studied four years in college. After finishing my theological course, Dr. Shedd and Dr. Cochran wished me to study medicine, but I refused, because I wanted to take the place of my father and preach salvation in Jesus Christ.

The first year after I finished college, I was sent to examine the schools in all towns in the plains of Urmia. The plains of Urmia are divided into three Rivers: City River, Nazloo, and Borandoose River. I had to go to all these rivers walking with a full bag of copy books for the schools and churches to keep the records. I had to go through snow and I was very much afraid. I finished my work, and then went into the house, which was so cold as there was no fire inside. The only kind of furnace was in the ground and ladies were sitting there, so I had to sit under the wall, so from that day until now, I suffer great pains with my back.

The second year, I was teaching and preaching in a village near the college. I had a congregation of over 150 persons and a school of from 40 to 50 children.

The third year, I was sent to Turkey to teach in the High School. It was a journey of four days on foot from Urmia. After I got there, I had a great deal of opposition. I only stayed there two months as I was afraid of being arrested by the Turks. I left the town at night, going back to Urmia. I was walking the whole night, all alone. I was near to a Kurds town The sun came out; suddenly I was held by two Kurds who tried to rob me. I did not surrender. Then one of them hit me under the ear with the handle of his dagger. I fell down unconscious. While I was lying there, they took all my clothes and some money that I had and put some of their clothes on me. After a long time, I regained consciousness. Shivering from the cold, I prayed for God's help, and started for Urmia City with great difficulty. I reached an Assyrian village where I asked for some bread and told them who I was. They gave me some clothes to put on, and after three days and nights, I reached Urmia City sick, bruised, and wounded.

The fourth year, again I was sent toTurkey to teach and preach. Again I was not successful. There had been some murder there and the head of the town was arrested by the Turks and the people could not do anything without him. Also there were some hindrances on account of religion but I stayed all that winter, in a cold house, preaching the gospel and in the Spring went down to Urmia and gave my report to the missionaries. It was nearing the time when I should begin my real service for the Lord. The next summer I was ordained a minister to preach in the town of Seir, a place on the slope of the mountains. A summer town for all missionaries and landlords. Here I began to build the church of our Lord. The church was full every Sunday and the landlords were coming to hear God's word. The first year, I rested although I had too many guests. The second year, the Kurds knew that I was there and every night I had from 10 to 100 Kurds in my house; they were eating and sleeping in my house for days and weeks, and when they left, they would take anything in my house that they wanted for themselves.

Difficulties increased in my service from time to time between Christians and Islam. Many times they came to kill me and my family. I had to flee for my life to another town where the Kurds could not reach me. On this flight it was a dark night and I went through the mountains and valleys which were full of thorns. My face, hands, and feet were bleeding and my body was scratched.

So in my 39 years of service before and after I was ordained to the ministry, I always have been in danger. One hand has always been on the gun and the other on the

REV. DAVID JACOB BENJAMIN'S RESUME. This pamphlet served as an introduction to Reverend Benjamin's evangelical ministry. It also served as a resume, with an autobiographical sketch and personal references from other Presbyterian ministers. (Both, courtesy of Nicholas Benjamin.)

Bible. Three times I was wounded on both sides, have been hurt many times, and many times left without anything and always fleeing here and there for fear of being murdered. One of our good people from Kurdistan heard that the Kurds had decided to capture all of my family and torment us bitterly until they were freed. Word was sent to Dr. Cochrane that I could never stay in Seir, so when I received this word, I left immediately and came to America with nothing, leaving my family behind. I did not intend to stay in this country, but I found I could not go back.

PERSONAL REFERENCES

AS a missionary of the Presbyterian Board of Foreign Missions, stationed in Persia for over forty years, I have personally known my friend and brother, Rev. David Benjamin for many years. He was educated in the Presbyterian Schools of Urmia and is a graduate of our Theological Seminary. Later he was ordained and stationed in various fields where he did most faithful work for our Board. His own father was killed by the Kurds while preaching the gospel.

I gladly commend him to the churches. He himself was persecuted and injured by the Kurds. He comes from a family which has done marvelous missionary work.

REV. FREDERICK COAN, D.D.
2315 Irving Avenue
South Minneapolis, Minn.

PERMIT me to say that the Rev. David J. Benjamin is a most effective speaker. I commend him favorably to the churches and missionary societies who desire a speaker to present the work among the Assyrians or the Orient. For some years he was in charge of our Persian-Assyrian Mission in Philadelphia where he rendered most efficient service.

WILLIAM P. FULTON, D.D.
Supt. of Church Extension
Philadelphia Presbytery.

I AM glad to commend the Rev. David Benjamin to any church or women's missionary societies which would like to hear a thrilling and stirring message. To few is given the glory of bearing on their bodies wounds received in trying to win others to Christ. Rev. Benjamin is a commanding speaker and our congregation were both instructed and inspired by his message.

DOUGLASS BUCHANAN, D.D.
South Presbyterian Church
Yonkers, N. Y.

The Rev. Benjamin Will Give Any One of the Following Addresses:

Habits and Customs in Persia
Presbyterian Work Among the Assyrians
The Story of My Life and Work Among the Kurds
The Problem of The Far East
The Crucified Nation

FINANCIAL:—An Offering of Appreciation is the only Financial Requirement.

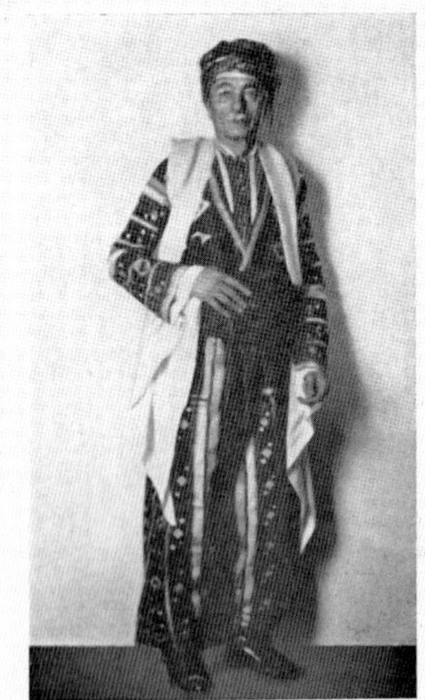

Photo by P. Stephens, Yonkers, N. Y.

REV. DAVID J. BENJAMIN
Assyrian Missionary — Evangelist
389 Riverdale Avenue
YONKERS, N. Y.

Available for Missionary Societies, Prayer Meetings or Evening Services

The History of Missionary Rev. David Jacob Benjamin. This page indicates the religious suffering at the hands of the Kurds and the difficult journey that Assyrian evangelist Rev. David Jacob Benjamin from Urmia experienced as he created an international network in support of his religious school for Assyrian and Kurdish boys in the Kurdistan mountains. His travels to Holland, Sweden, Wales, and the United States furthered his mission. The network of ministers he created also helped him eventually come to preach in the United States. (Author's collection.)

INTRODUCTION

Missionary and Evangelist, Rev. Jacob is the son of late Pastor Jacob, the native pioneer missionary of Tagawar, Kurdistan, who labored in his Master's cause for fifty-five years, when he indured many persecutions and hardships, and lately been killed with his wife for the sake of his Master, by these cruel kurds, and his property plundered and his house burned. The history of the family and labors with many severe experienced persecutions, hardships and sufferings, reads like a romance.

Rev. Jacob visited Holland in 1906 in the hope to interest the Christian friends in the work for which his father suffered so much. He was warmly received by the Christian friends and was greatly encouraged when he returned to his country, and he became engaged by preaching the Gospel only for Kurds, and in opening a school to educate them to Christianity.

In 1910 he added a new branch to his work by opening a school for persecuted Christians in Russia Armawir, with a congregation to whom he was preaching and teaching for two years, with great sufferings and hardships. The work has been generously and voluntarily supported by the Christian friends in Holland for the last seven years.

3

Kurds, by teaching them a profession in Christ Jesus as their Saviour and Redeemer, and to save many precious souls from under the power of Mohamed and bring them to Jesus.

Rev. Jacob is hoping to extend this much valued work of preaching and teaching the Christ Jesus among the Kurds Mohamedans having faith in God and His people who are anxious for God's Kingdom to come among the Kurds too, as they also have precious and eternal souls. To assist this great cause, read Matthew 28, etc.

Present needs: A sum of $8000 is urgently needed and $1000 annually is wanted, to have some more schools, teachers, and school house, etc.

Rev. Jacob is at present in this country endeavoring to enlist the sympathy of the Christian friends in this new and blessed work for the Kurds. He will be glad to address meetings in the churches and drawing-room meetings with the purpose of getting friends to help him in his work. He will be also glad to get some annual subscribers, and some individual who would undertake to keep and support one of the teachers of the school. $30 will support one teacher for six months and $120 for one year.

The prayers of the Christian friends are asked in behalf of this branch of work of the spreading of the Word of salvation to those dark Kurds, who are still sitting and dwelling in the valley of sin and death.

Rev. David Jacob's letter and appeal to Christian friends

Address in care of Rev. J. E. Davies, Nanticoke, Pa.

Dear friends:

In presenting to you this little report of my work, may I have the favour to ask your kind perusal of it, which I hope you will find interesting. I will be very glad to meet with the Lord's people who would be glad to encourage and help me in my work of faith

8

for Kurds Mohamedans. First of all I need your earnest prayer that the Lord may according to His will direct me to carry on His work; and I also need your sympathetic assistance to go on with this work of establishing schools and preaching the Word of God among the Kurds Mohamedans." Let God's ways be opened in Kurds also" as they are a wild tribe, and dark people in the world of God. Annual subscriptions and special donations will be thankfully received and acknowledged by me in this country to the care of Rev. T. E. Davies, Walsh Baptist minister, Nanticoke, Pa. Also please send to Mr. Thomas W. Boettner, Wyoming, Pa.

Yours in Christ,

Rev. David Jacob.

Rev. David Jacob's School—Hydarloowi, Kurdistan, Persia

9

Reverend Benjamin's Call for Support. This page continues the letter found on the previous page describing Reverend Benjamin's mission, travels, and fundraising efforts to build schools in Urmia, to staff them, and to stock them with school supplies. Reverend Benjamin made it his personal mission to educate Assyrian and Kurdish children and to bring them to salvation. (Author's personal collection.)

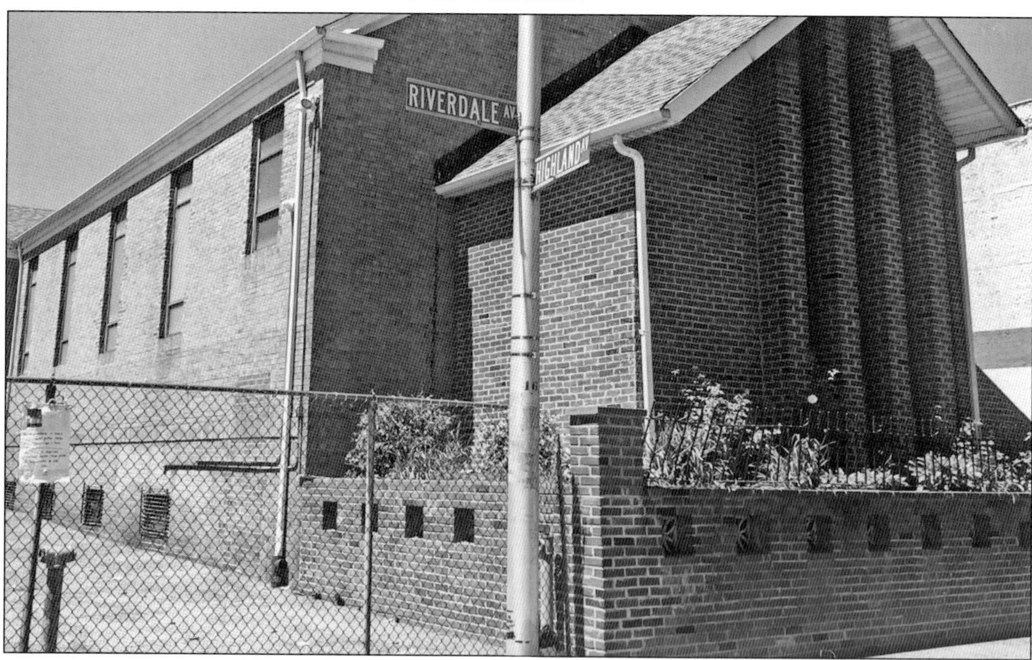

Yonkers Church at the Corner of Riverdale and Highland Avenues. Rev. David Jacob Benjamin held services in Assyrian at this church. Before coming to Yonkers, he preached at Gaston Presbyterian Church in Philadelphia. He also preached at the site of the first Assyrian Presbyterian Church on Jackson Street in Yonkers. (Author's collection.)

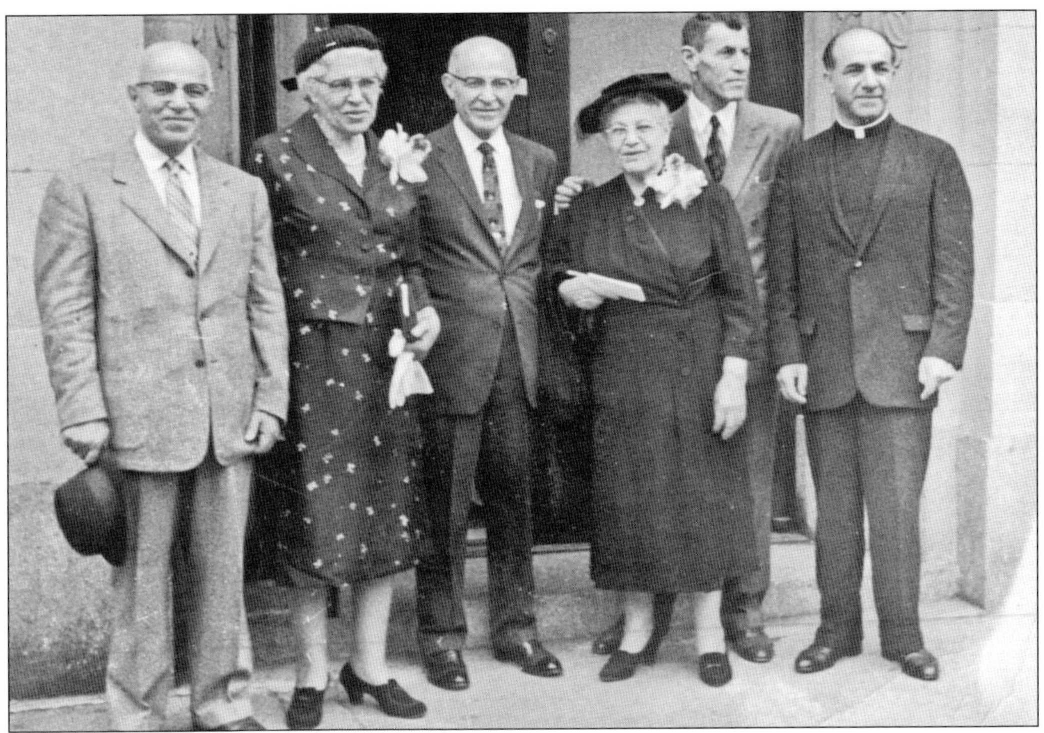

Dedication of the Assyrian Presbyterian Church, 355 South Broadway. Pictured here from left to right are Eshoo, Shalem, Rev. Marshall Yacoe (Qasha of the Assyrian Presbyterian Church), Shushan, her son Jesse, and Rev. Richard Pera on October 8, 1961. (Courtesy of Kathy Yacoe.)

THE CHURCH DIRECTORY

REVEREND MARSHALL YACOE, *Minister*

MRS. WILLIAM H. DAVIDSON, *Choir Director*

THE BOARD OF ELDERS

EPRIM AMEER	BABA DAVID
DARIUS BABA, SR.	ROBERT NWEEIA, *Clerk*
NATHANIEL BABA	WILLIAM SARGIS
THEODORE BENJAMIN	JOSEPH P. SARGIS

T. M. SOLEIMAN, *Treasurer*

THE BOARD OF TRUSTEES

NORMAN BABA	BISMARK MALICK
NICHOLAS BENJAMIN	JOSEPH P. SARGIS, *Secretary*
NORMAN DAVID	T. M. SOLEIMAN, *President*

THE WOMEN'S MISSIONARY SOCIETY

MRS. SHALEM BADEL .... *President*
MRS. LOUISE JACOBS .... *Vice President*
MRS. KATE BADAL .... *Secretary*
MRS. EMMA JACOBS .... *Treasurer*

THE YOUTH FELLOWSHIP

FRANKLIN AMEER .... *President*
FRED SOLEIMAN .... *Vice President*
NANCY BADAL .... *Secretary*
MARY SOLEIMAN .... *Corresponding Secretary*
NORMAN DAVID .... *Treasurer*

Dedication Bulletin of the Assyrian Presbyterian Church, October 9, 1961. Listed here are the church clergy, officers, and members of the missionary and youth organizations. (Courtesy of the William and Lilly Sargis family.)

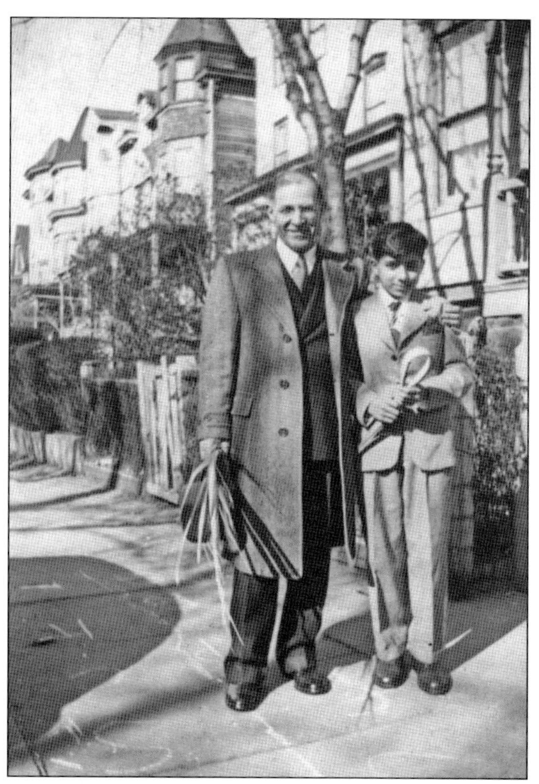

Palm Sunday and Confirmation Day, Yonkers. Rev. Marshall Yacoe (left) is pictured with John Ameer on the day of his confirmation in 1948. (Courtesy of Kathy Yacoe.)

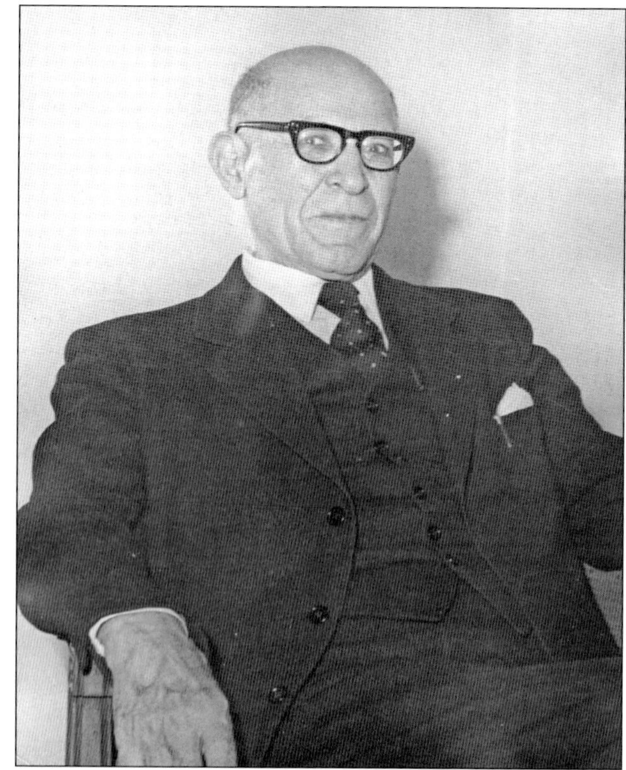

Qasha Marshall Yacoe. Marshall Yacoe, the minister of the Assyrian Presbyterian Church on South Broadway, is pictured in the home of William and Lydia Kambar in Yonkers in the 1960s. (Author's collection.)

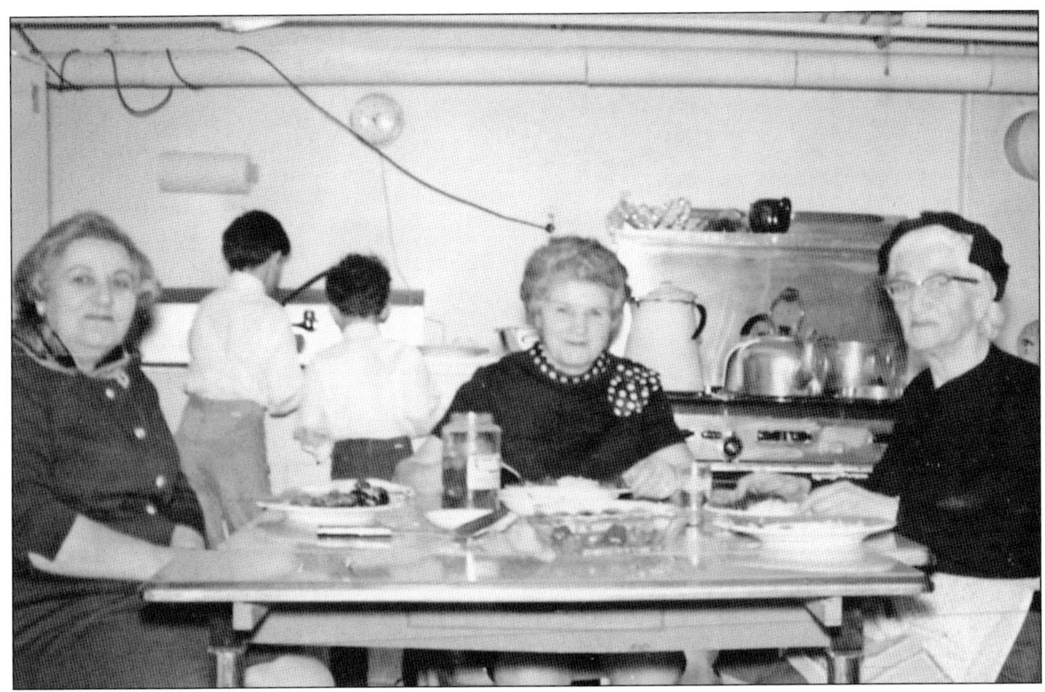

Assyrian Presbyterian Church Kitchen, Yonkers. From left to right are Suria Soleiman, Blandina Benjamin, and Louise Jacobs. In the background are two unidentified boys. The congregation often enjoyed Assyrian meals prepared in this kitchen. (Author's collection.)

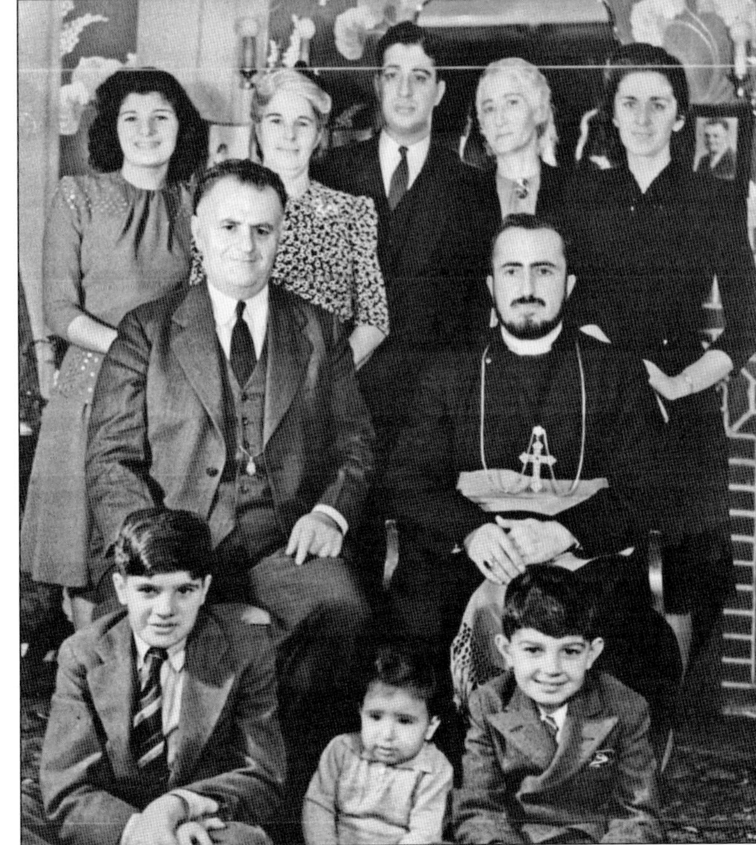

His Beatitude Mar Eshai Shimun XXIII with the Jacobs Family, 1940. From left to right are (first row) John, Roger, and Eugene Jacobs; (second row) David Jacobs and Mar Eshaii Shimun XXIII; (third row) Elizabeth, Emma, Clarence, Louise, and Margaret Jacobs. (Courtesy of Shirley Benjamin.)

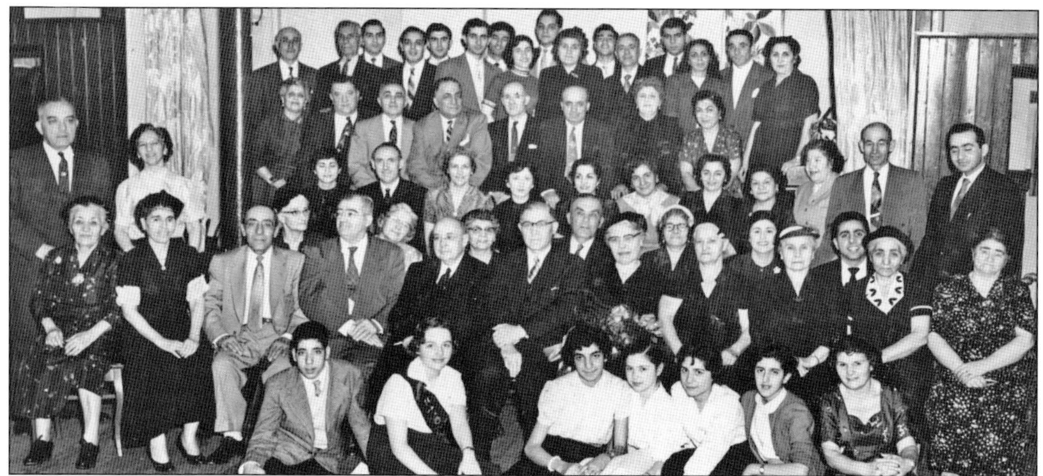

The Assyrian Presbyterian Church Congregation, 1955–1956. From left to right are (first row) Franklin Ameer, Leslie Davidson, Eleanor Ameer, Carol ?, Marleen Oushalim, Estelle Vitti, and Blandina Benjamin; (second row) Elizabeth "Isha" Sargis, Esther Baboo David, Baba David, Theodore Benjamin Ardashier, Qasha Dalyawish, Qasha Marshall Yacoe, Shalem Yacoe, two unidentified, and Terlan Elia; (third row) Darius Baba, Emma Kambar, Louise and Emma Jacobs, Elizabeth "Bessie" Baba, Nathaniel (Tom) Baba, Sophie Nweeia, and Lilly and Bill Sargis; (fourth row) Sue Nweeia, William Davidson, Jane Davidson, Norma and Irene Baba, Agnes Ameer, Judith Caram, Elizabeth Baba, Miriam Hasrato, Yonan Kambar, and Andrew Soleiman; (fifth row) Zenhela and Jimmy Vitti, John Yohannan, Luther George, Nicolai Benjamin, Eprim Ameer, Alice Yohannan, and Almas Benjamin; (sixth row) Elisha Yohannan, unidentified, Joe Eshoo, Philip, Charlotte, Suria, and Timothy Soleiman, Katherine Sargis Vesio, and Nanajan Yohannan; (seventh row) Norman Baba, Norman Baboo-David, Robert Kambar, Danny Baba, Kenny Kambar, John Ameer, and John J. Vesio. (Courtesy of Shirley Benjamin.)

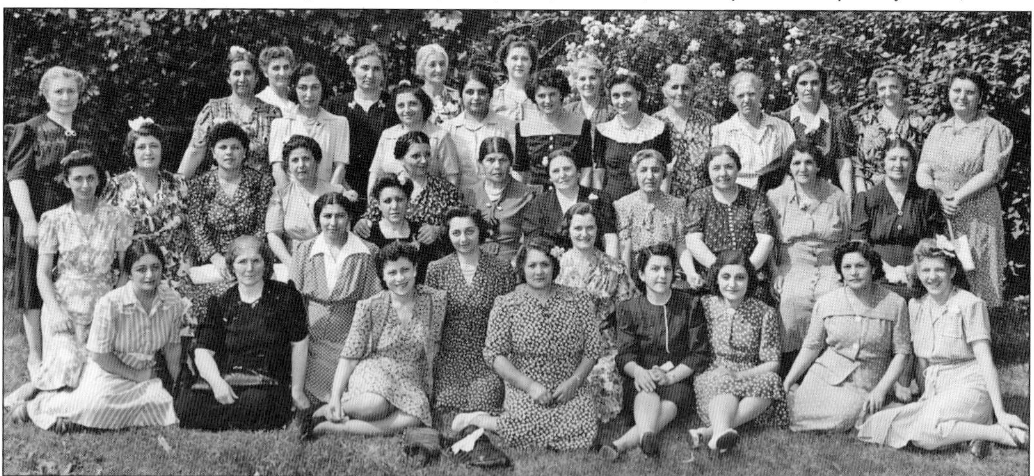

The Assyrian National Women's Association, June 1943. From left to right are (first row) Lucy Sarmast, Rabbi Lucy Shlimoun, Ketro Aziz (kneeling), Shami Yonan, Judith Caram, Khanito George, unidentified, Lucy Jacobs, Susie Yonan, Elizabeth Baba, and Margie Eshoo; (second row) Margaret Jacobs, Alice Yohannan, two unidentified, Nazlu Jacobs, Sue Nweeia's grandmother, and three unidentified; (third row) two unidentified, Almas Benjamin, Alice Eshoo, Marusa Jacobs Aslan, Florence Jacobs Gabriel, Blandina Paulus Benjamin, and Rebka Yohannan; (fourth row) Julia Ameer, unidentified, Louise Benjamin Jacobs, Lucy Aivaz Benjamin, Emma Benjamin Jacobs, and two unidentified. (Author's collection.)

TESTIMONIAL DINNER PROGRAM, DECEMBER 1940. The cover shows the Lamassu, the Assyrian winged bull, commemorating the visitation of Mar Shimun. (Courtesy of Shirley Benjamin.)

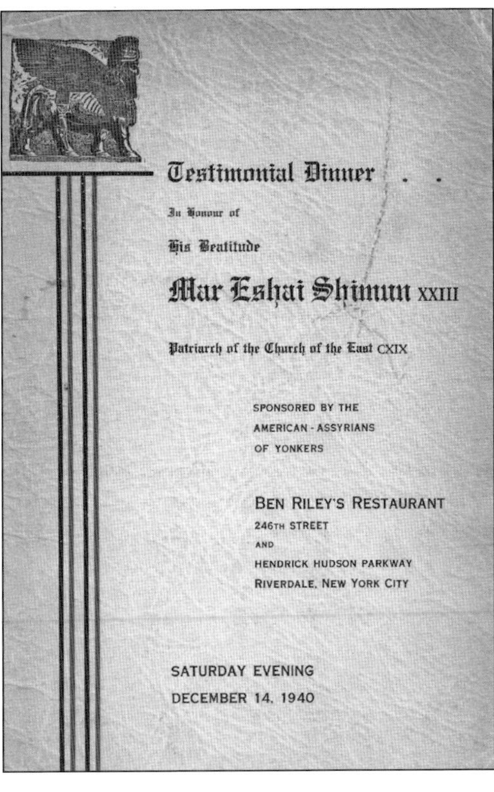

Testimonial Dinner . .

In Honour of

His Beatitude

Mar Eshai Shimun XXIII

Patriarch of the Church of the East CXIX

SPONSORED BY THE
AMERICAN - ASSYRIANS
OF YONKERS

BEN RILEY'S RESTAURANT
246TH STREET
AND
HENDRICK HUDSON PARKWAY
RIVERDALE, NEW YORK CITY

SATURDAY EVENING
DECEMBER 14, 1940

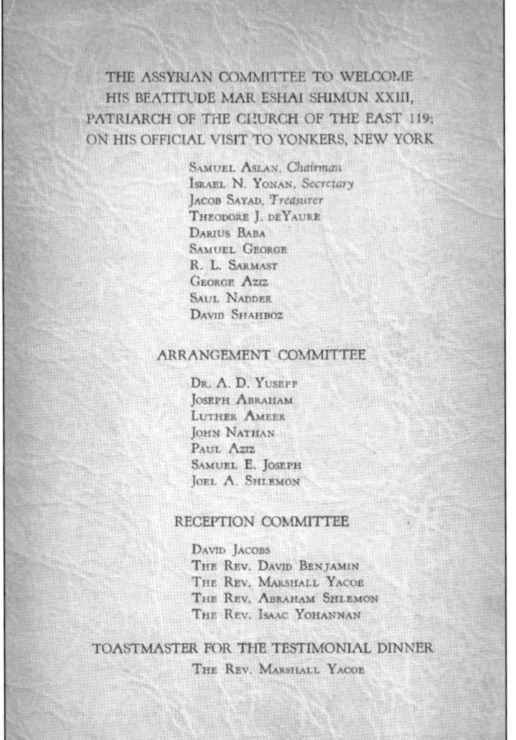

THE ASSYRIAN COMMITTEE TO WELCOME
HIS BEATITUDE MAR ESHAI SHIMUN XXIII,
PATRIARCH OF THE CHURCH OF THE EAST 119;
ON HIS OFFICIAL VISIT TO YONKERS, NEW YORK

Samuel Aslan, *Chairman*
Israel N. Yonan, *Secretary*
Jacob Sayad, *Treasurer*
Theodore J. deYaure
Darius Baba
Samuel George
R. L. Sarmast
George Aziz
Saul Nadder
David Shahboz

ARRANGEMENT COMMITTEE

Dr. A. D. Yuseff
Joseph Abraham
Luther Ameer
John Nathan
Paul Aziz
Samuel E. Joseph
Joel A. Shlemon

RECEPTION COMMITTEE

David Jacobs
The Rev. David Benjamin
The Rev. Marshall Yacoe
The Rev. Abraham Shlemon
The Rev. Isaac Yohannan

TOASTMASTER FOR THE TESTIMONIAL DINNER

The Rev. Marshall Yacoe

TESTIMONIAL DINNER PROGRAM, DECEMBER 1940. This page lists the large committee of men, including clergy and other Yonkers Assyrians, who prepared and carried out the dinner honoring Mar Shimun. The affair was held in Riverdale at Ben Riley's Restaurant. (Courtesy of Shirley Benjamin.)

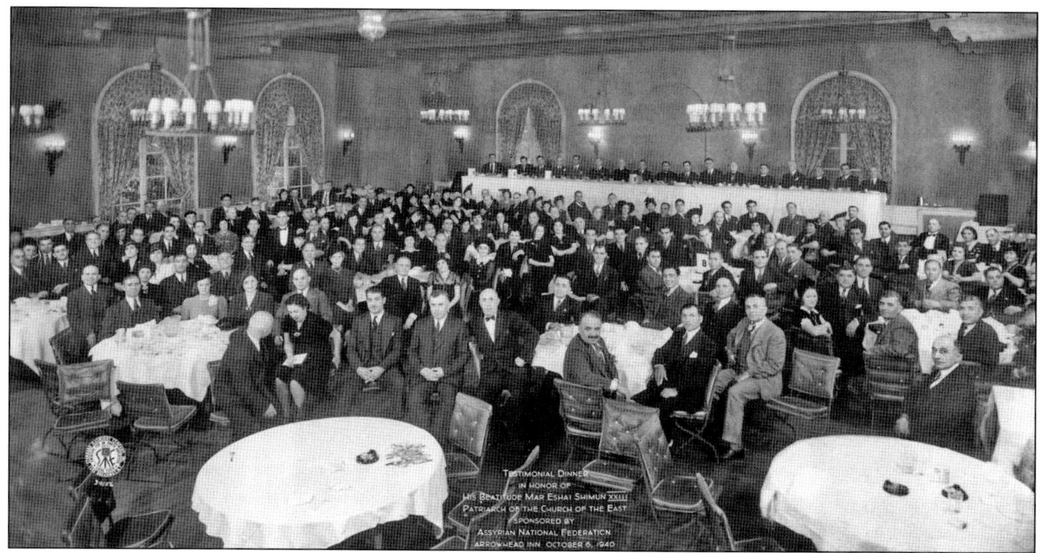

TESTIMONIAL DINNER HELD IN HONOR OF MAR SHIMUN, OCTOBER 6, 1940. This affair was held at Arrowhead Inn and included Assyrians from the metropolitan area. (Courtesy of Shirley Benjamin.)

SHOOKHA (DOXOLOGY)

L'kha Allaha Baba oo Broona,
Oo rookha D'Koodsha Tletayoota;
Tishbookhta ooeakara Yahwey,
Koolay D'burrah Beshmaya Hawey. Amen.

Praise God from whom all blessings flow;
Praise Him, all creatures here below;
Praise Him above, ye heavenly host;
Praise Father, Son, and Holy Ghost. Amen.

* * * * * * * * * *

MHEMNEENAN D'SHLEEKHI (APOSTLES' CREED)

Hamoonewekh b'Allaha Baba Akheed D'kool, Baryana D'Shmaya oo urra; oob'marran Esho Msheekha Brooni Ekhedaya; Ow D'pishly Bteena Min Rookha D'Koodsha, oopishly Leeda Min Maryam D'Toolta; Koobily Kehesha Min Pontius Pilatoos; Pishly Mikhya L'Skeepa; Mitly, oopishly Kweera, oo sleely L'sheool; B'yooma D'tlah Kimly Min gawa D'meety, Sekly L'Shmaya; oo tivly min Yameena D'Allah Baba Akheed K'hool; oomin Tawma bit atti lidyana l'khyayi oo L'meety.

Hamoonewekh Brookha D'koodsha; B'eata Kadishta Catoolecata; Bsharikoota D'kadishy; B'shwaka D'khtiyati; D'kyamta D'paghry oo khayi Abadenayi. Amen.

I believe in God The Father Almighty, Maker of heaven and earth: And in Jesus Christ His only Son our Lord; who was conceived by the Holy Ghost; born of the Virgin Mary; suffered under Pontius Pilate; was crucified, dead, and buried; He descended into hell; the third day He rose again from the dead; He ascended into heaven; and sitteth on the right hand of God the Father Almighty; from thence He shall come to judge the quick and the dead.

I believe in the Holy Ghost; the holy Catholic Church; the Communion of Saints; the Forgiveness of sins; the Resurrection of the body; and the Life everlasting. Amen.

NEO-SYRIAC, ASSYRIAN, AND ENGLISH TRANSLATIONS OF THE DOXOLOGY AND APOSTLES' CREED. This page from the Assyrian Presbyterian Church in Yonkers was inserted in the Psalms of David. Services were conducted in English and Assyrian. (Author's collection.)

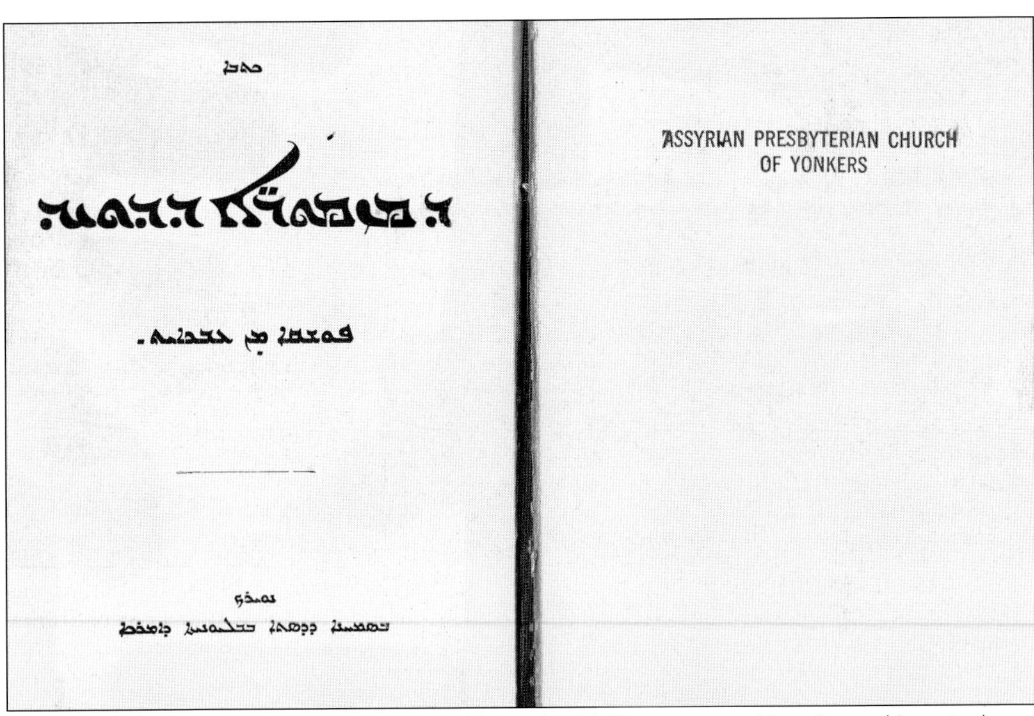

THE PSALMS OF DAVID. This book, translated from the Old Testament to Neo-Syriac (Assyrian), was donated to the Assyrian Presbyterian Church in Yonkers by Suria Soleiman. (Author's collection.)

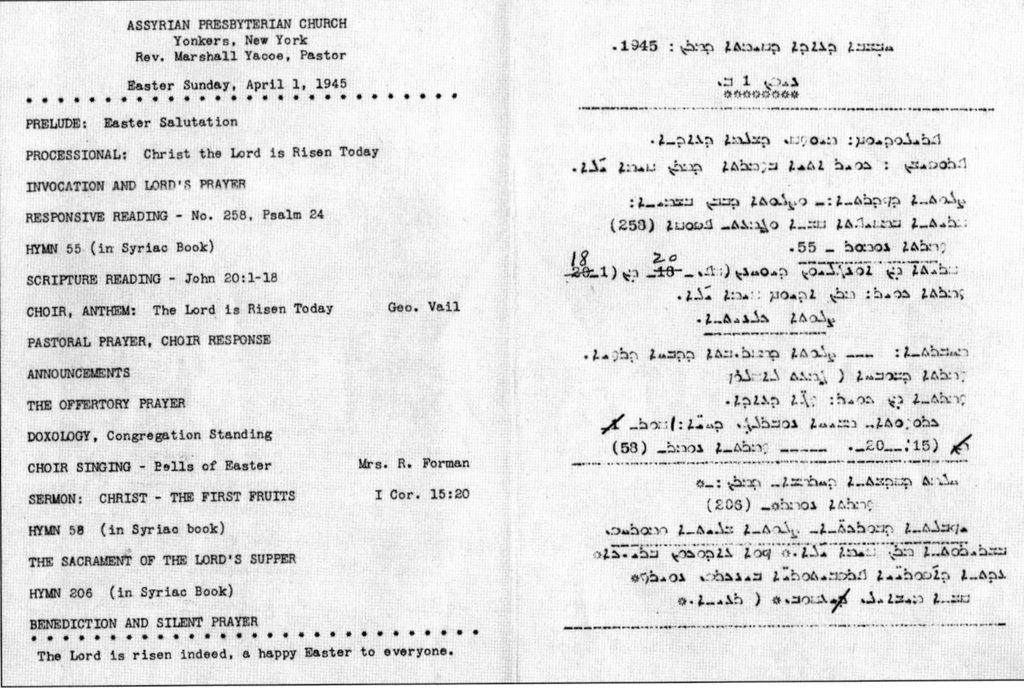

ASSYRIAN PRESBYTERIAN CHURCH
Yonkers, New York
Rev. Marshall Yacoe, Pastor

Easter Sunday, April 1, 1945

PRELUDE: Easter Salutation

PROCESSIONAL: Christ the Lord is Risen Today

INVOCATION AND LORD'S PRAYER

RESPONSIVE READING - No. 258, Psalm 24

HYMN 55 (in Syriac Book)

SCRIPTURE READING - John 20:1-18

CHOIR, ANTHEM: The Lord is Risen Today — Geo. Vail

PASTORAL PRAYER, CHOIR RESPONSE

ANNOUNCEMENTS

THE OFFERTORY PRAYER

DOXOLOGY, Congregation Standing

CHOIR SINGING - Bells of Easter — Mrs. R. Forman

SERMON: CHRIST - THE FIRST FRUITS — I Cor. 15:20

HYMN 58 (in Syriac book)

THE SACRAMENT OF THE LORD'S SUPPER

HYMN 206 (in Syriac Book)

BENEDICTION AND SILENT PRAYER

The Lord is risen indeed, a happy Easter to everyone.

EASTER SUNDAY BULLETIN. This bulletin is from the Assyrian Presbyterian Church in Yonkers on April 1, 1945. The left page is in English, and the right is the Neo-Syriac translation. (Courtesy of the William and Lilly Sargis family.)

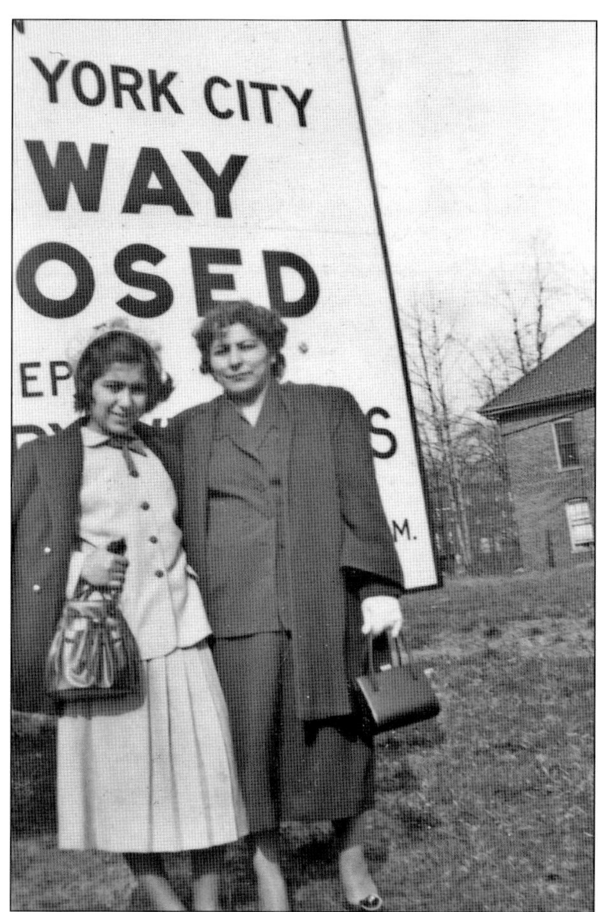

EASTER SUNDAY. Alice Aziz (left) and her mother, Ketro Aziz, are pictured in Riverdale in front of a sign that announces the closing of the parkway on Easter Sunday, April 5, 1953. (Courtesy of Alice Aziz David.)

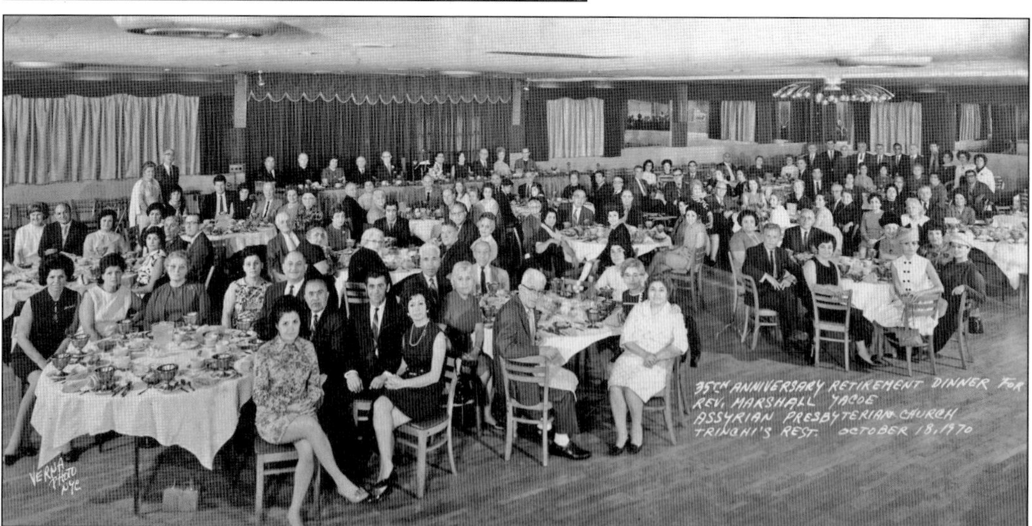

QASHA YACOE'S RETIREMENT PARTY. Members from several Assyrian churches in the area joined to celebrate Reverend Yacoe at his 35th anniversary and retirement dinner at Trinchi's Restaurant (formerly Steve Phillips Restaurant) at 1144 Yonkers Avenue on October 18, 1970. (Courtesy of the William and Lilly Sargis family.)

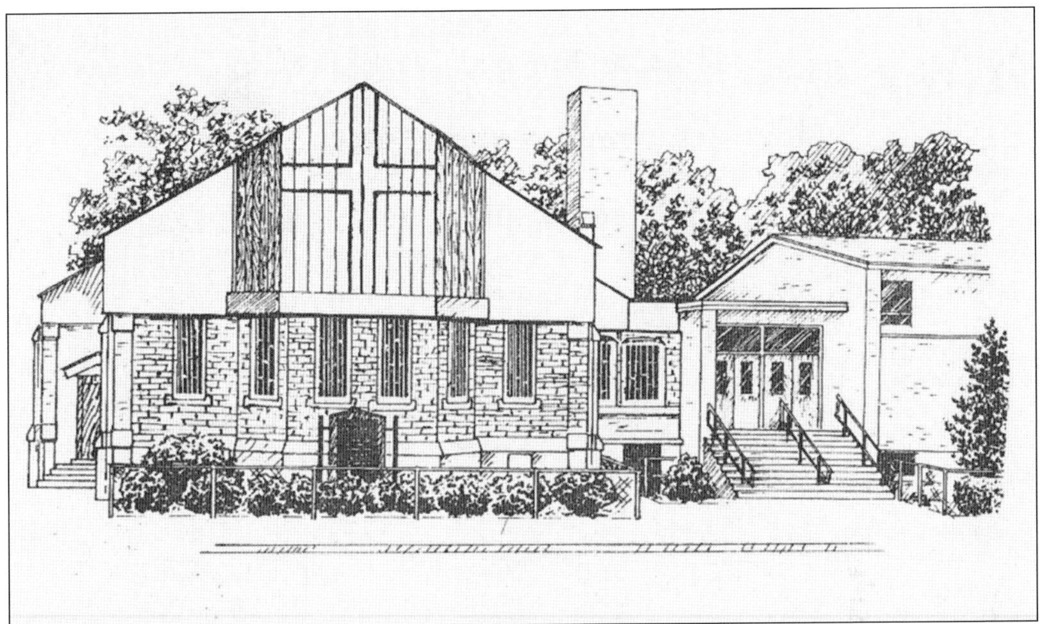

SOUTH PRESBYTERIAN CHURCH, 112 RADFORD STREET, YONKERS. Because the membership of the Assyrian Presbyterian Church aged and many parishioners moved out of Yonkers, the church closed its doors in the 1970s. The remaining congregation merged with the South Presbyterian Church on Radford Street. The edifice was razed in April 2002 to make room for a Portuguese church. (Courtesy of Lydia Kambar.)

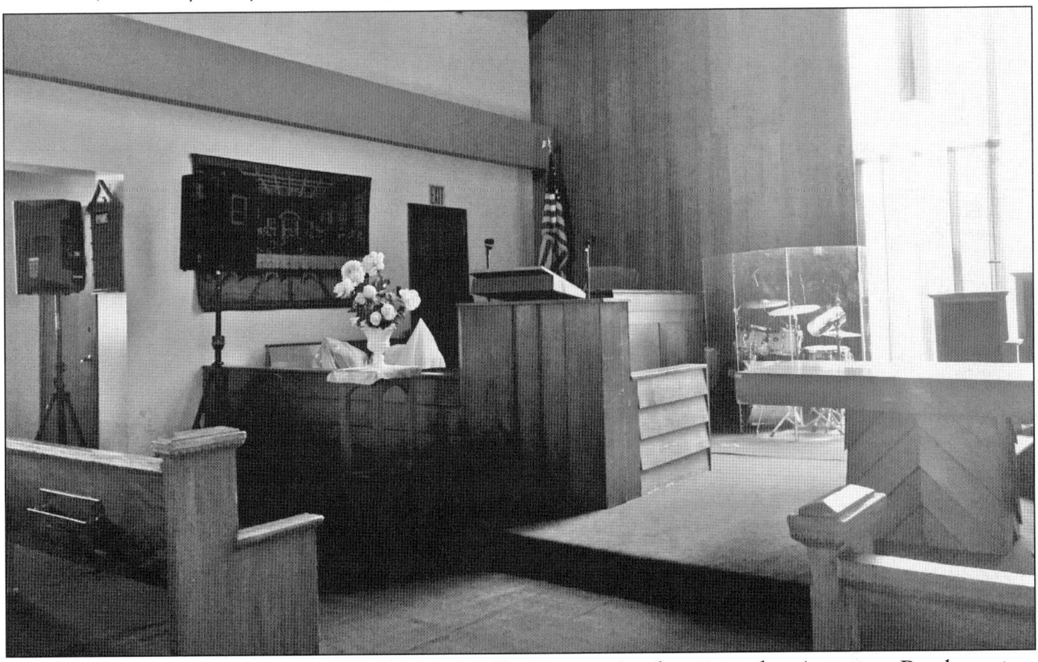

PULPIT OF SOUTH PRESBYTERIAN CHURCH, YONKERS. At the time the Assyrian Presbyterian Church merged with South Presbyterian Church, it brought gifts of a Persian carpet woven to produce the image of the Last Supper, pictured on the wall behind the pulpit, and its pews. (Author's collection.)

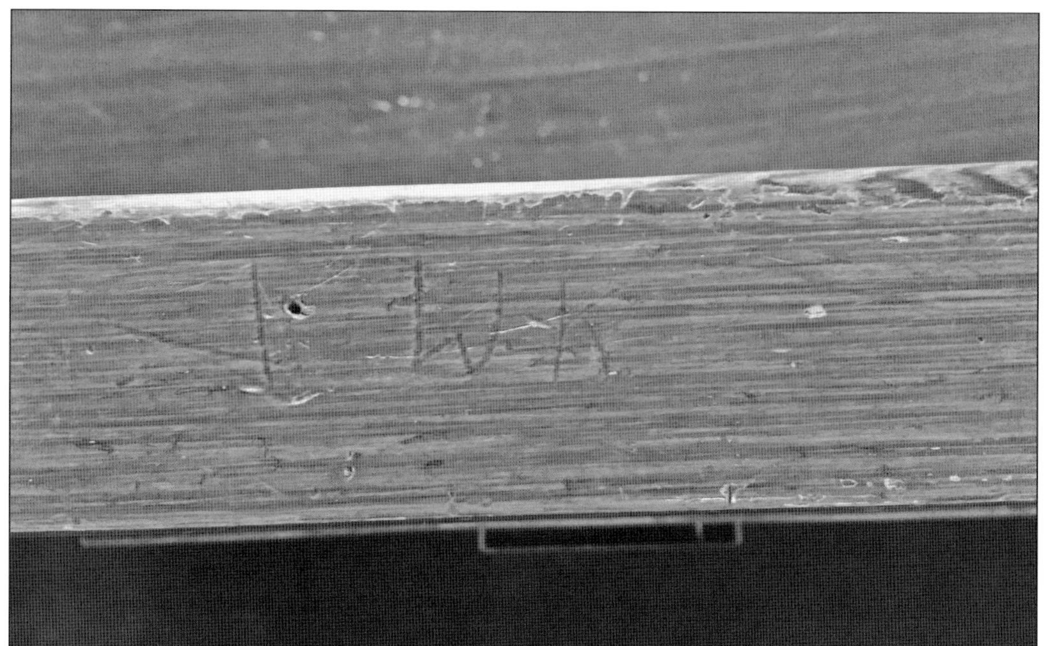

PEW CARVED WITH INITIALS W.K. The new church bore signs of the old congregation. When William Kambar of the Assyrian Presbyterian Church carved his initials in the pew as a little boy, he never imagined that they would still exist and be carried into the South Presbyterian Church on Radford Street. (Author's collection.)

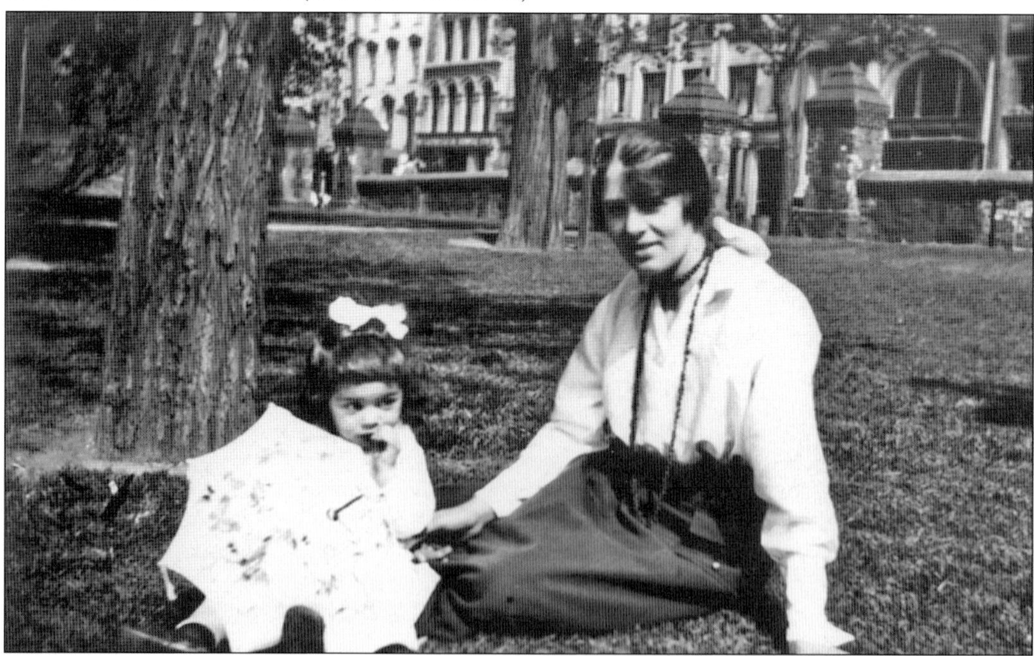

COURTYARD OF ST. JOHN'S EPISCOPAL CHURCH. Emma Jacobs is pictured with her daughter Elizabeth in 1918. Elizabeth died not long after this photograph was taken. She was two and a half years old. Because she preferred the attention of her uncle Sam Jacobs to anyone else's and rarely left his side, she died from influenza three days after he did. (Courtesy of Shirley Benjamin.)

Stained-Glass Window. This window in St. John's Episcopal Church at 1 Hudson Street in Yonkers was dedicated in loving memory of Clarence Jacobs. He and his wife, Margaret, were married at St. John's and remained faithful active parishioners. Many Assyrians worshipped at St. John's. In fact, in the 1930s, the church had an Assyrian minister, Rev. Isaac Yohannan, who held services on Sunday afternoons in Assyrian. (Author's collection.)

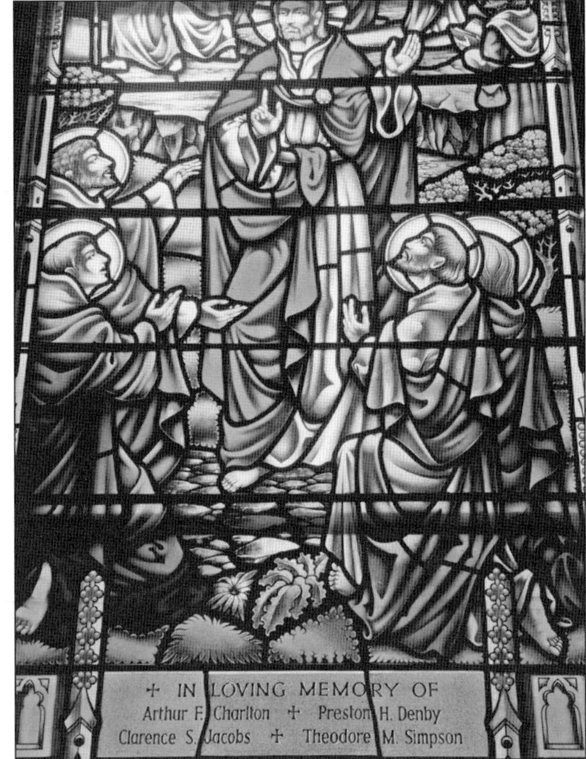

Pew Marker. The family of David Jacobs (1898–1971) has memorialized him in St. John's Episcopal Church in Getty Square. (Author's collection.)

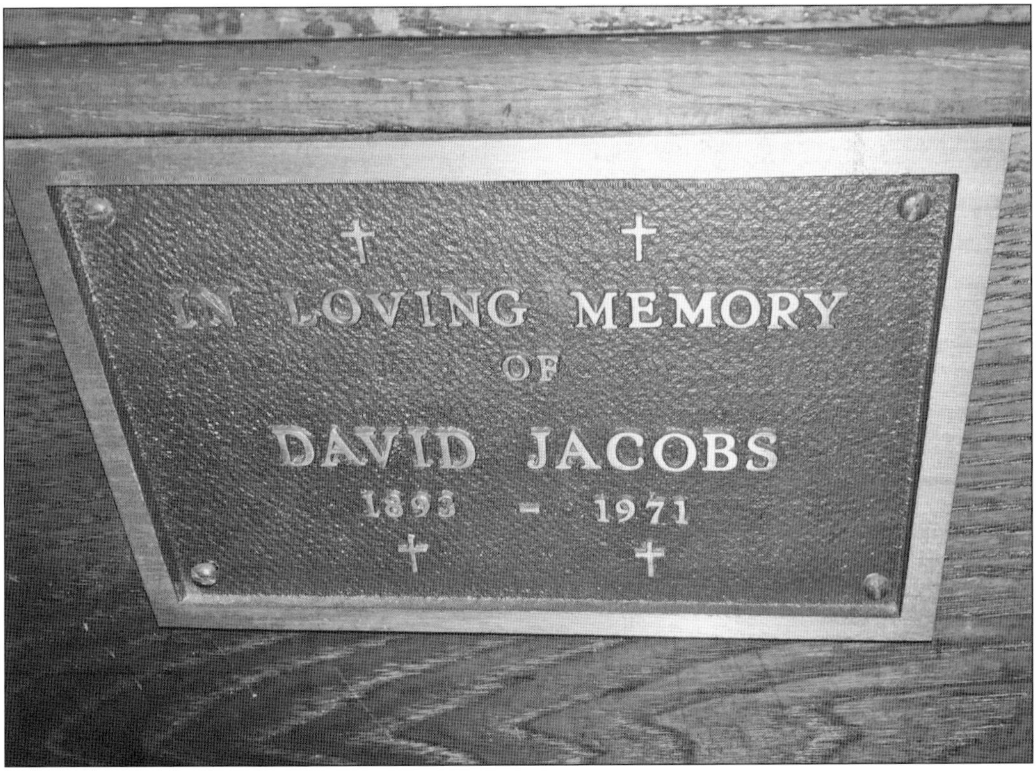

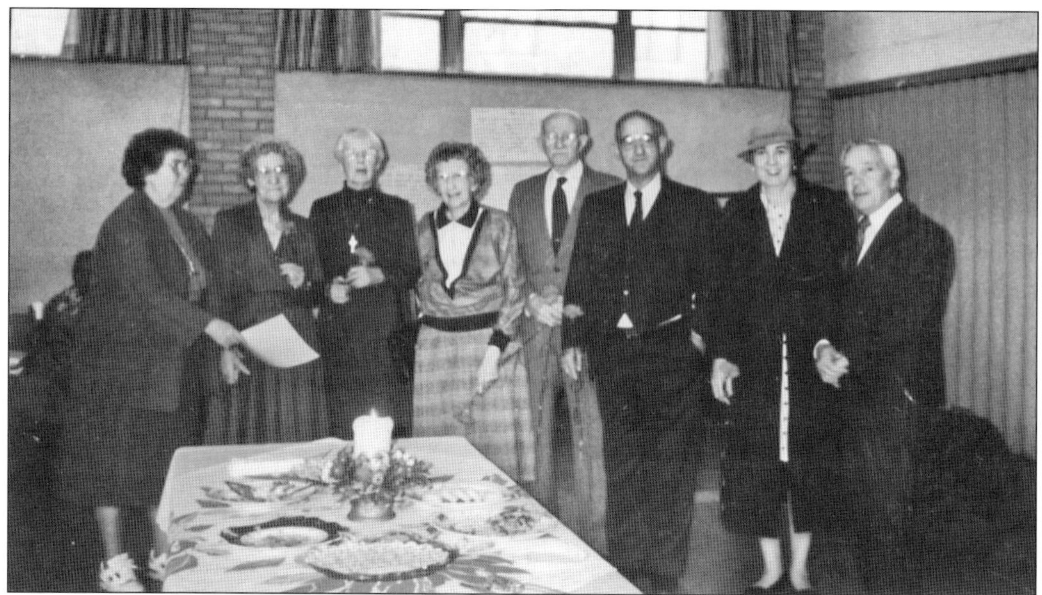

Merging of the Assyrian Presbyterian Church with South Presbyterian Church. When the Assyrian Presbyterian Church closed its doors, the remaining Assyrians joined the South Presbyterian Church. Scottish Presbyterians founded this church. Pictured here is the joint session comprised of elders from both churches. From left to right are Rev. Margaret "Peggy" Howland, May Whalen, Agnes Ross, Gladys Nicol, former Assyrian church members Nicholas Benjamin and William Kambar, Shirley Benjamin, and Rene Morgante in the South Presbyterian Church's fellowship hall on December 12, 1994. (Author's collection.)

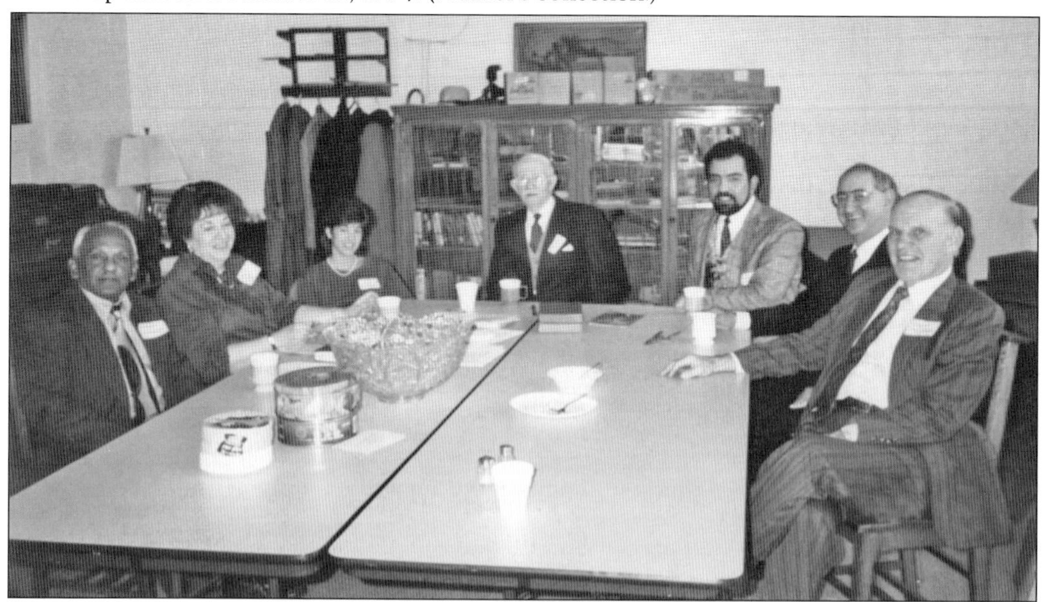

South Presbyterian Church Session Meeting. From left to right on December 6, 1992, are church elder Rupert Singh, former Assyrian Presbyterian Church member Ruth Hasrato Kopp, Assyrian Kim Kambar; former Assyrian Presbyterian Church member Nicholas Benjamin, unidentified church elder, former Assyrian Presbyterian Church member William Kambar, and Wally Coleman. (Author's collection.)

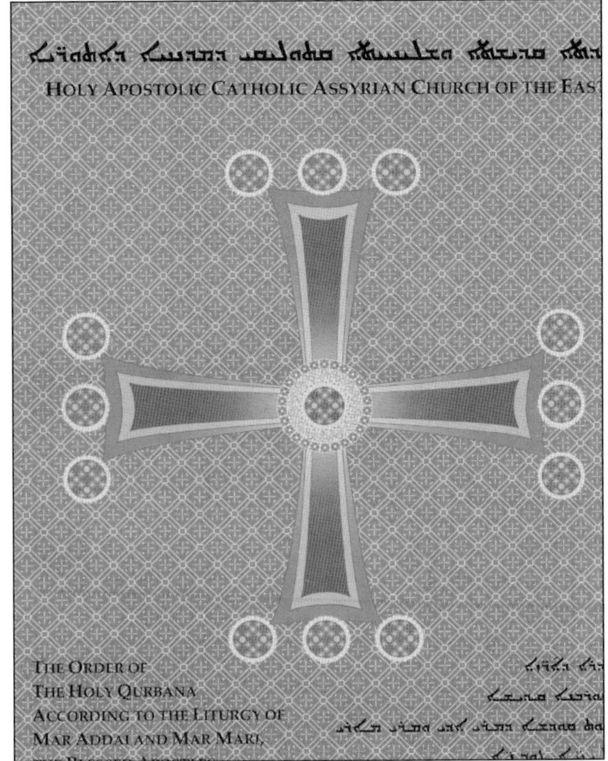

MAR MARI PARISH LITURGY. This book's cover features the Assyrian cross, the oldest Christian cross, which dates to 33 AD. It contains the readings for Sunday services in Assyrian with English translations. (Author's collection.)

MAR MARI CHURCH YOUTH ASSYRIAN DANCE GROUP. This c. 1983 photograph includes, from left to right, (first row) Joanne David, Vilma Mazzei, Diane Michaels, Violet Ishoo, and Valentine Eshaya; (second row) Jackie Ishou, Linda Mikhail, Rosana Mirza, Lida Zarvand, Shamiran Atoori, and Smetic Lazari; (third row) William Mikhail and John Brakhia (fourth row) Alfred Oushanani, Vova Ayvaz, William Ishoo, Charlie Youhan, Edward Sarkiso, and Wilson Oushanani. (Courtesy of Nancy Mirza Multari.)

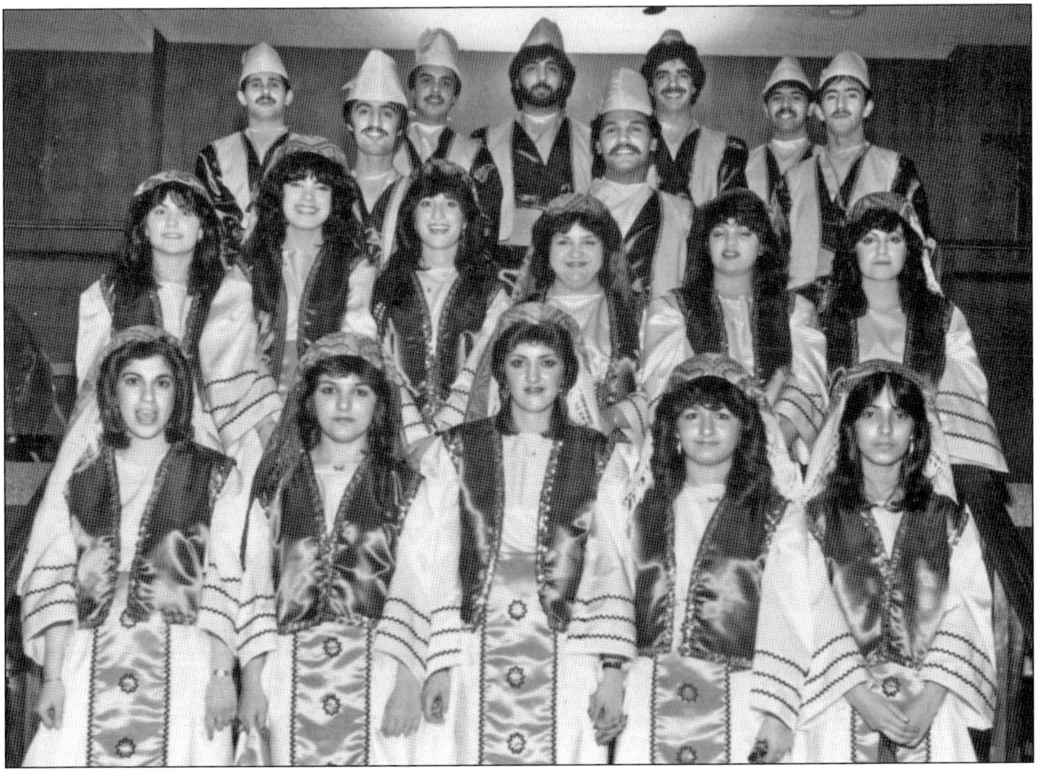

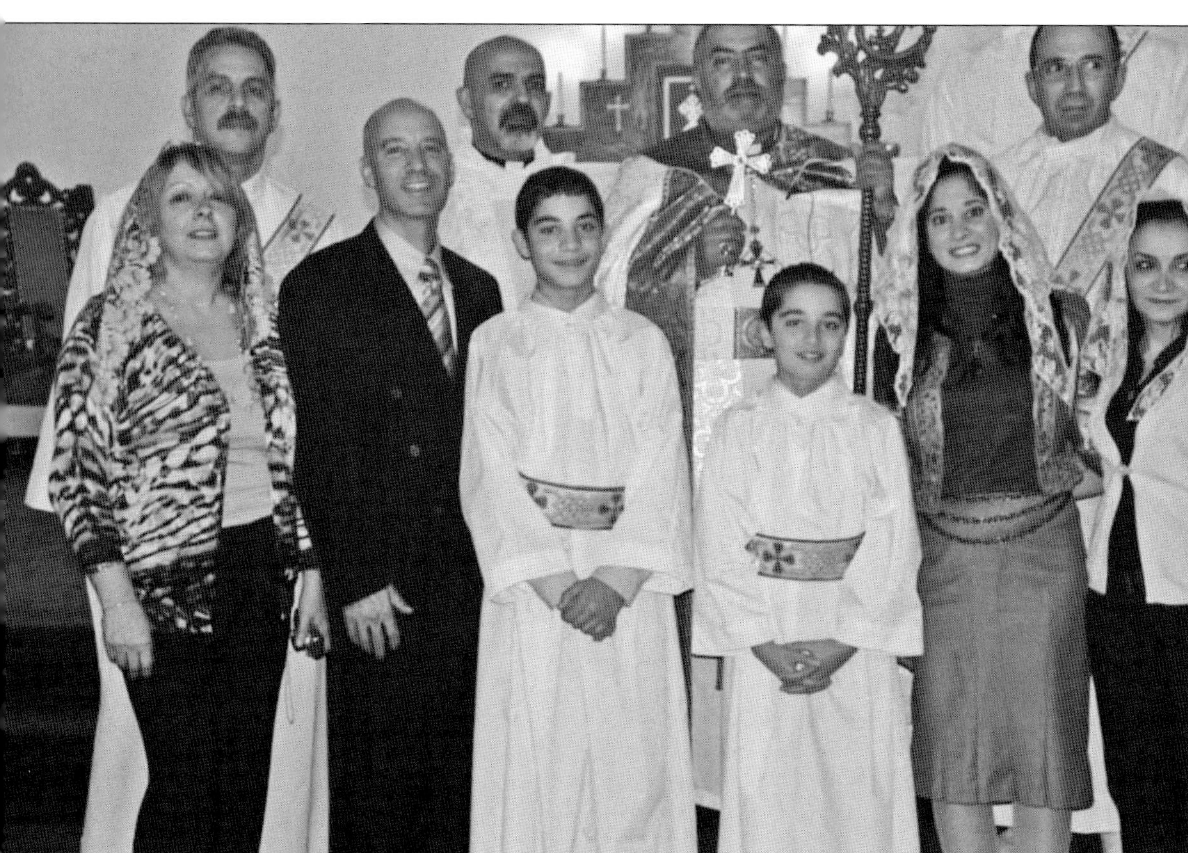

Mar Mari Church Congregation. In the 1950s, the Assyrian Apostolic Catholics worshipped at the Mar Mari Church, the Church of the East, which was housed in the rectory on Buena Vista Avenue. In 1966, the congregation held a ground-breaking ceremony for the church that exists today. The church was established in 1970. It currently houses Assyrians from several Middle Eastern countries who have immigrated for generations to Yonkers and the surrounding area. Current members of the congregation in 2018 include, from left to right (first row) Josephine Ishoo, Lorans Francis, Ralph Multari, Lector Matthew Multari, Nancy Mirza Multari, and Janeet Yousif Francis; (second row) Deacon Edmond Oushanani, Rev. Addai Francis, Bishop Mar Paulus Benjamin, and Lector Peter Multari. (Courtesy of Nancy Mirza Multari.)

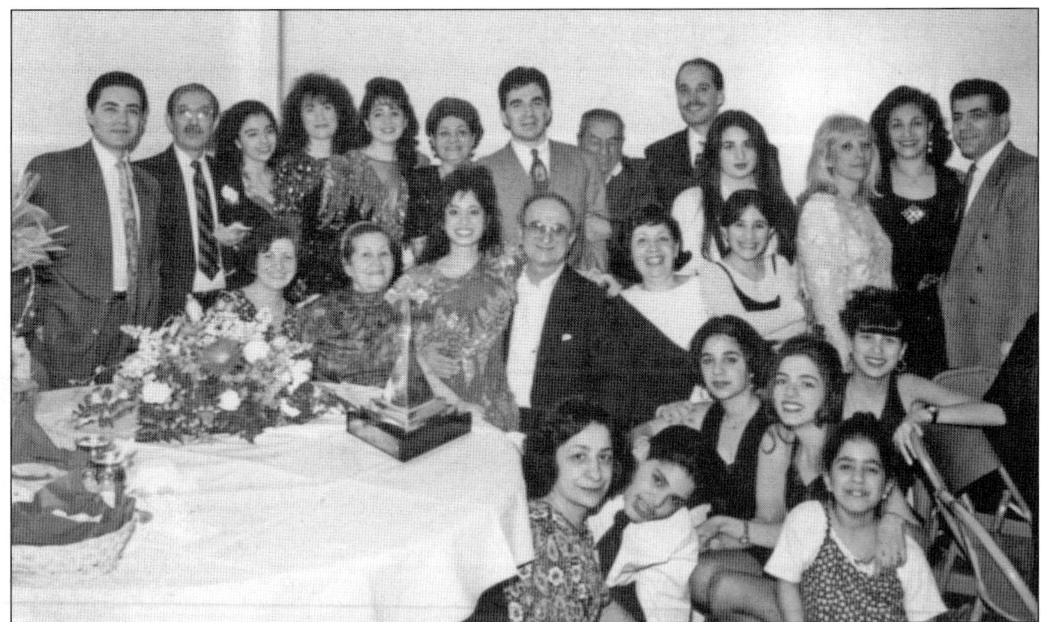

Ivan Mirza, Honoree of the Mar Mari Church of Yonkers Epiphany, 1995. Pictured here are, from left to right, (first row) Diana Mirza, George Shumunnejad, Dominique Mirza, Rachel Shumunnejad, Rosalie Shumunnejad, and Atorina Mirza; (second row) Jenny Mirza, Victoria Yeldalo, Nancy Mirza. Ivan Mirza, Nina Mirza, Pauline Shumunnejad, Maxine Crea, Jeanette Shumonnedzad, and Robert Shumunnejad; (third row) Joseph Shumunnejad, Boris Mirza, Daniella Mirza, Rosana Mirza, Renee Mirza, Zina Shumunnejad, Joseph Akalski, Lazar Youhan, Ralph Multari, and Valentine Shamoon. (Courtesy of Nancy Mirza Multari.)

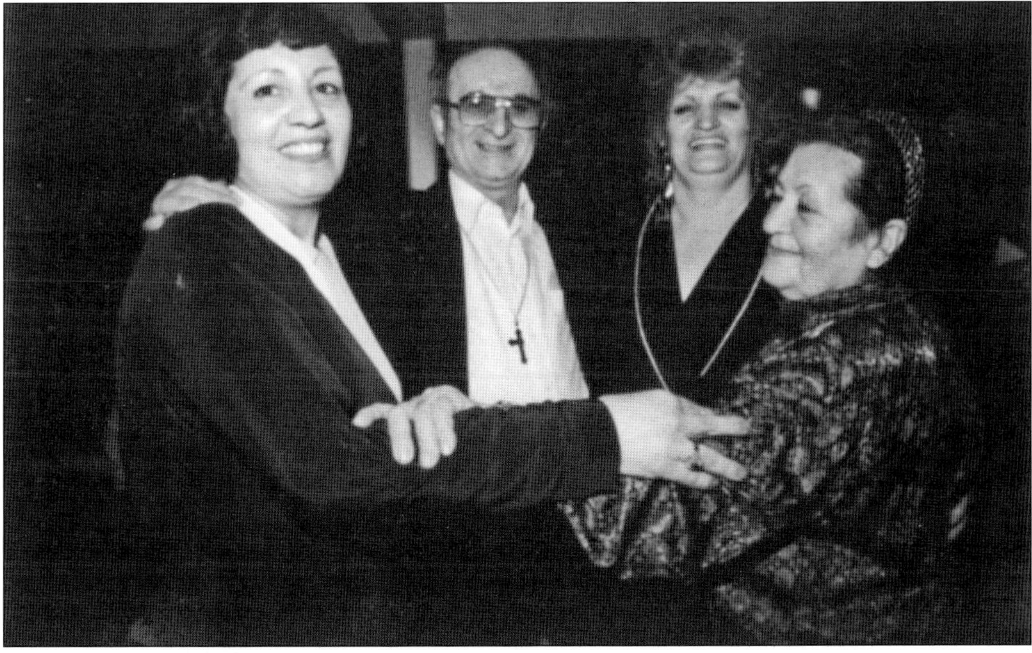

Mar Mari Church Party. From left to right are Nina Mirza, Ivan Mirza, Daisy Tatari, and Victoria Yeldalo in 1995. (Courtesy of Nancy Multari.)

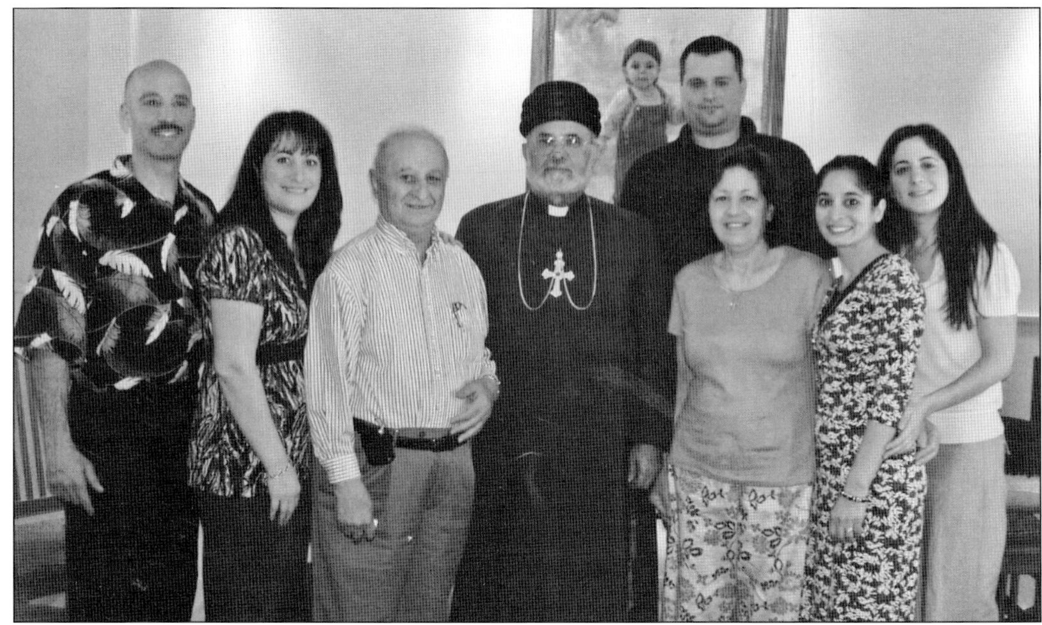

Mar Dinkha IV Visits Mar Mari Church Parishioners. From left to right are Ralph Multari; Rosana Carravone; Ivan Mirza; his Holiness Mar Dinkha IV, Catholic patriarch of the Assyrian Church of the East; Nina Mirza; Nancy Mirza-Multari; Renee Orscher; and Christian Orscher (in back) at the Multari home in Pound Ridge, New York, in 2015. (Courtesy of Nancy Multari.)

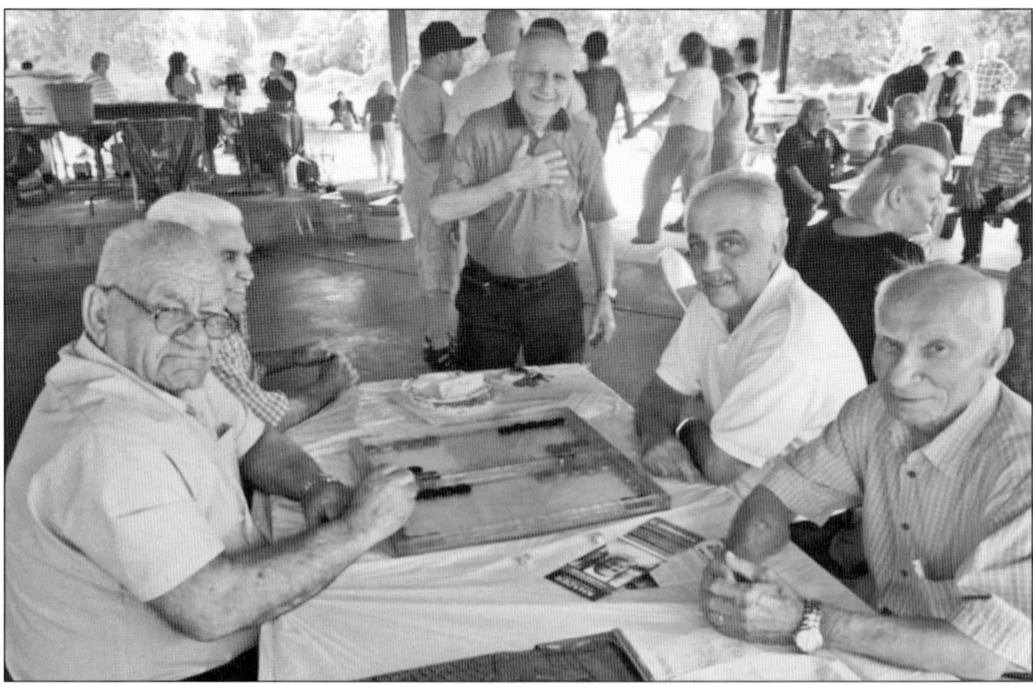

Mar Mari Assyrian Church Picnic. Picnic-goers play backgammon and chess. Seated from left to right are Younathan Shamoeilzad, Zhoura Khoshaboo, Edmond Essapour, and Youra Belvarmorood. The man standing nearby is Boris Ishoo. The picnic was in V.E. Macy Park in Ardsley, New York, in July 2018. (Courtesy of Nancy Multari.)

Five

Secular Life

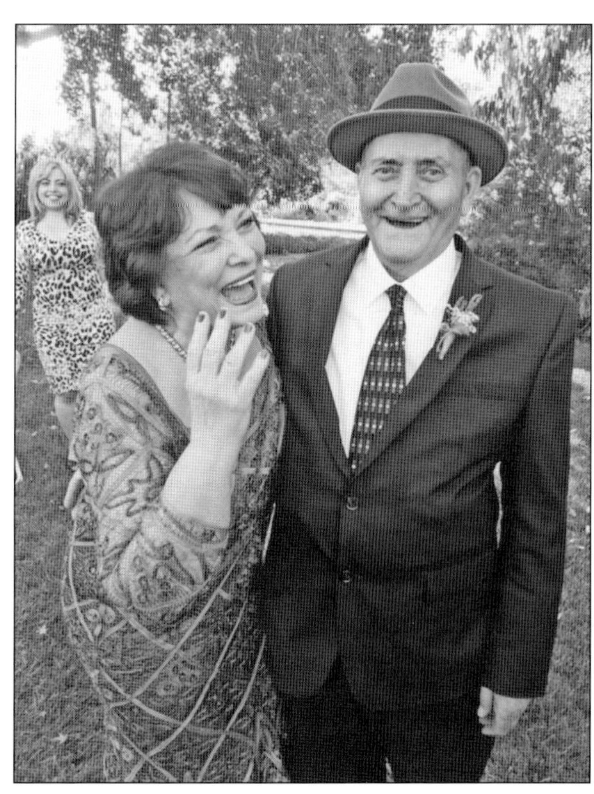

The Beitdashtoos. Lola Beitdashtoo-Michaels and her brother Andre are pictured at his granddaughter's wedding in 2013. In the background is cousin Claudine Barin. (Courtesy of Fiona Michaels-Lazar.)

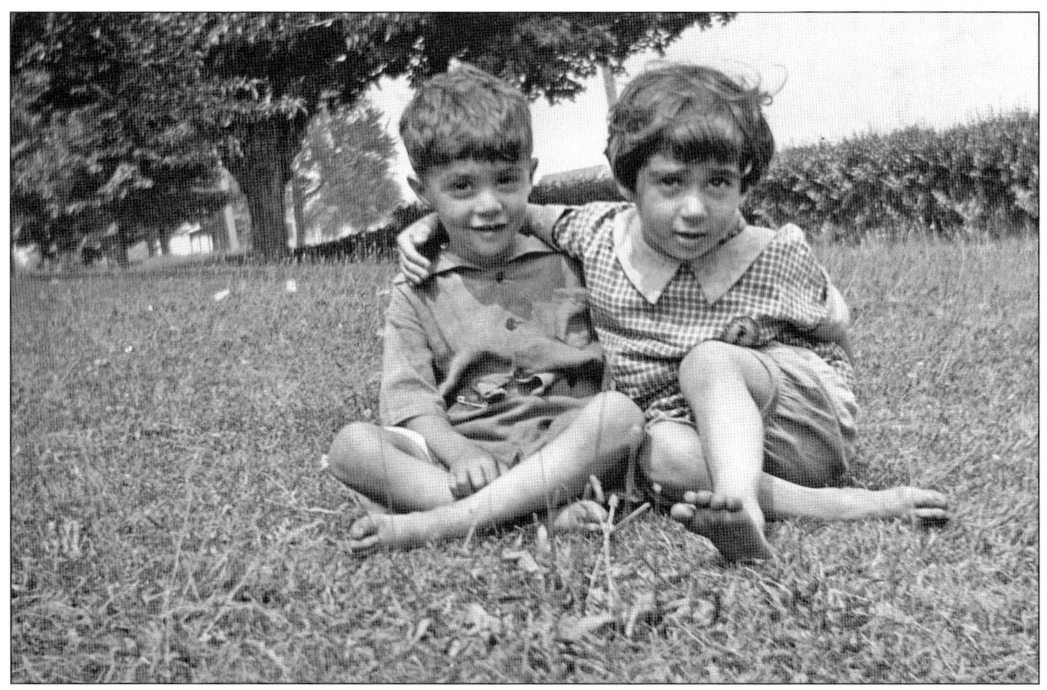

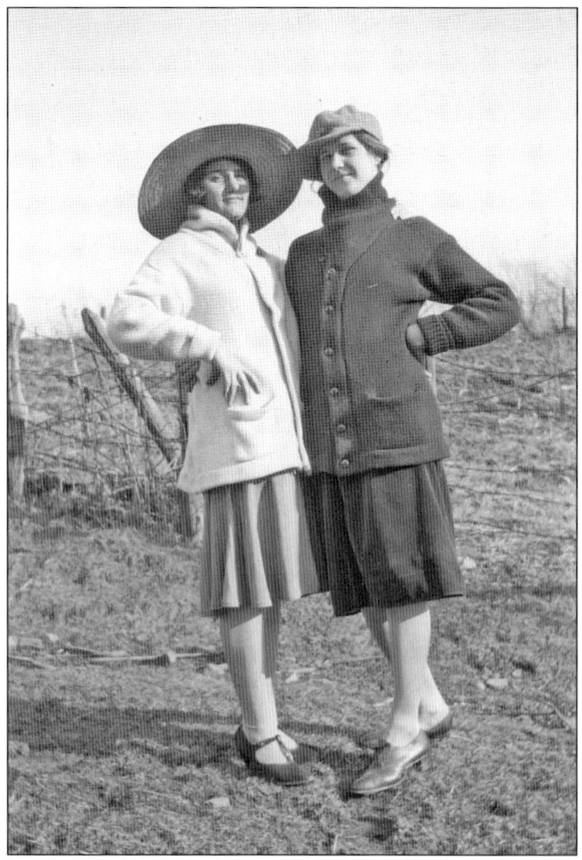

New Britain, Connecticut. Cousins Sammy Jacobs and Betty Benjamin pose in the 1920s on the family farm in New Britain. (Author's collection.)

Sisters-in-Law. Blandina Benjamin (left) and Lucy Benjamin are pictured at the family farm in Kensington, New Britain, Connecticut, in the 1920s. (Author's collection.)

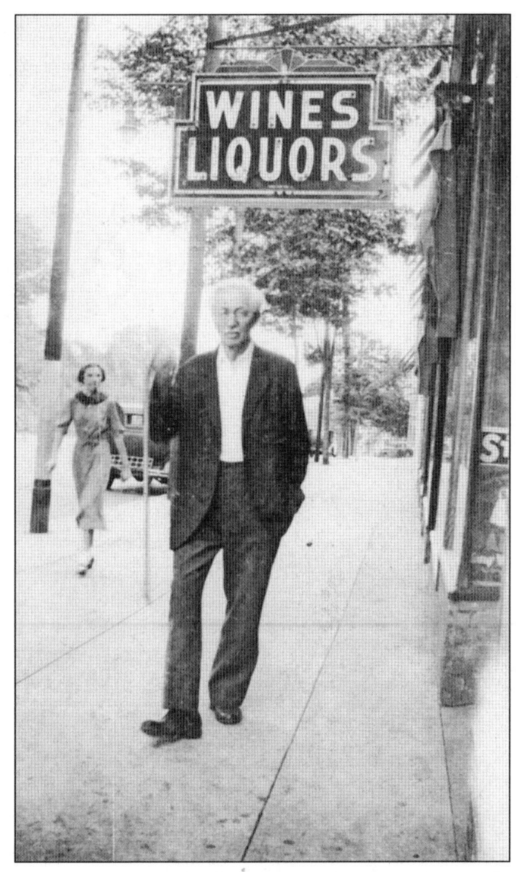

REV. DAVID JACOB BENJAMIN. The reverend is pictured on Riverdale Avenue walking past one of Dave Jacobs's liquor stores, near his son Nathan's candy store, on May 10, 1931. (Courtesy of Shirley Benjamin.)

NEW BRITAIN, 1920S. After initially settling in Philadelphia, the family moved to New Britain and then to Yonkers. From left to right are (first row) unidentified, Nathan Benjamin with unidentified child on his shoulders, Nick Benjamin, Teddy Benjamin, and Jacob Benjamin Ardashier; (second row) Julia Benjamin holding Margaret Ardashier in her lap, unidentified, Clarence Jacobs, unidentified girl, and Almas Benjamin; (third row) unidentified woman holding an unidentified baby, Rev. David Jacob Benjamin, and his daughter Louise Benjamin Jacobs. (Author's collection.)

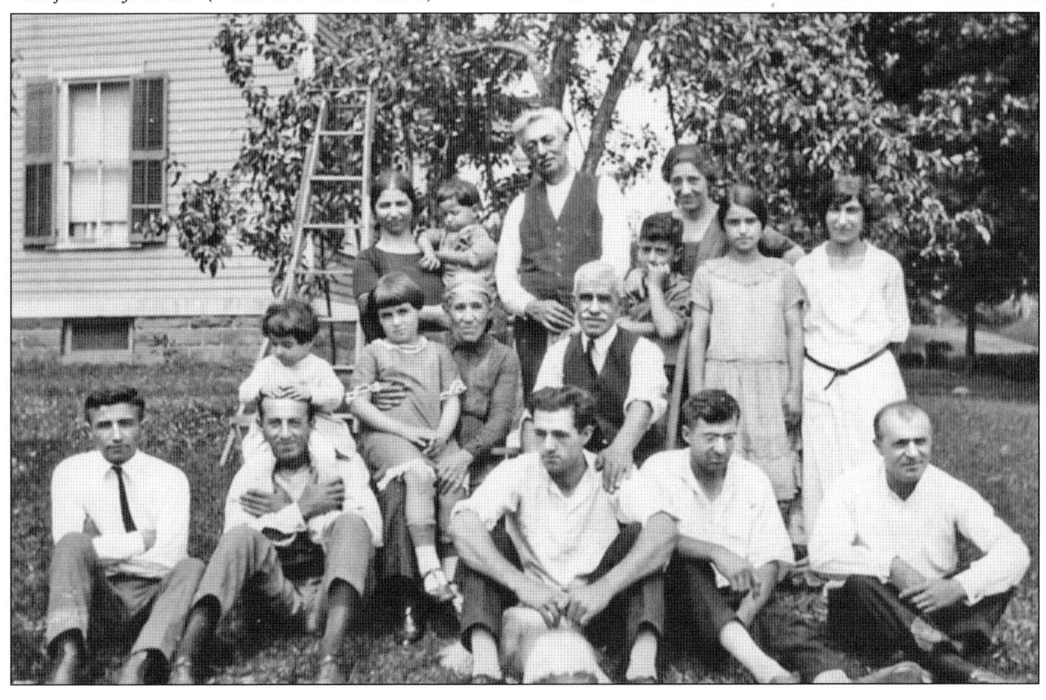

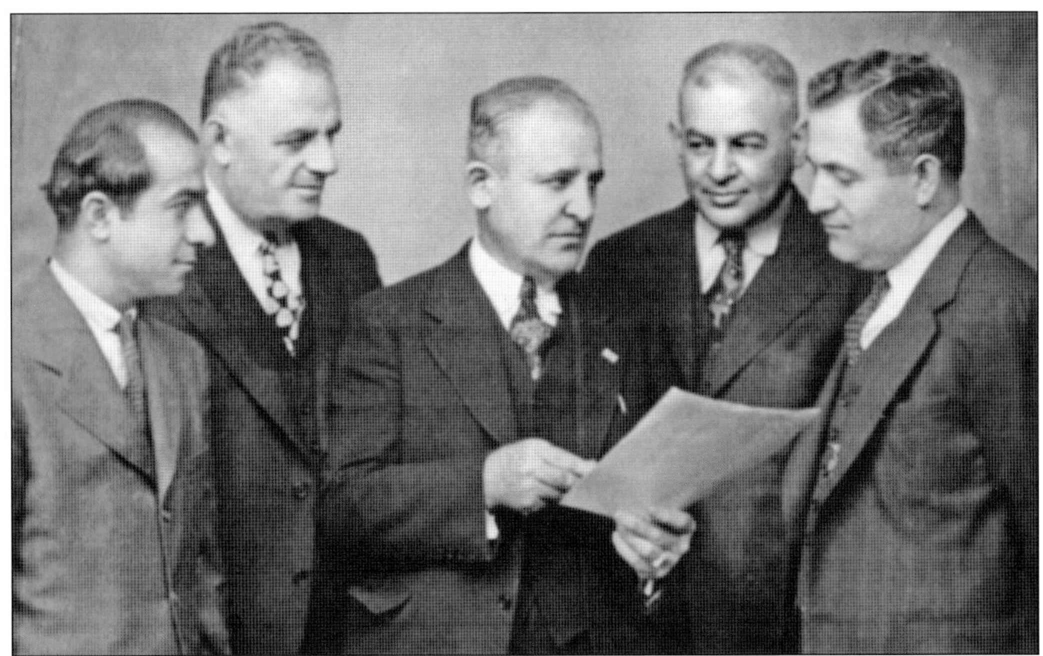

Assyrian American Federation Members. From left to right are Isaac Yonan, David Jacobs, unidentified, Sam Aslan, (husband of Marusa Jacobs Aslan and father of Willie, Victor, Emmy, and John), and unidentified. The federation members from New Jersey were Assyrian but spoke a different dialect from the Assyrians of Yonkers. (Courtesy of Jean Jacobs Correa.)

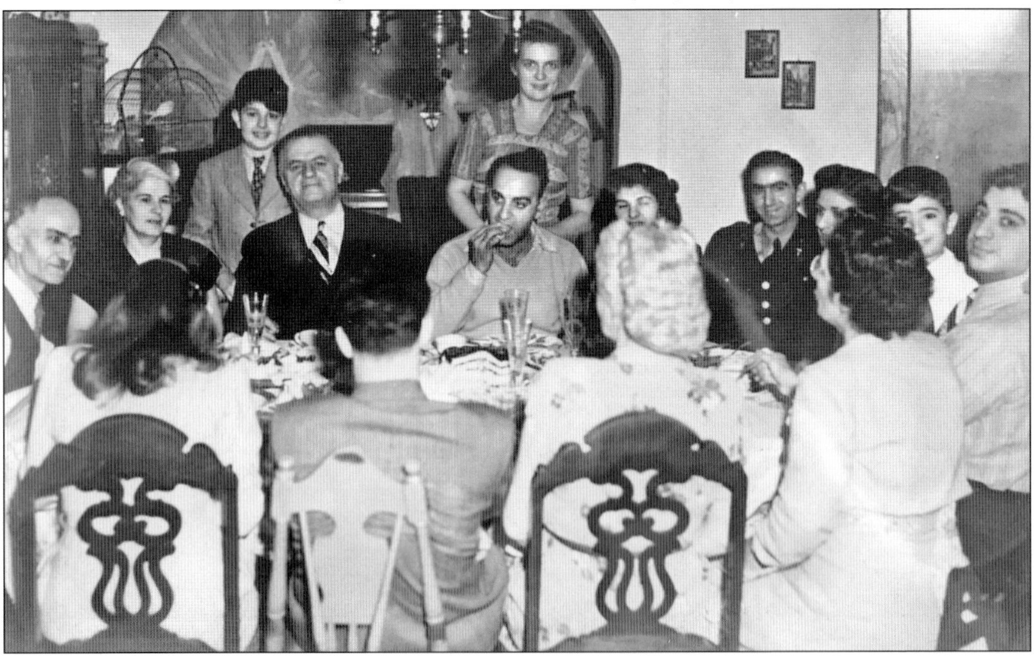

Dinner in New Jersey. Pictured during the 1940s are, from left to right, Benjamin Isaac David (at the head of the table), Emma Benjamin Jacobs, Eugene Jacobs, David Jacobs, Theodore Benjamin David, Helen David, Elizabeth Jacobs, Arthur David (in uniform), Margaret Jacobs, Roger Jacobs, Clarence Jacobs, Batishva David, Louisa Jacobs, and two unidentified. (Courtesy of Joe David.)

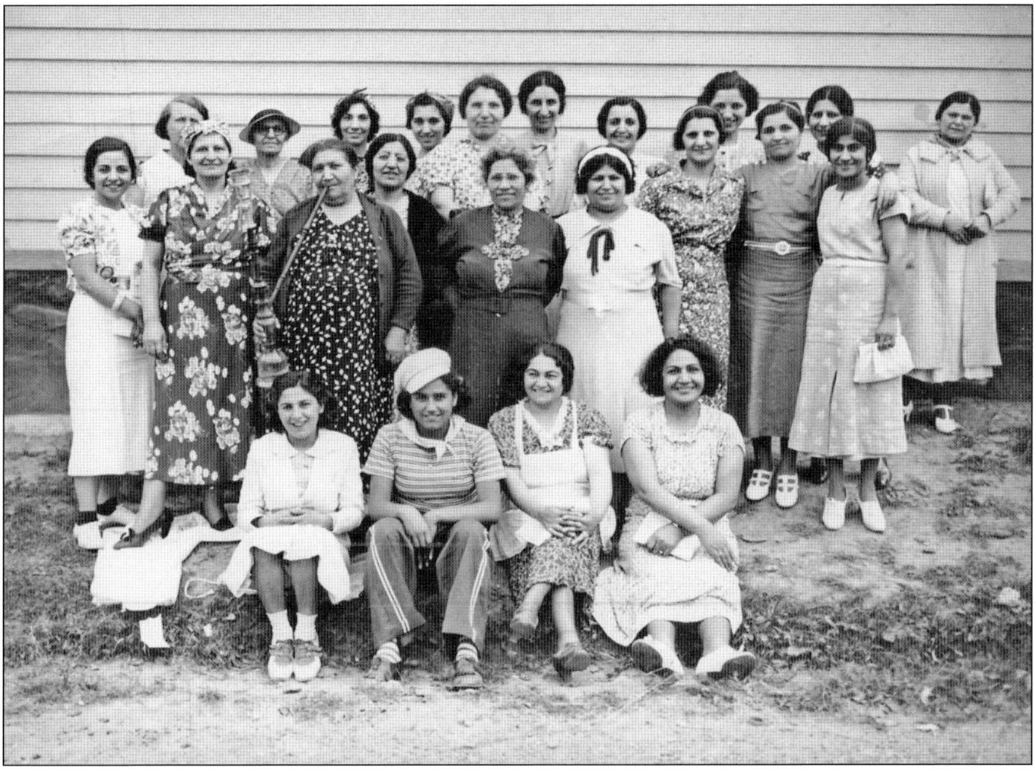

Batishva David Joins the Assyrian Women in Elizabeth, New Jersey. Eventually Benjamin Isaac David and Batishva David, sister of Elizabeth and Saul David, moved to Elizabeth, New Jersey. (Courtesy of Joe David.)

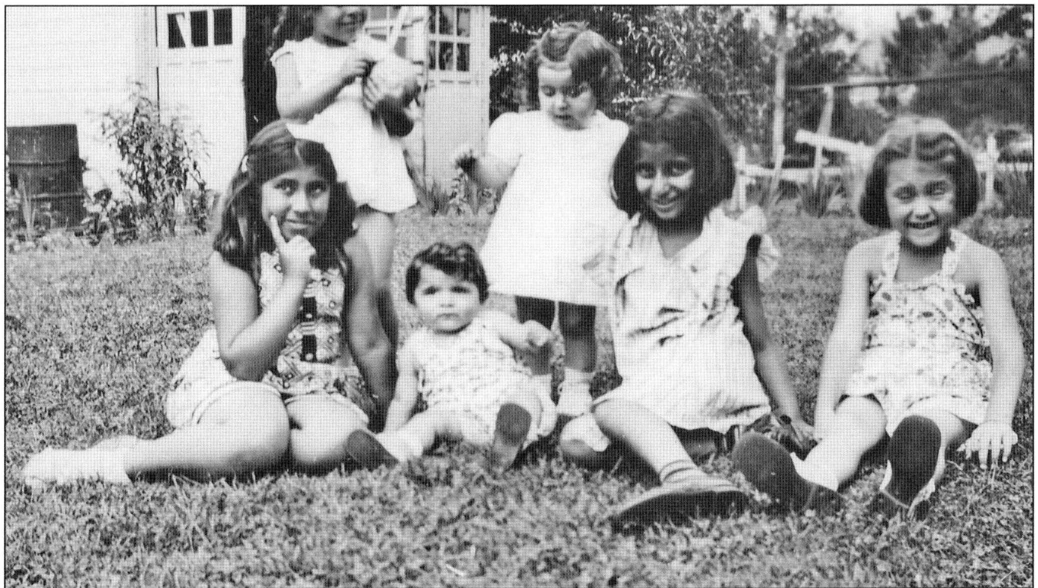

Cousins. From left to right, cousins Sarah Benjamin, Elaine Benjamin, Marion Aziz, Margaret Moses, Maryanne Benjamin, and Alice Aziz play in the yard of Gibbo Aziz's home on Smith Street in New Britain in 1940. (Courtesy of Alice Aziz David.)

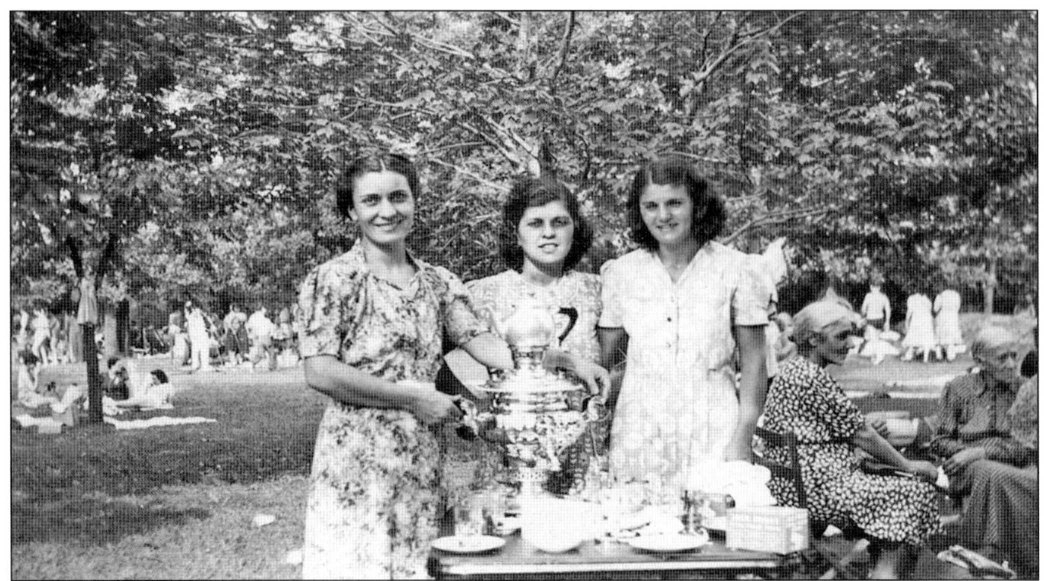

Assyrian Picnic with Samovar. From left to right are Rebekah Yohannan, Mary Benjamin, and Blandina Benjamin. Assyrian picnics were held once a year. Historically, they have been at Trevor Park on Warburton Avenue, Glen Island Park in New Rochelle, Tibbetts Brook Park on Midland Avenue, and Sullivan's Oval on Van Cortlandt Park Avenue and Spruce Street in Yonkers. Today, the picnics are held at Macy Park in Ardsley. (Courtesy of Shirley Benjamin.)

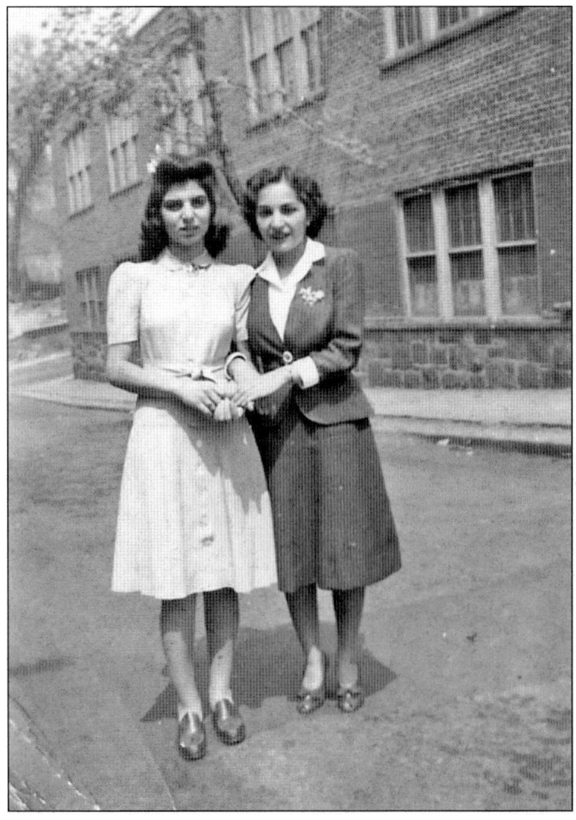

Baba Family. Mary and Irene Baba pose in the schoolyard in Yonkers. (Author's collection.)

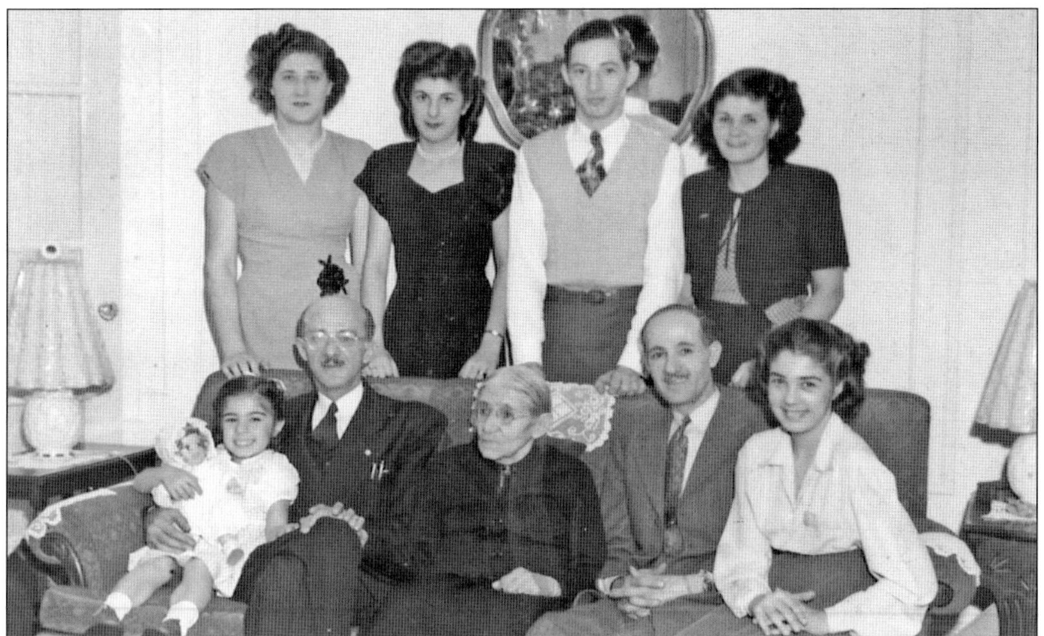

Julia Benjamin with Her Sons' Families. On Christmas in 1944 or 1945, the Benjamin brothers (seated from left to right) Nathan and Nick join their mother, Julia, with (left to right) Joanne (Nick and Blandina's daughter, holding a doll) and her sister Shirley at Nick's side. Standing is Lucy, Nathan's wife, with Lydia (her niece), son David, and sister in-law Blandina, wife of Nick. (Author's collection.)

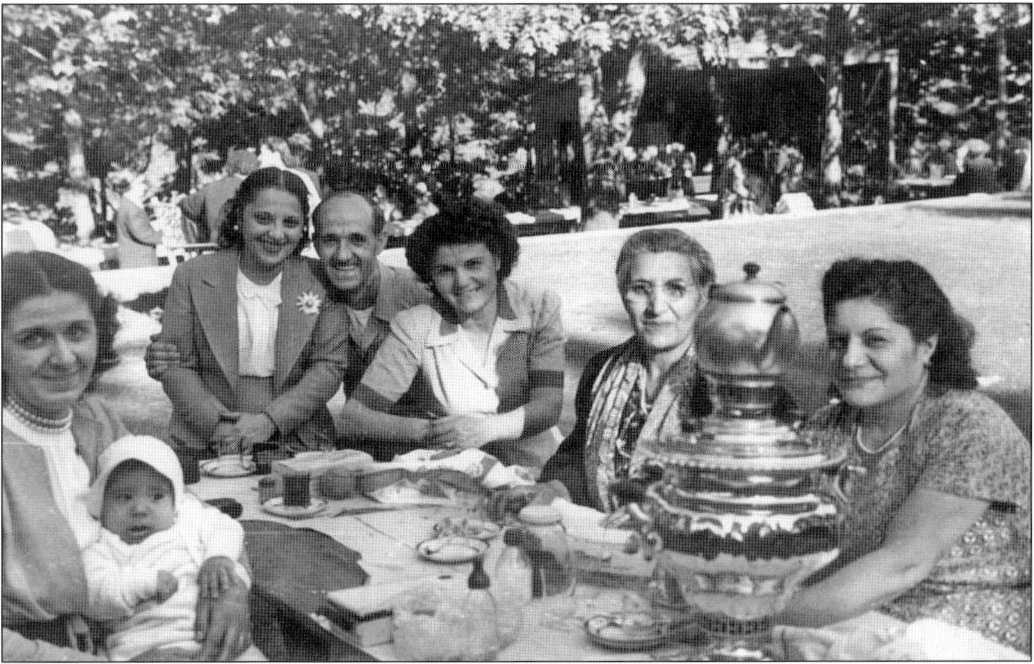

Picnic Assyrian Style. Pictured here are (from left to right) Margaret Jacobs and her son Roger, unidentified, Nicolai Benjamin, Blandina Benjamin, Elizabeth Sargis, and Elizabeth Baba at Glen Island Park in New Rochelle. (Courtesy of Shirley Benjamin.)

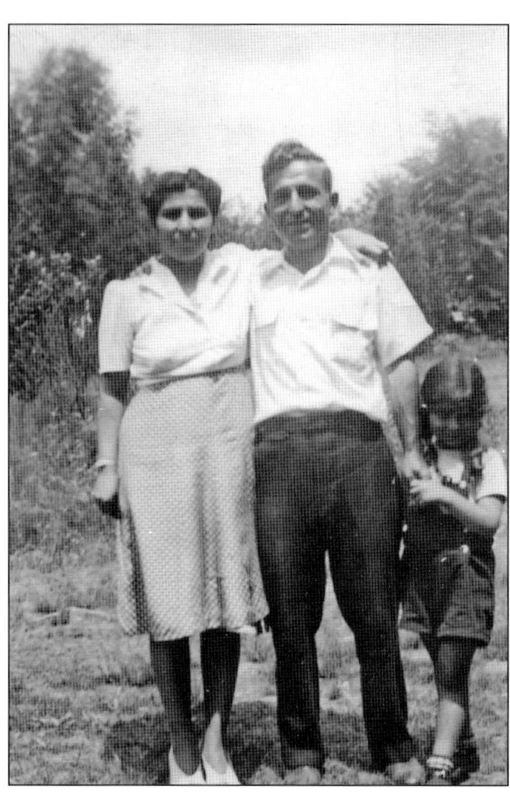

The Aziz Siblings with Niece. Ketro Aziz is with her brother Gibbo and her niece Elaine Benjamin at Gibbo's home on Smith Street in New Britain in 1943. (Courtesy of Alice Aziz David.)

Red Cross Volunteerism. From left to right, Darius Baba, Nazlu Jacobs, and Louisa Jacobs donate a quilt to sell to raise money for the Red Cross during World War II. (Courtesy of Nancy Lee Jacobs.)

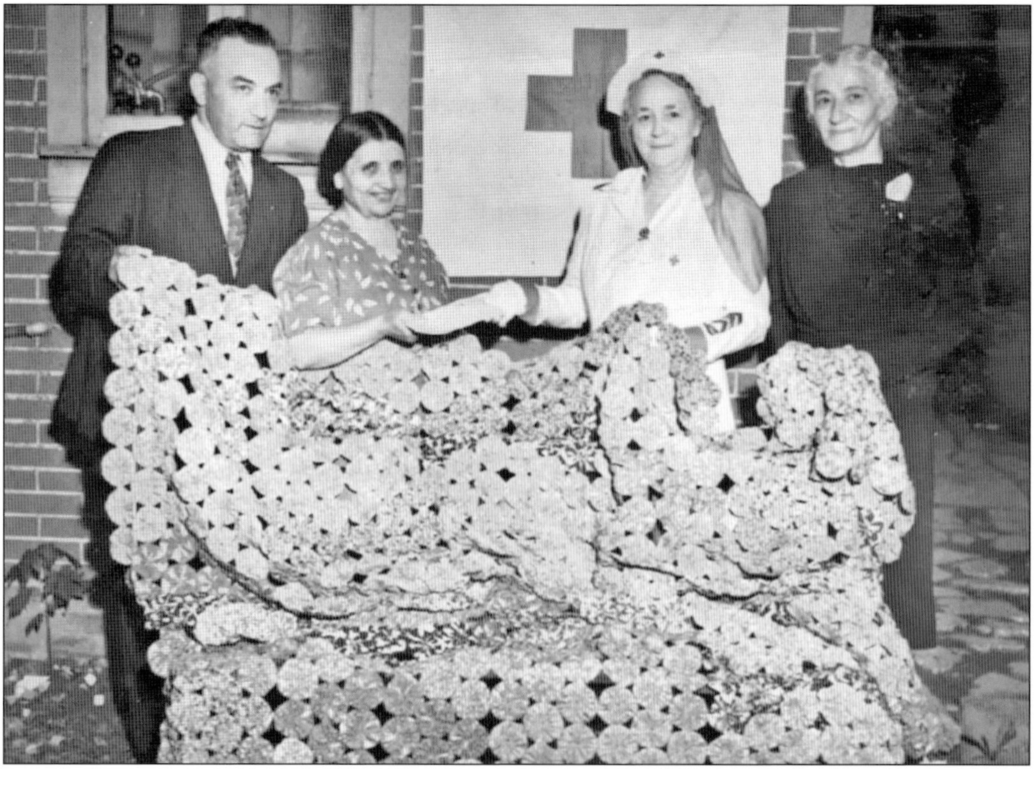

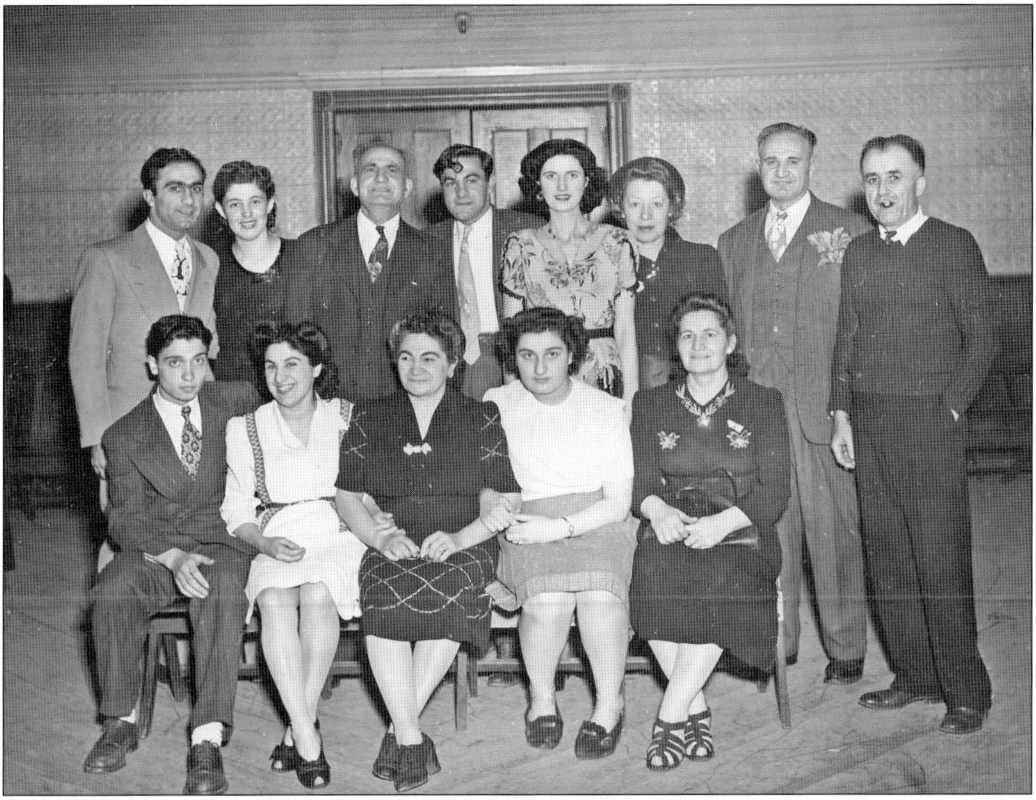

Benny David. The people in this group picture are unidentified except for Benny David (second row, far left). (Courtesy of Joe David.)

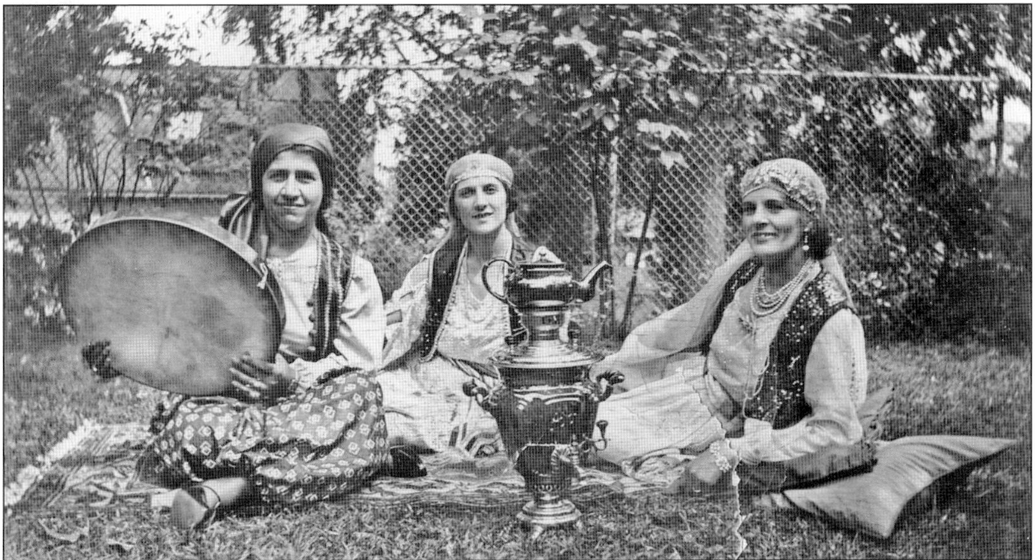

Assyrian Costumes for Show. Assyrians often performed pageants at Fernbrook Hall on Lawrence Street in Yonkers. From left to right are Nanajan Gabriel (Unna), Nancy Eddy, and Emma Benjamin Jacobs. The picture was taken in Emma's yard on Belvedere Drive in the 1940s. (Courtesy of Shirley Benjamin.)

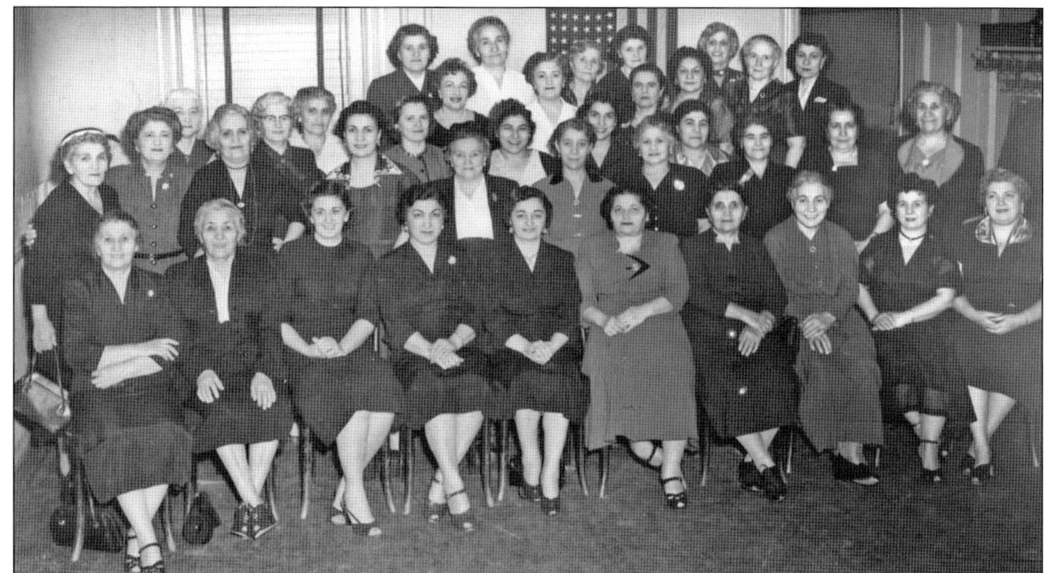

The Assyrian Women's Association, 1954. From left to right are (first row) Asyet Sargis, Elizabeth "Isha" Sargis, Margaret Jacobs, Almas Benjamin, Judith Caram, Marusa Jacobs Aslan, Nazlu Jacobs, Julia Baboo, and an unidentified woman who lived on Knowles Street; (second row), Mrs. Joseph Abraham, Alice Yohannan, Helen Badal, Rebekah Yohannan, Margaret Benjamin, Asley Yonan, Khanitu George, Mrs. Nweeia, Mrs. Joseph, and Mrs. Karaman; (third row) Louise Benjamin Jacobs, Emma Benjamin Jacobs, Margie Eshoo, Ketro Aziz, Florence Jacobs (wife of Jimmy), and Sophia Ameer; (fourth row) Julia Ameer, unidentified, Lucy Sarmast, Miriam Hasrato, Elizabeth Baba, Rabbi Lucy Shlimoun, and Shami Yonan; (fifth Row) Suria Soleiman, Alice Eshoo, unidentified, Blandina Paulus Benjamin, and Zenhela (Zella) Vitti. (Author's collection.)

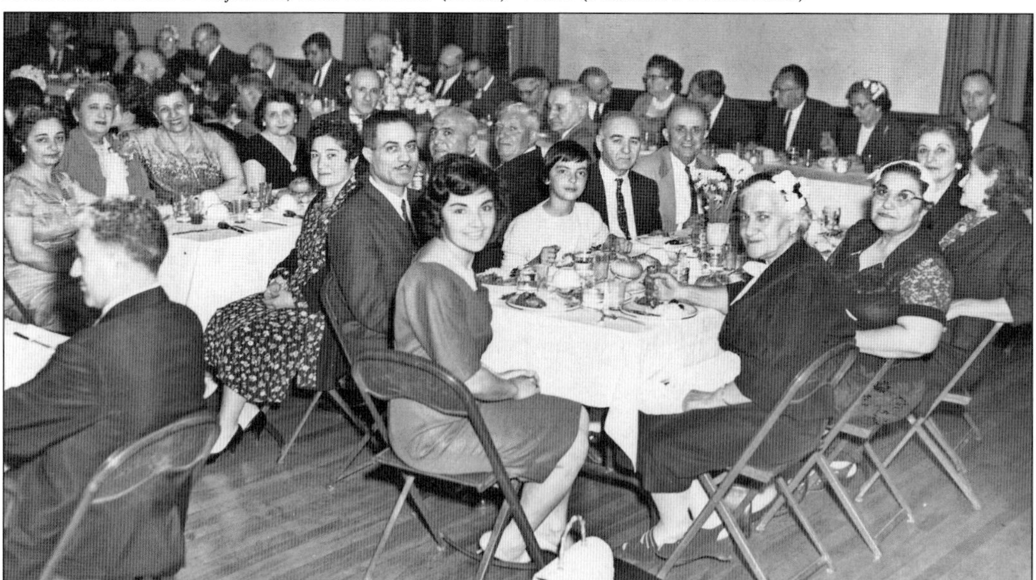

Assyrians with Susanne Ameer Monasa. Pictured are (from left to right) Susanne, Homer Malek, Arabella (Susanne's daughter), Abie David, unidentified, Mary Abraham, and three unidentified. The picture was taken in Yonkers around 1961–1963. The Ameer family came to this country on March 20, 1960, the first day of the Persian New Year. (Courtesy of Susanne Ameer Monasa.)

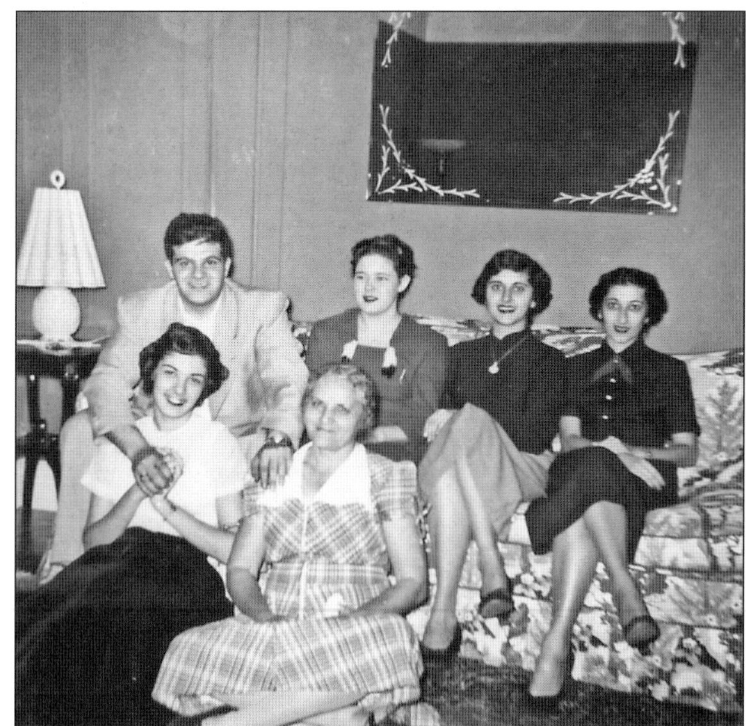

Before the Wedding. Family and friends gather before the wedding of Johnny Jacobs and Susanne Ameer in October 1958. From left to right are (on floor) Shirley Benjamin and Nano Paulus; (on couch) Johnny Jacobs, Joan Benjamin, and Terry and Katherine Bacus. (Author's collection.)

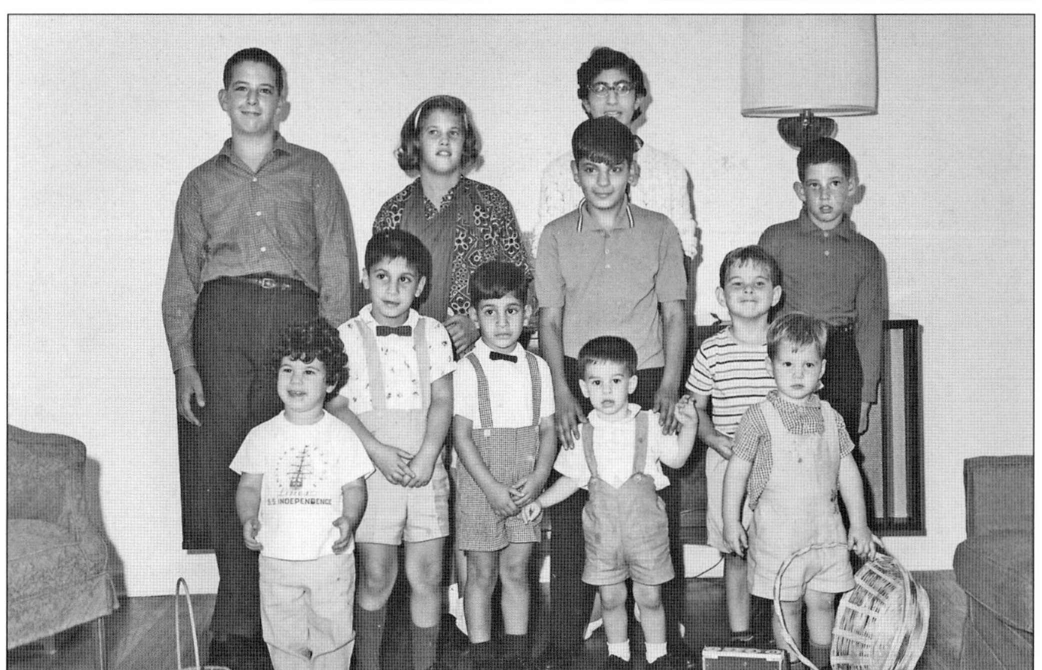

The Benjamin, Jacobs, Shank, and Kambar Children. From left to right are (first row) toddlers Ruth Kambar, Mark and John Jacobs, Gregory Shank, and David Jr. and Gregory Benjamin; (second row) Gilbert and Nancy Benjamin, Karl Jacobs and Liz Jacobs (behind Karl), and Gary Benjamin. This photograph was taken in September 1965 at 89 Travers Avenue in Yonkers. (Author's collection.)

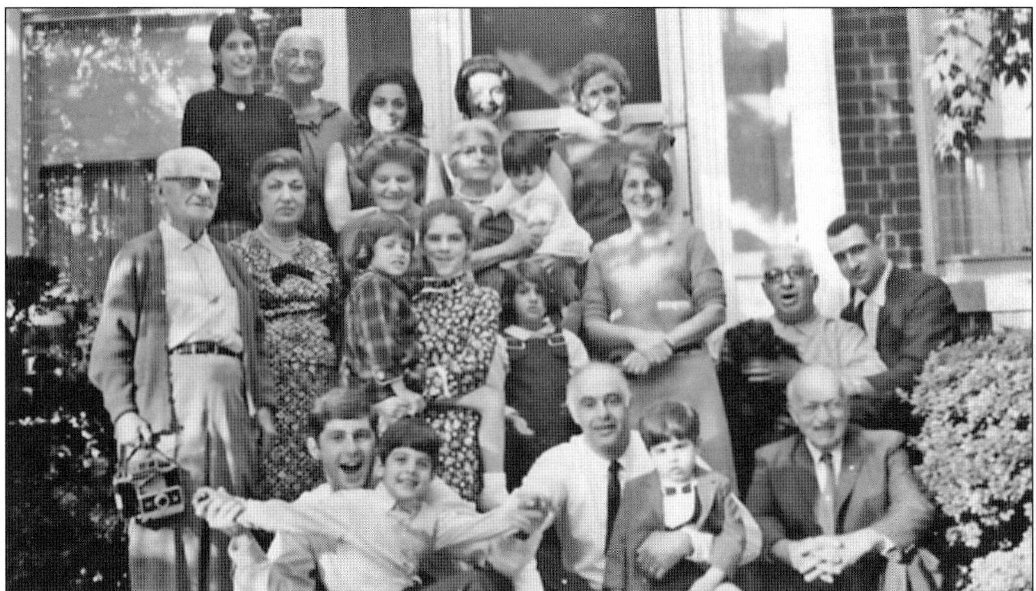

The Jacobs Family. From left to right are (first row) David holding Eugene, Sammy holding Chris, and Jacob Benjamin Ardashier; (second row) Jean Jacobs holding Te-See Bender, Beth Bender, Elizabeth Jacobs Bender, Clarence Jacobs, and Fred Benjamin; (third row) David, Almas Benjamin, Blandina Paulus Jacobs Benjamin, and Emma Benjamin Jacobs holding Leah Jacobs; (fourth row) Louise Jacobs, Louisa (Mahti) Jacobs, Gloria Jacobs, Jean Jacobs, and Margaret M. Yonan Jacobs. This picture was taken in 1969 or 1970 on Belvedere Drive. (Courtesy of Shirley Benjamin.)

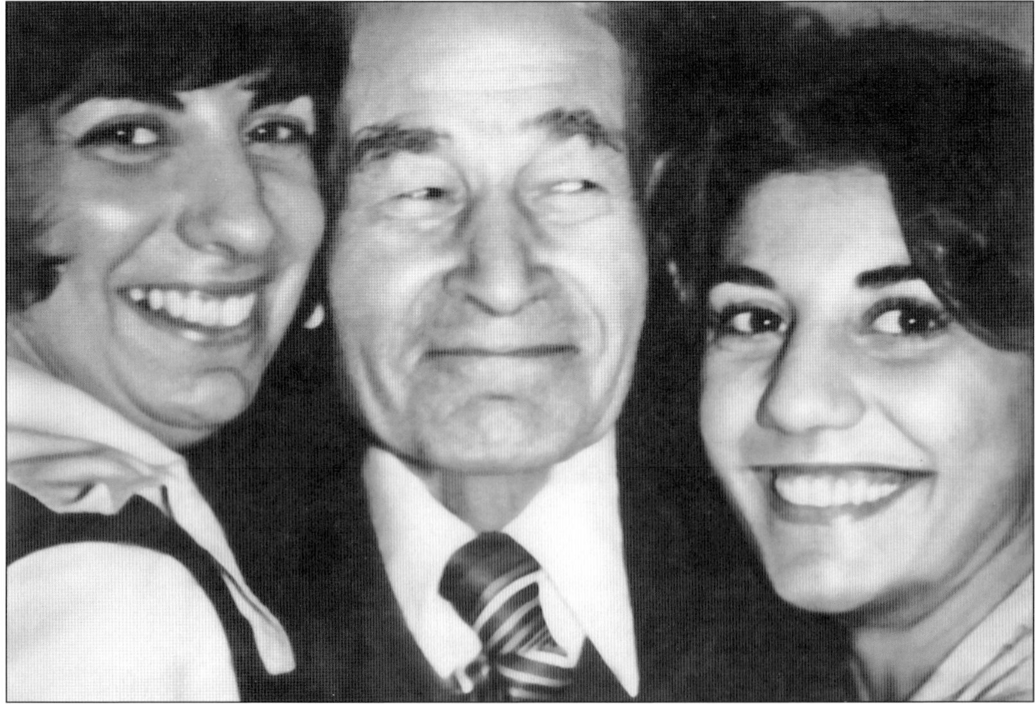

For the Love of Uncle. From left to right are Shaaron Yohanna, her uncle Yonan Kambar, and her sister Michele Yohanna in the 1970s. (Courtesy of Michele Yohanna.)

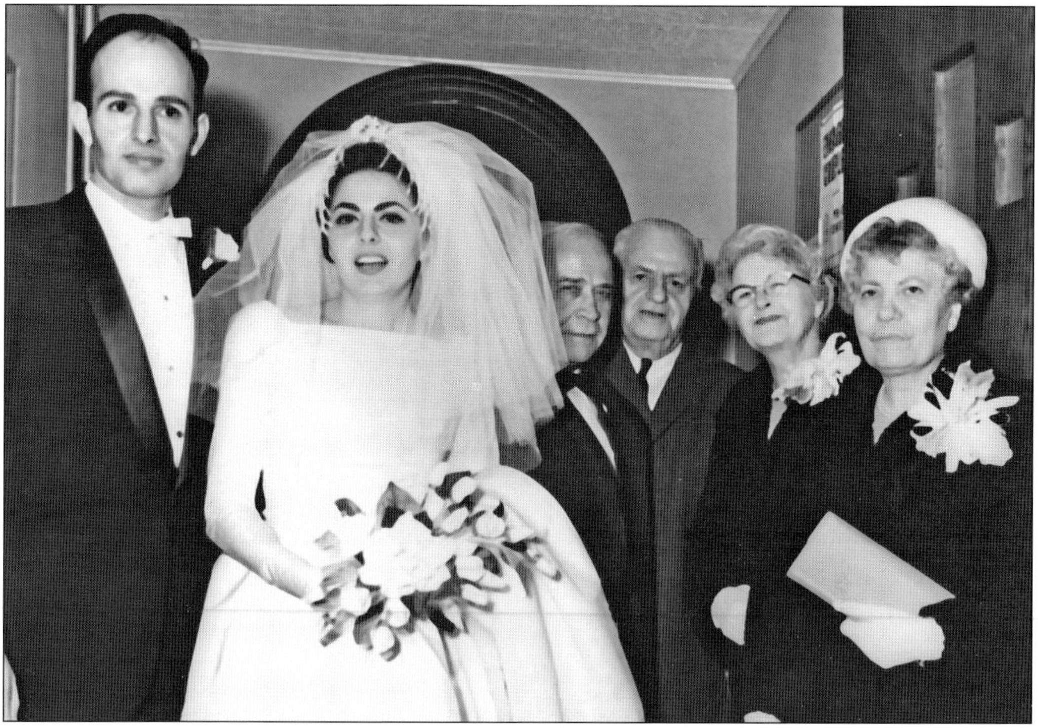

Mr. and Mrs. Jacobs, January 27, 1963. Pictured at the wedding of Eugene and Gloria Jacobs are (from left to right) Eugene and Gloria Jacobs and Gloria's father, Frank Greco; Eugene's parents, David and Emma Jacobs; and Gloria's mother, Virginia Greco. The wedding took place at St. Margaret's Church in Riverdale. (Courtesy of Jean Jacobs Correa.)

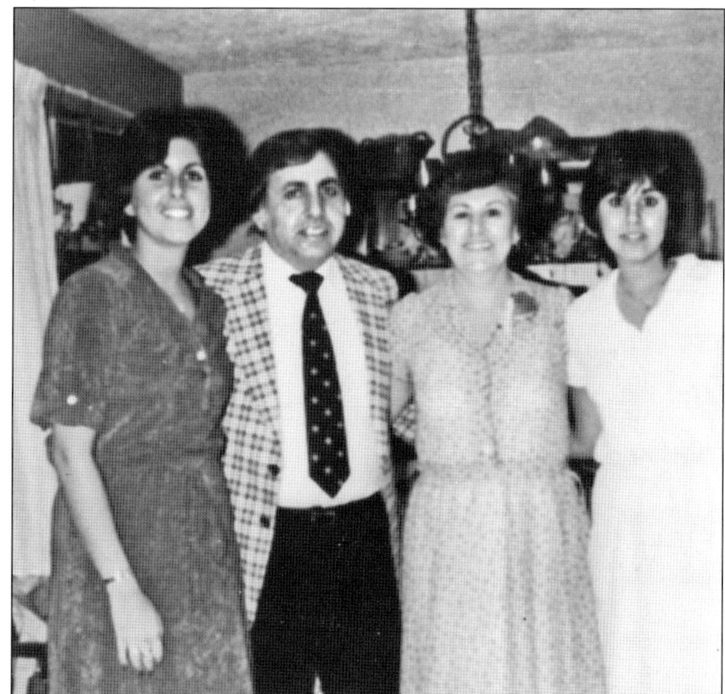

The Sargis Family. Pictured here from left to right are Billy, Karen, Lilly, and Elizabeth Sargis at their home in Yonkers in the 1970s. (Courtesy of the William and Lilly Sargis family.)

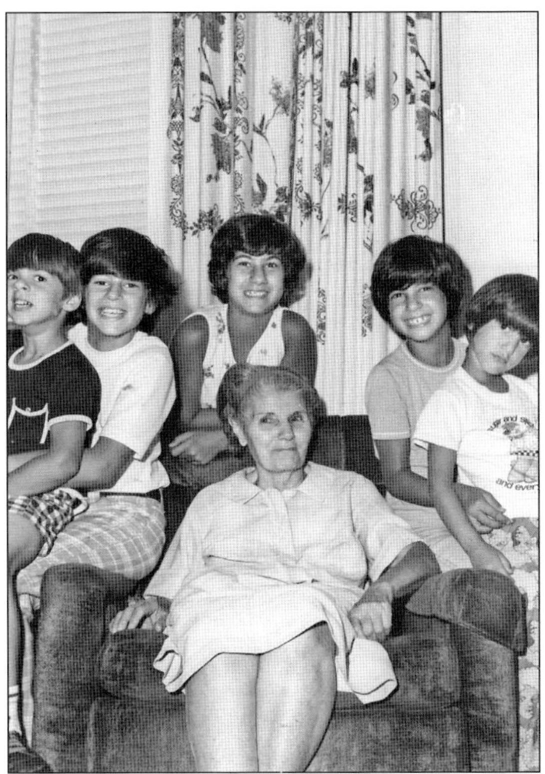

Visiting Nana. From left to right are Richard and Gregory Shank, Ruth Kambar, Blandina Paulus Jacobs Benjamin, and Carol and Kim Kambar at 34 Pier Street in Yonkers in 1975 or 1976. (Author's collection.)

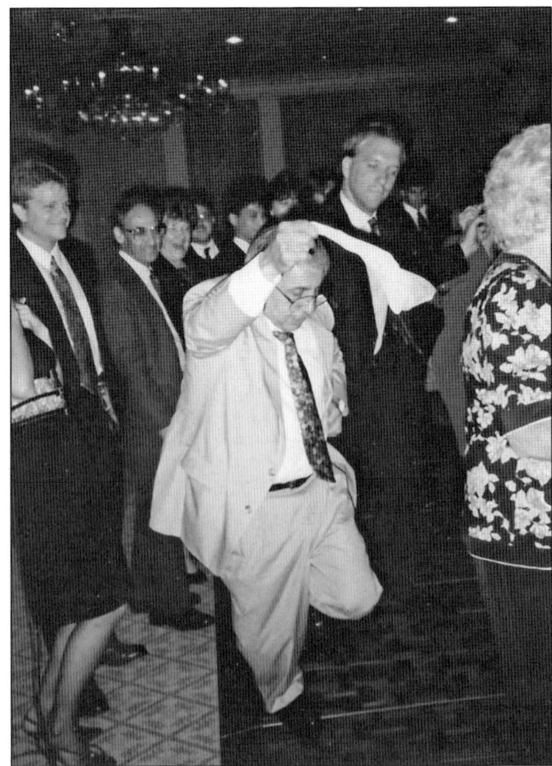

William Sargis and Michael Kikkert. Billy (left) and Michael are dancing the *sheikhani* at Kellyanne Kambar's wedding in June 1992. Directly behind Michael are Bob and Jean Kambar. (Author's collection.)

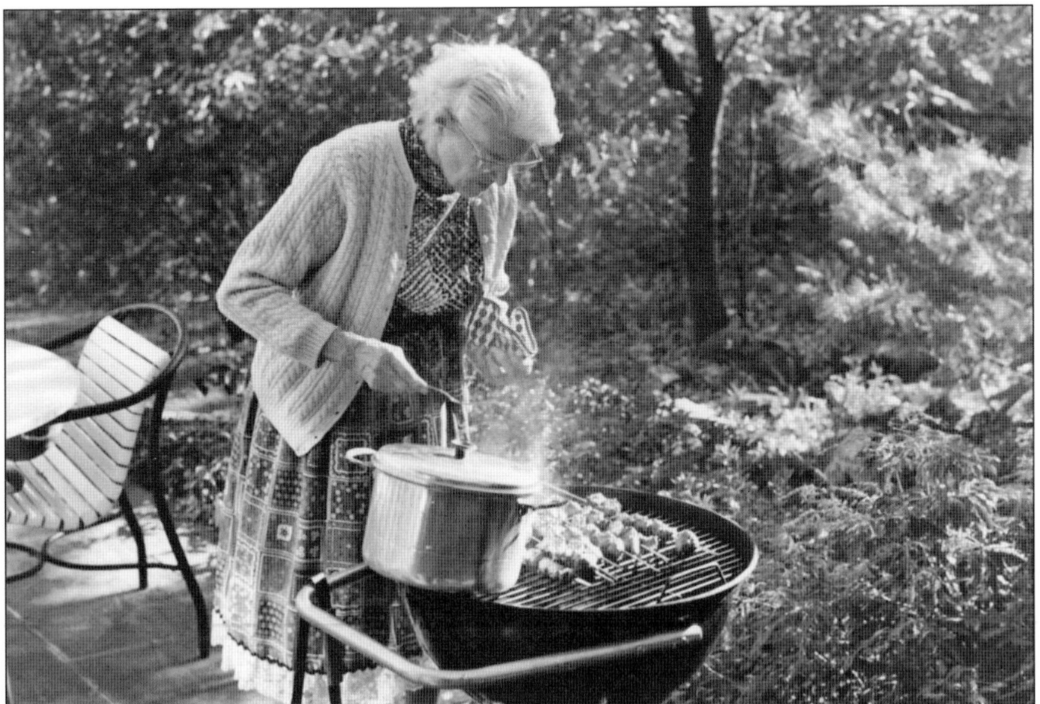

Emma Jacobs Makes Shish Kabob. Emma Jacobs is pictured in the backyard of her daughter Elizabeth's home in Chappaqua, New York. (Author's collection.)

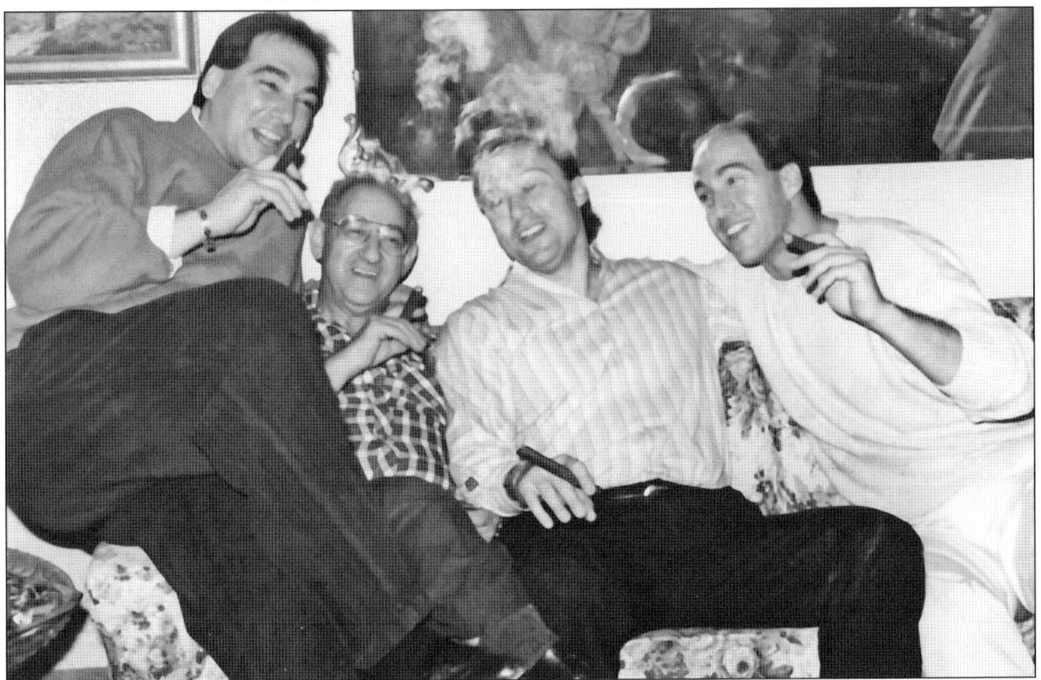

Family Bonding. From left to right are Robbie Muldoon, William Kambar, John Muldoon, and David Muldoon at Nick Benjamin's 90th birthday party in Yonkers in December 1990. (Author's collection.)

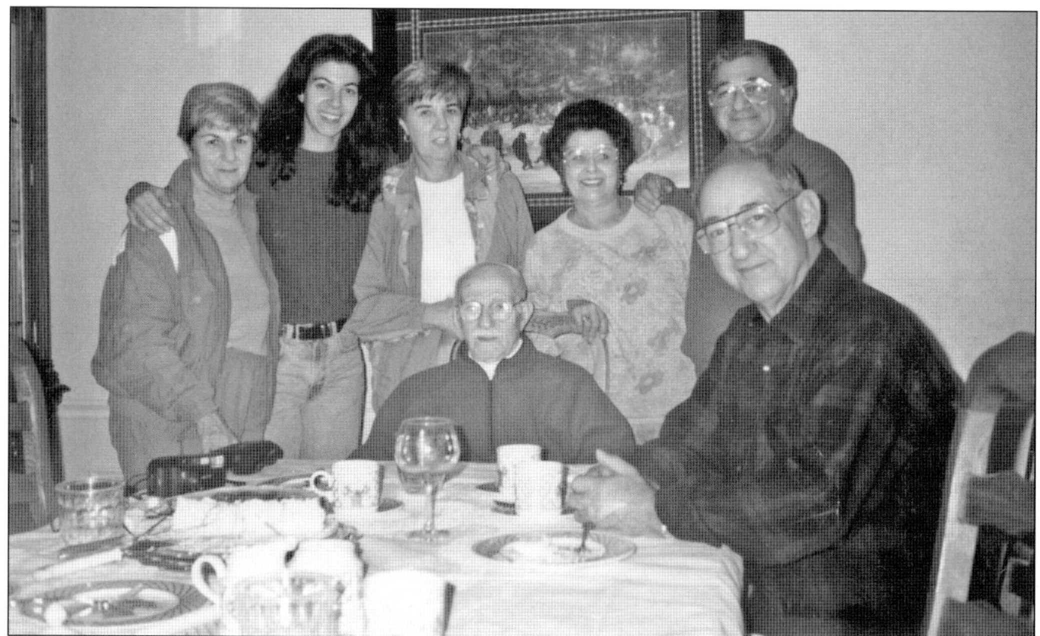

Yonkers Family Visits Alice in Dallas. From left to right are Lydia Kambar, Carol Silvestri Kambar, Shirley Benjamin, Alice Ameer Hurmis, Dave Hurmis, and William Kambar. Seated is Nicholas Benjamin at 94 years old in January 1995. Alice was from Yonkers but had moved to Dallas. This reunion took place after Carol Silvestri moved to Plano. Lydia and Alice hadn't seen each other in 30 years. Soon after, Alice delivered homemade *dolma* to Carol at work. (Author's collection.)

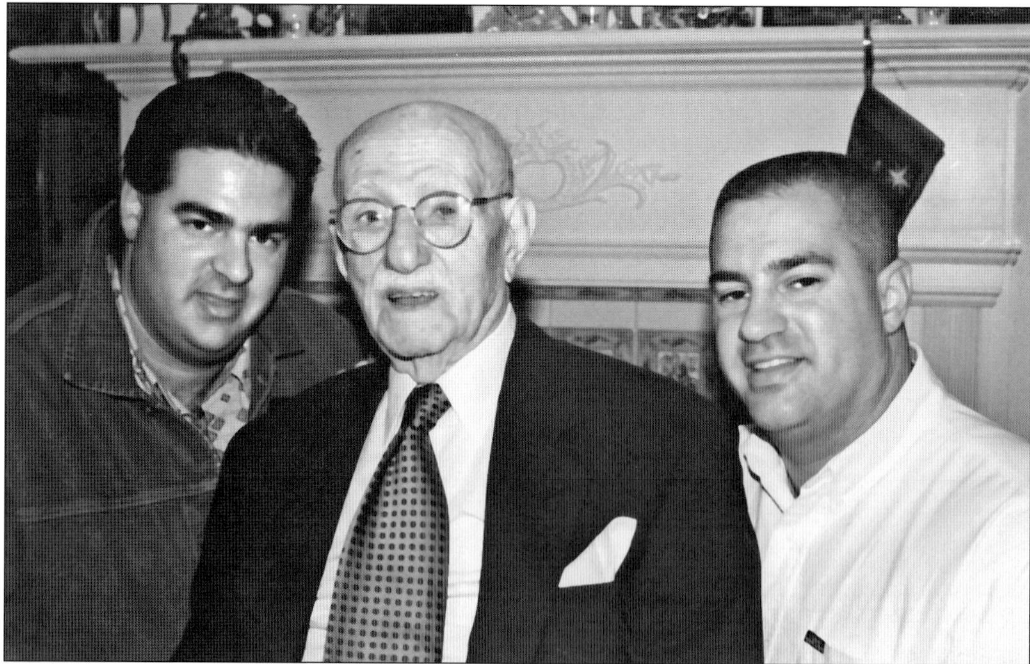

Nick Benjamin's 100th Birthday. Nick is pictured on December 3, 2000, with his daughter Joanne's sons Richard (left) and Gregory Shank. Both grandsons were raised in Yonkers. (Author's collection.)

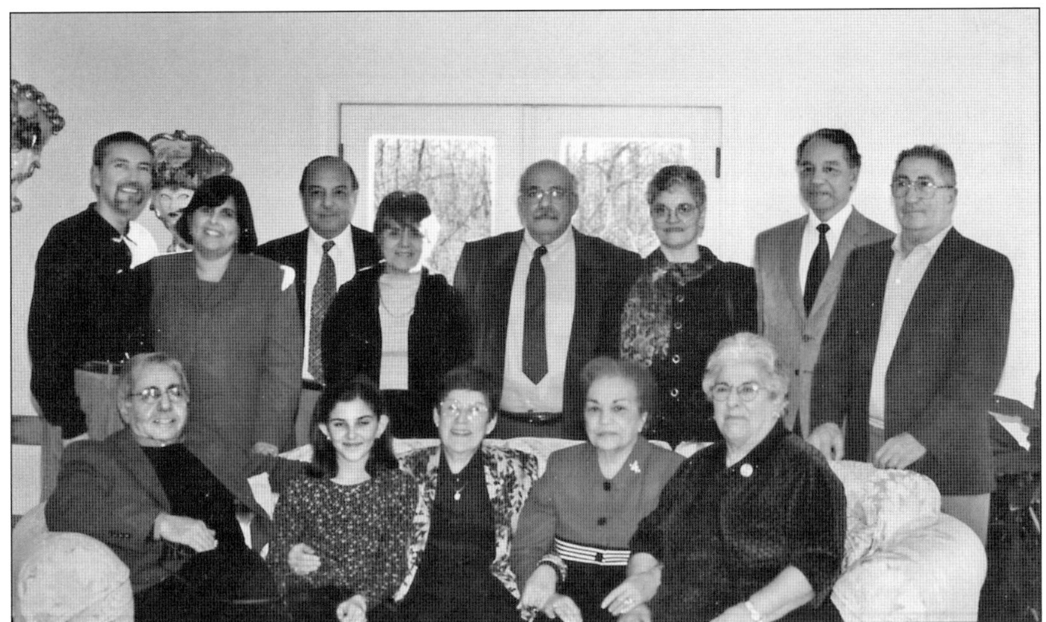

Yonkers Friends. The families celebrate Nick Benjamin's 100th birthday on December 3, 2000, two days before his actual birthday. Seated from right to left are Billy Sargis, his granddaughter Kathryn McCarthy, Lilly Nweeia Sargis, Irene Baba, and Dottie Eshoo Dalia; (second row) Andrew Shimrock (husband of Karen Sargis), Karen Sargis, Darius and Barbara Ovanes Baba, John and Margarita Ameer, Danny Baba, and David Dalia. The gathering was at Nick's granddaughter's home in Pawling, New York. (Author's collection.)

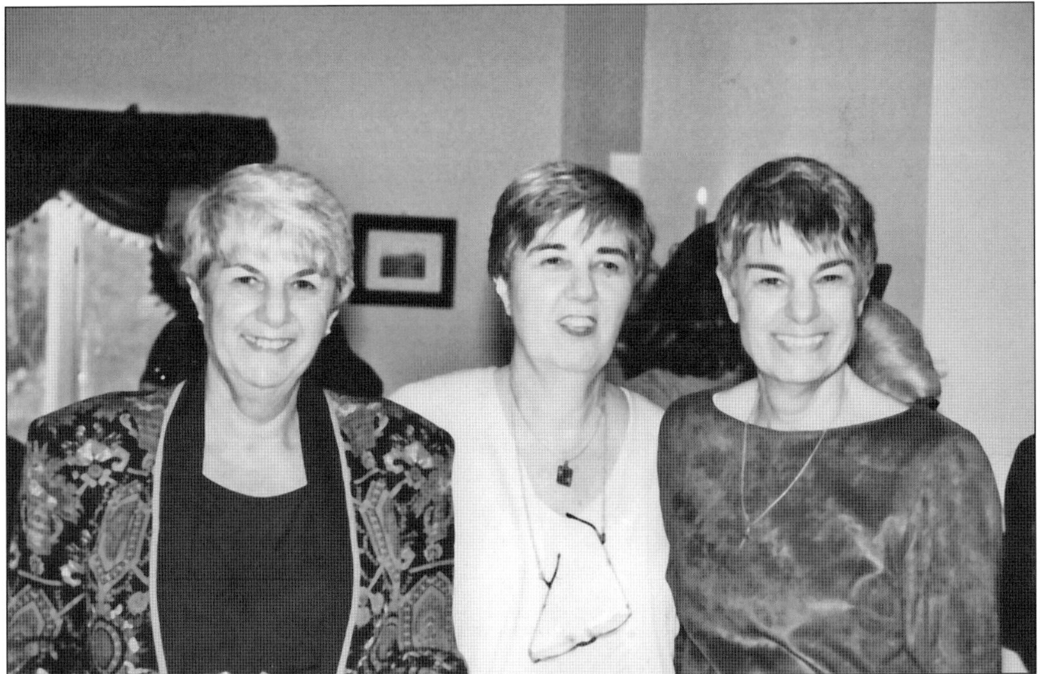

The Benjamin Sisters. From left to right are Lydia Kambar, Shirley Benjamin, and Joanne Shank at the 100th birthday celebration of their father, Nick, in December 2000. (Author's collection.)

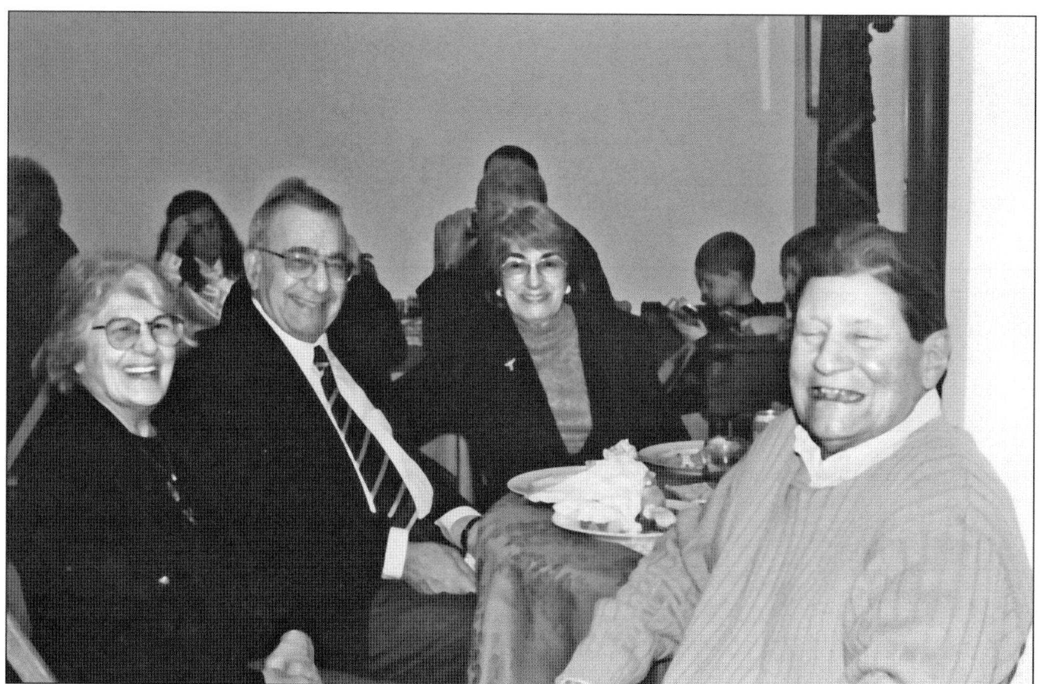

NICK'S 100TH. From left to right are Elizabeth Jacobs Bender, Sam Jacobs (the son of Lucy and Samuel Jacobs), Betty Benjamin Muldoon, and Jerry Bender at Nick Benjamin's 100th birthday celebration in December 2000. (Author's collection.)

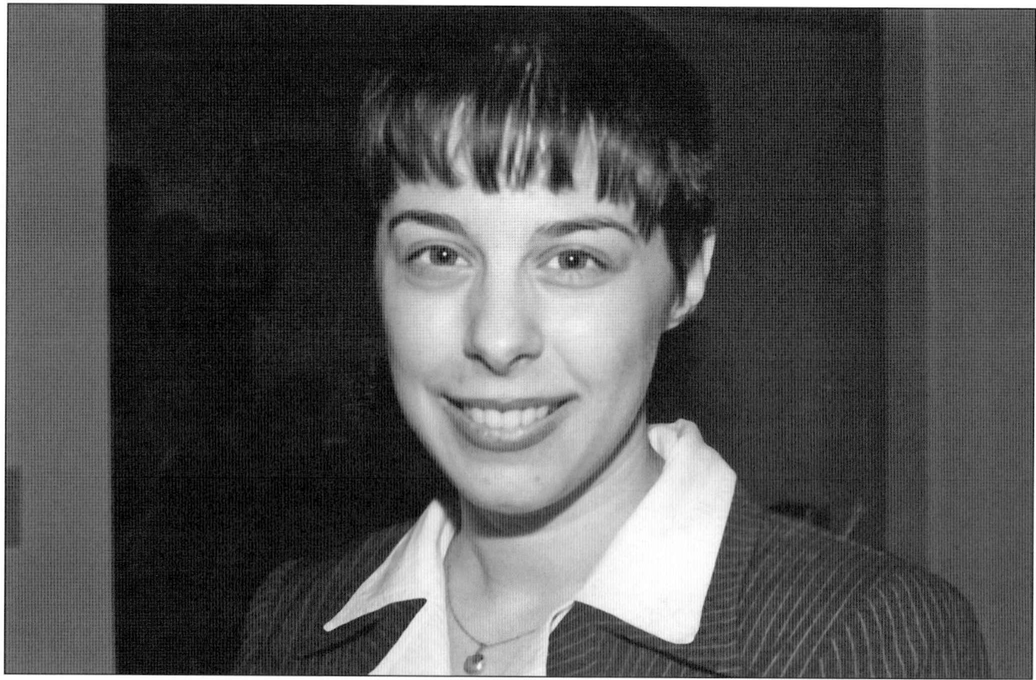

VICTORIA BLANDINA SHANK. Victoria, daughter of Joanne Benjamin Shank and George Shank, is pictured at her grandfather Nick Benjamin's 100th birthday party on December 2, 2000. (Author's collection.)

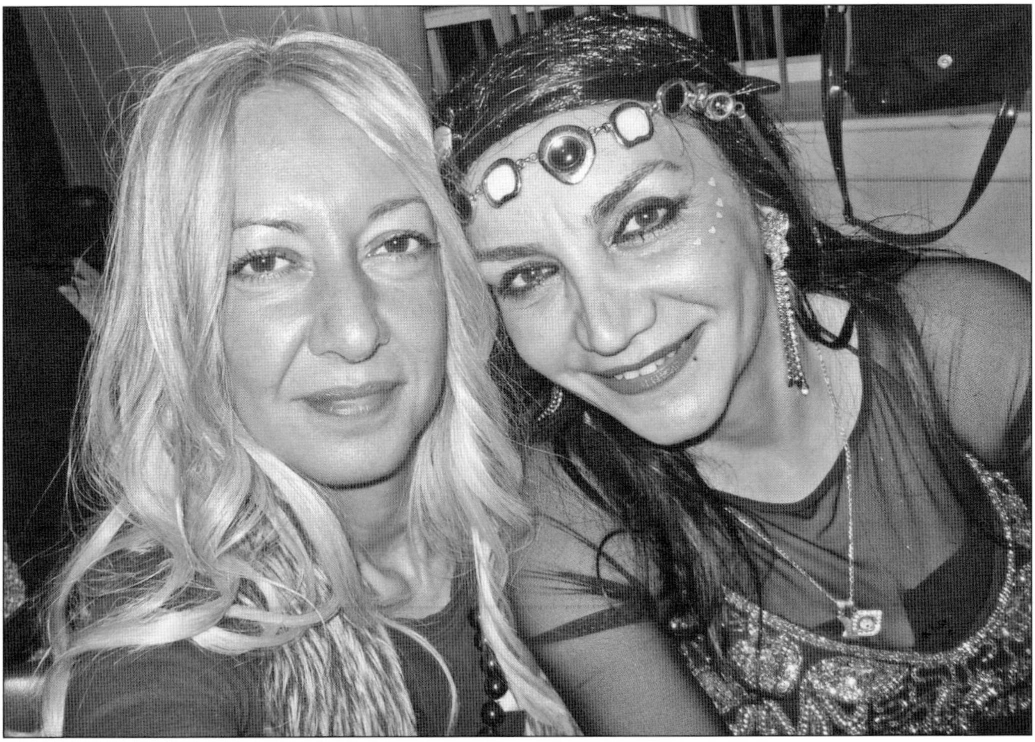

Assyrian American Association's Halloween Party. Fiona Michaels-Lazar (left) and Janeet Yousif Francis are pictured in 2014. (Courtesy of Fiona Michaels-Lazar.)

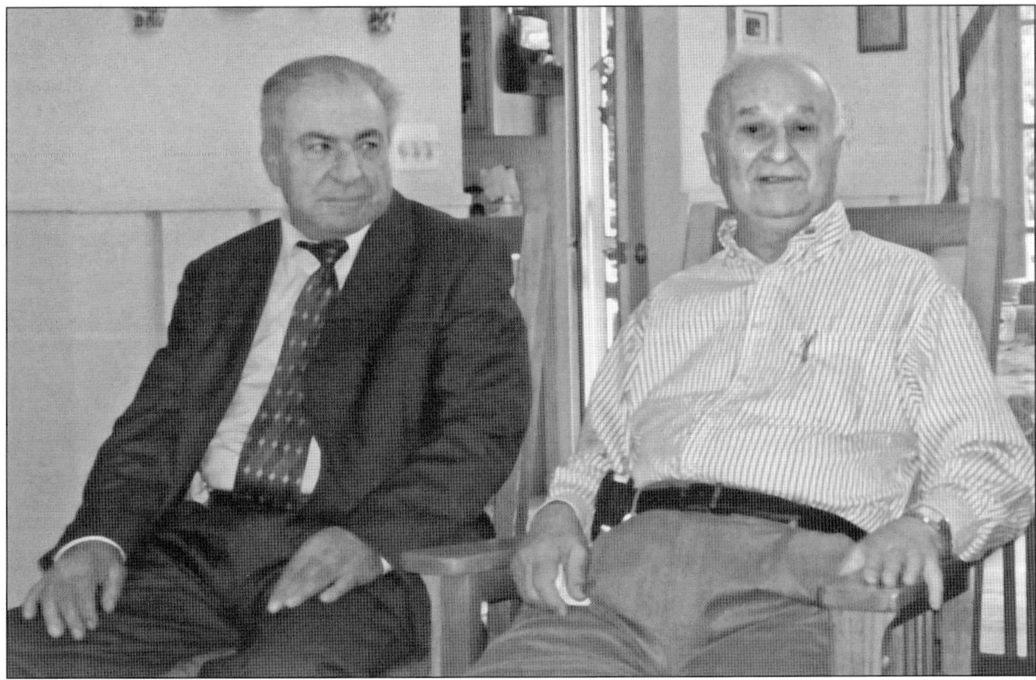

Tickran Naybeen (left) and Ivan Mirza. This picture was taken at the Multari home in Pound Ridge, New York, in 2005. (Courtesy of Nancy Multari.)

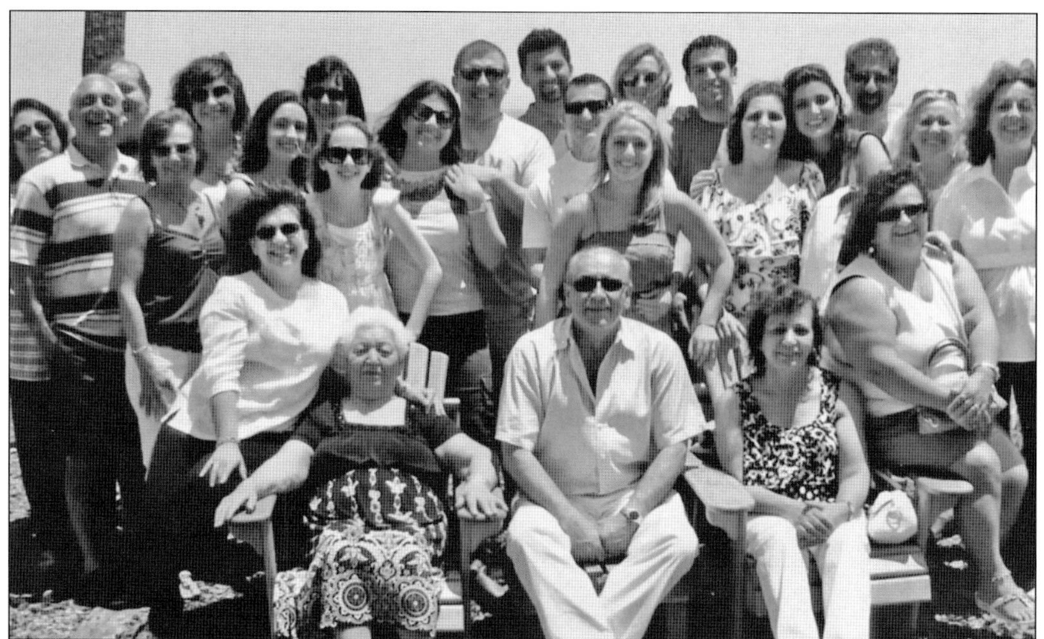

Amelia Island, Memorial Day Weekend, 2009. From left to right are (first row) Jacquie BabayiKunka (on edge of chair), Sara Jerjis Shabdin, Jonathan Shabdin, Mimi Shabdin, and Betty Mirza (on arm of chair); (second row) Connie Ameer, Jaime Kunka, Stephanie Ishoo, Juliet Gevargis-Mizimakoski, Marlene Ameer, Jennifer Ameer Farrell, Arni Sarbadian, and Zofia Gevargis; (third row) Jeff Ameer, Gina Marie Engels, Bale Mizimakoski, and Scott Farrell; (fourth row) Jeff's sister, unidentified, Gina Marie Engels, George Gevargis, two unidentified, and John Gevargis. (Courtesy of Jacquie BabayiKunka.)

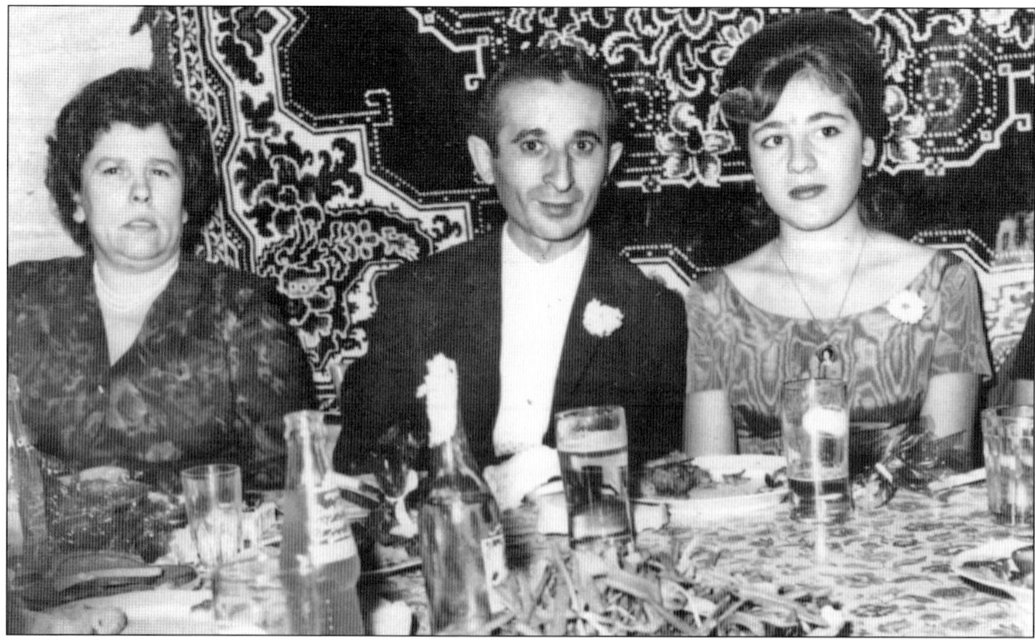

Mirza and Shumunnedjad Engagement Party. From left to right are unidentified, Ivan Mirza, and Nina Shumunnedjad in 1963. (Courtesy of Nancy Multari.)

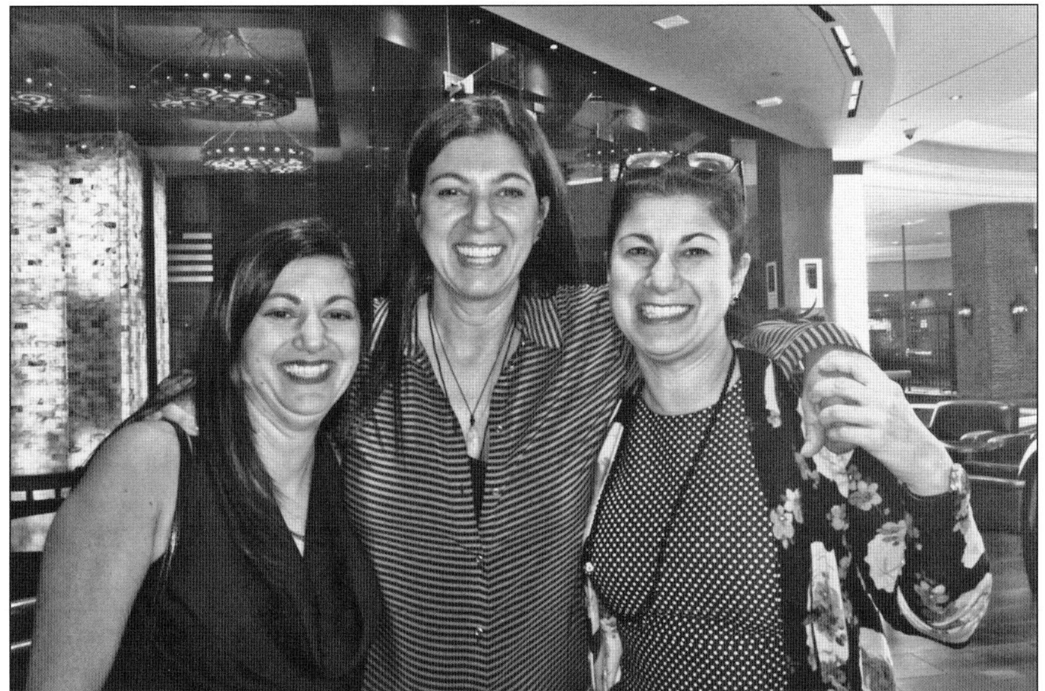

The Kambar Sisters. The sisters are celebrating Shirley Benjamin's birthday at Foxwood Casino in Connecticut. From left to right are Kim, Carol, and Ruth in November 2013. (Author's collection.)

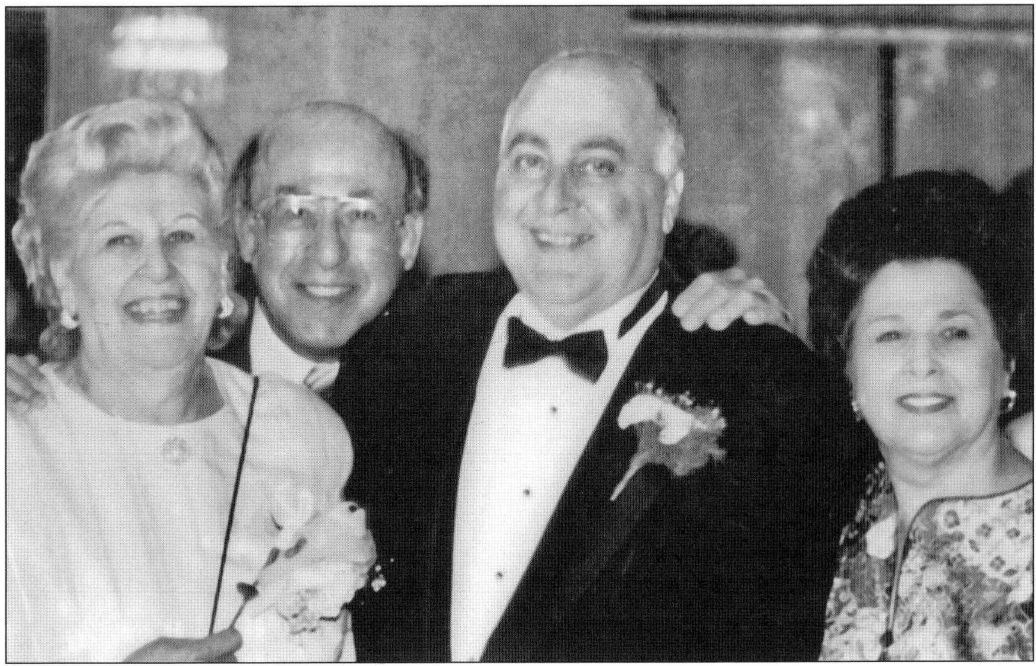

The Ameer and Sargis Families. From left to right, Sadie Ameer Sargis, Robert Ameer, Sargis (Sonny) Ameer, and Alice Ameer Hurmis are pictured at John Ameer's wedding in Brooklyn in 1996. (Courtesy of David Odishoo.)

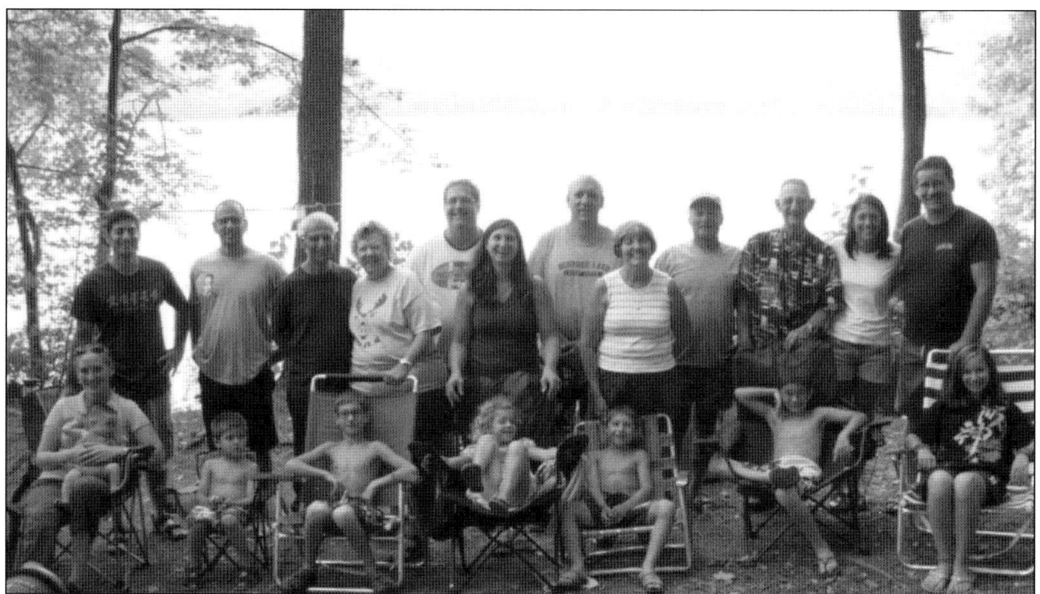

Kambar Family on Lake George. Most of the Kambar clan gathered on Labor Day weekend, September 4, 2011. From left to right are (first row) Rene, baby Emma, and Nathan Kambar; Jacob, Hannah, and Noah Szymanski; and Maxwell and Nicole Kambar; (second row) Christopher Kambar; Alexander Kambar; Bob and Jean Kambar; Chett Szymanksi; Kelly Anne Kambar Szymanski, Michael Kikkert; Diana and Ken Kambar; William Kambar; Kim Kambar Carpenter; and Bruce Carpenter.

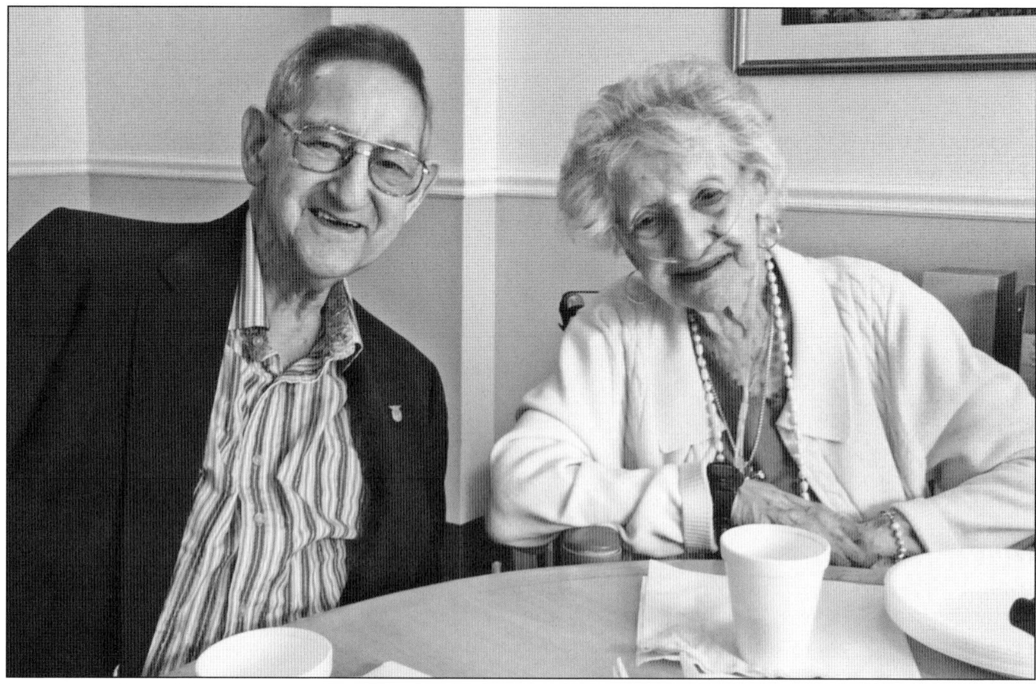

Bill and Jan. Ninety-year-old Bill Kambar visits his 100-year-old aunt Jan "Jennie" Moorad Kambar just four days before her birthday. The picture was taken in Ridgefield, Connecticut, in 2015. (Author's collection.)

Six

Contemporary Assyrian Life in Yonkers

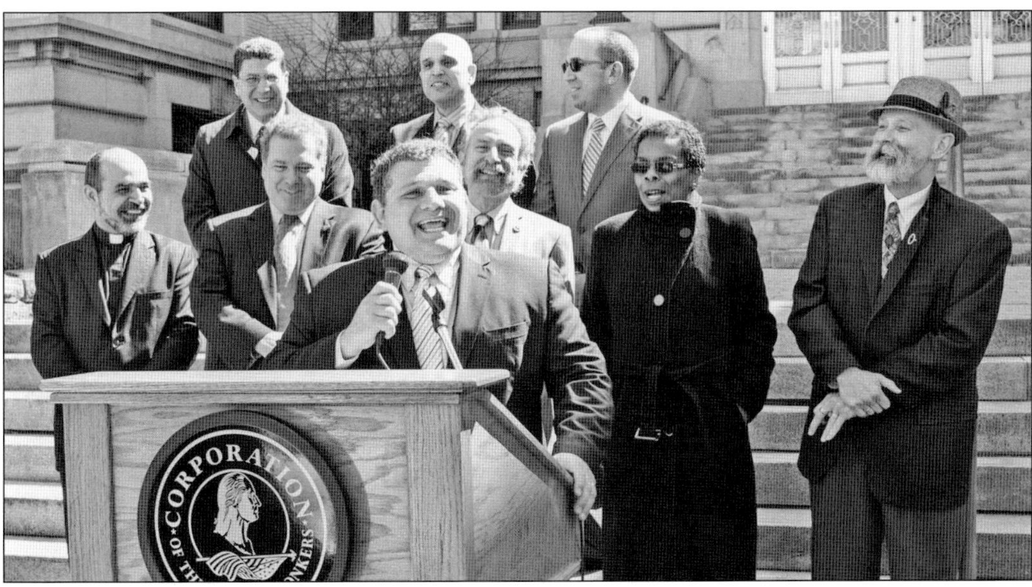

Assyrian Flag Raising, Yonkers City Hall, April 2017. In 1968, Assyrian artist George Bit Atanus of Tehran designed the Assyrian flag to represent the hope of returning to a unified community in Mesopotamia, the original homeland of the Assyrians. In 1974, the sixth congress of the Assyrian Universal Alliance met in Yonkers and approved the flag. The Assyrian National Federation and Bet-Nahrain Democratic Party adopted it. In 2015, this flag was raised at Yonkers City Hall to acknowledge the Assyrian New Year and the 100th anniversary of the Assyrian American Association, established by David Jacobs. Each year since, Mayor Michael Spano and city council president Liam McLaughlin have joined the Yonkers Assyrian community to celebrate. (Courtesy of Susy Gevarguize.)

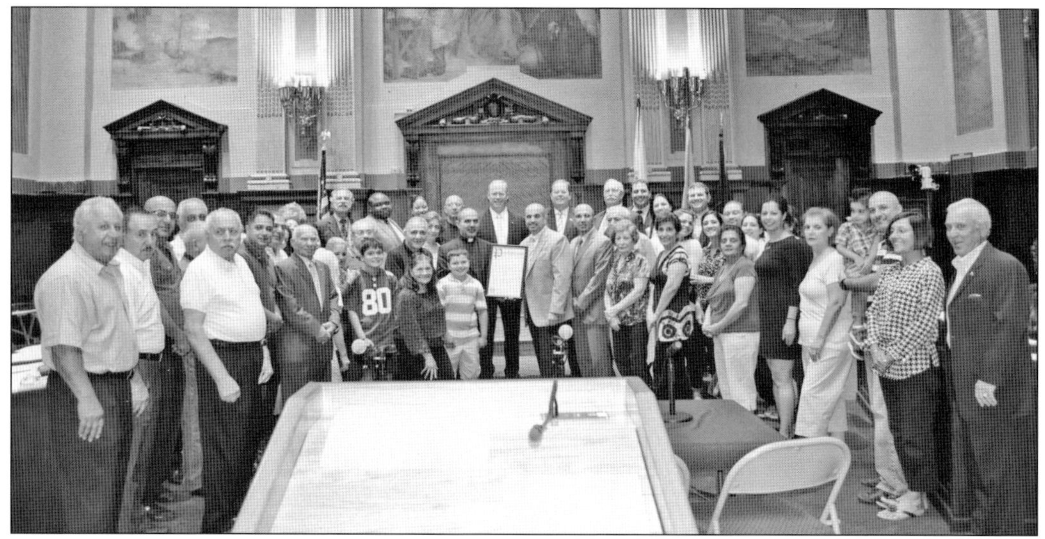

Assyrian Proclamation. This photograph was taken at Yonkers City Hall on September 10, 2014, at the presentation of the resolution supporting Assyrian Christians and condemning ISIS. From left to right are (first row) Vovo David Rafael, Gil Behpour, Youra Belvamrood, Valentine Shamoun, Lila Givargidze, Alex Gevarguize, Anna Constantine, Jacob Constantine, Sara Akalski, Valeh Ackerman, Marlene Eskander, Jennifer Danialan, Lily David, Zaya Brakhia, George Brakhia, Maxine Crea, and two unidentified; (second row) Edmond Constantine, Lova Atini, Joseph Lazar, Boris Eshoo, Edmond Essapour, Simon Lazar, Nancy Multari, Alice David, Souren Givargidze, Robert Shummunejad, Diane Mirza, Rev. Addai Francis, Fred Sarkiso, Joseph Akalski, Tikran Naybeen, Ashley Youhan, Pauline Shummunejad, Zaya Givargidze, and Rosalie Shummunejad; (third row) city council members Michael Sabatino, Christopher A. Johnson, Corazon Pineda-Isaac, Liam McLaughlin, John Larkin, Mike Breen, Jeanette Shummunejad, and Mark Constantine. (Courtesy of Susy Gevarguize.)

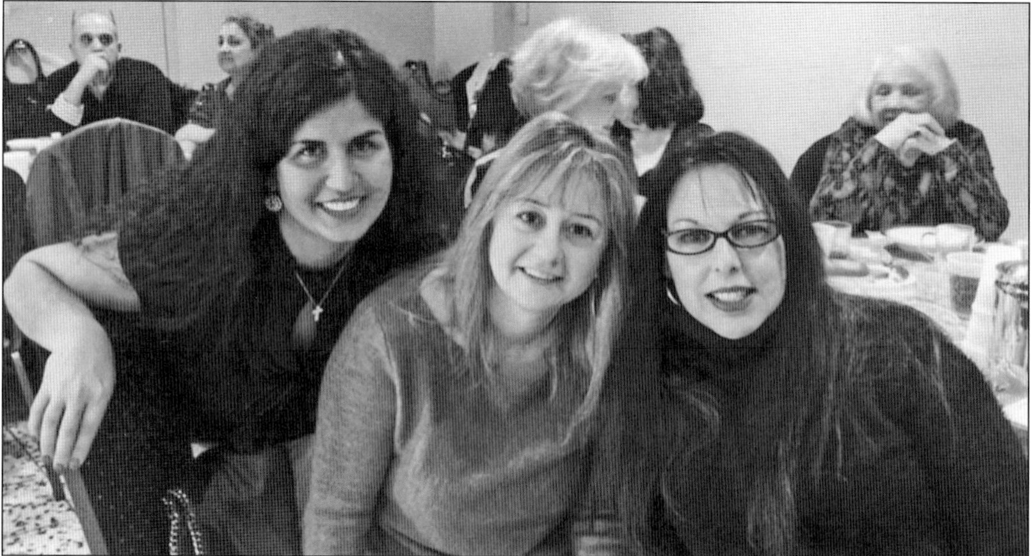

Mar Mari Members. From left to right, Jennifer Aiwazzi, Susy Gevarguize, and Denise Sargis are pictured in the fellowship hall of the Mar Mari Parish for Sunday breakfast after mass in 2017. (Author's collection.)

Assyrian Club Event. To kick off the opening of the gallery exhibit Assyrians in Yonkers, Jordan Allott and Helma Adde's film *Our Last Stand* drew 200 Assyrians and friends from throughout the country. Pictured here, Helma Adde and Dr. Sargon Donabed discuss the current plight of the Assyrians as they continue to face genocide in the Middle East. Valeh and Fred Sarkiso prepared the dinner and hosted the event on October 8, 2017, at the Assyrian Club on Ludlow Street. (Author's collection.)

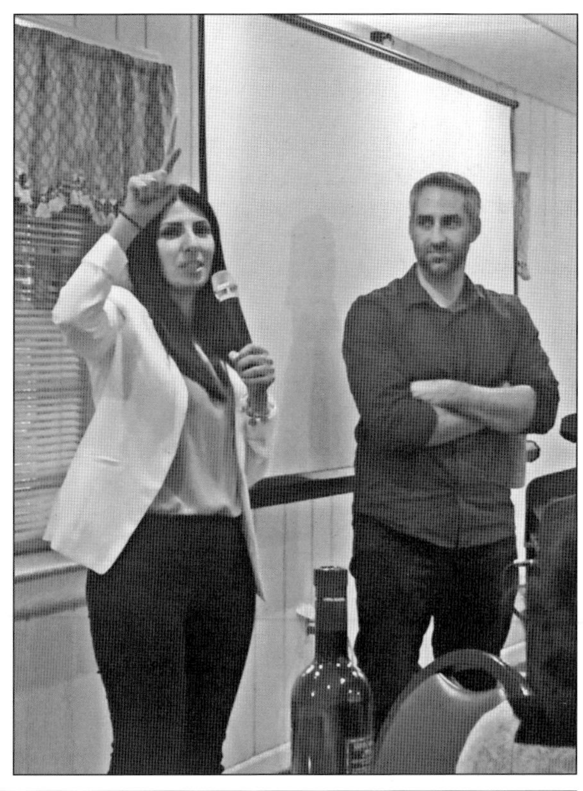

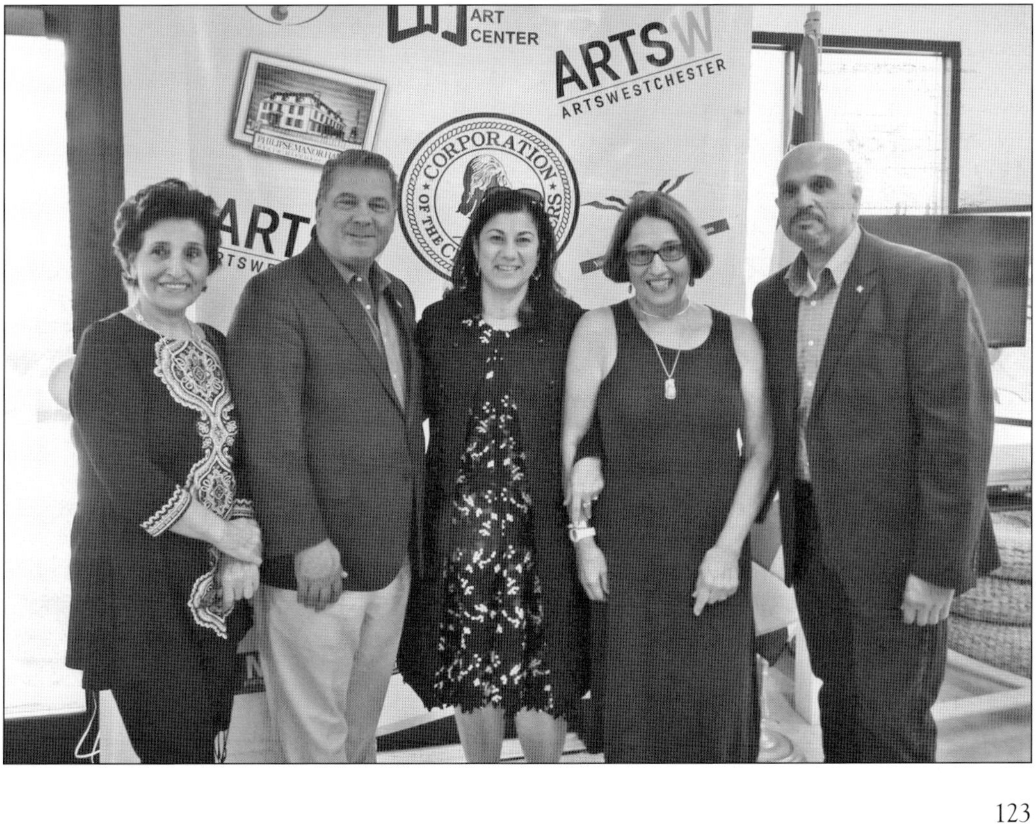

Assyrians in Yonkers Exhibit. On October 9, 2017, (from left to right) Valeh Sarkiso and Mayor Mike Spano join Ruth Kambar, curator of photography and narrative; artist Kathy Yacoe, curator of art and photography; and Fred Sarkiso, president of the Assyrian American Association, at the exhibit's opening ceremony, held at the Blue Door Gallery. (Courtesy of Jacquie BabayiKunka.)

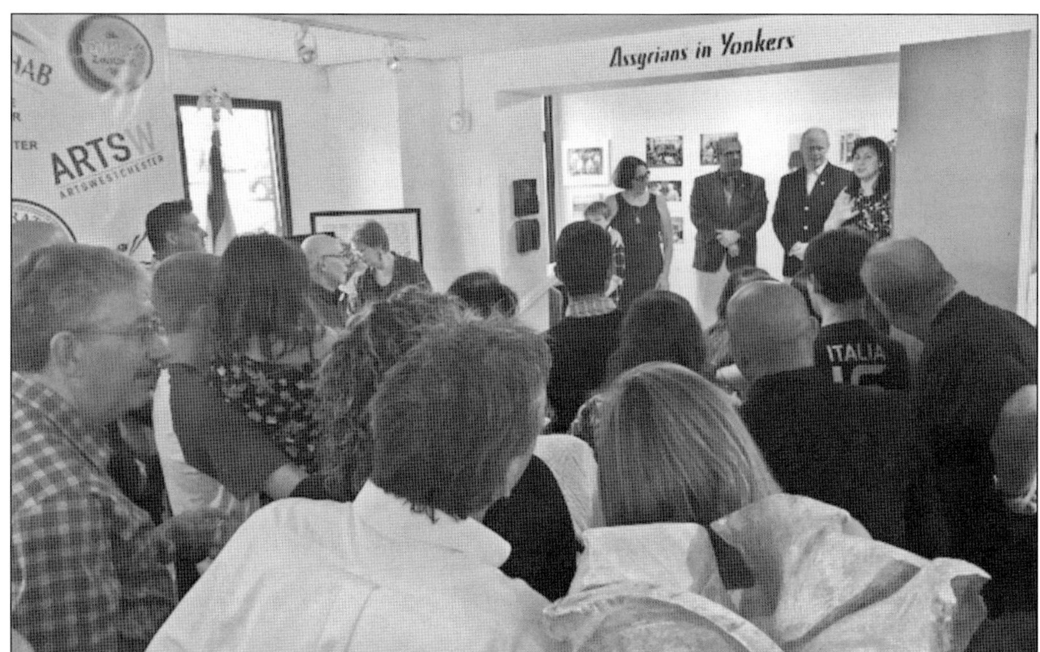

Addressing Gallery Visitors. At the opening of the Assyrians in Yonkers exhibit at the Blue Door Gallery on October 9, 2017, in front of the exhibit banner donated by Fred Sarkiso, (from left to right) Kathy Yacoe, Mayor Mike Spano, city council president Liam McLaughlin, and Ruth Kambar address their audience, telling the tale of the Assyrians in Yonkers. (Courtesy of Jacquie BabayiKunka.)

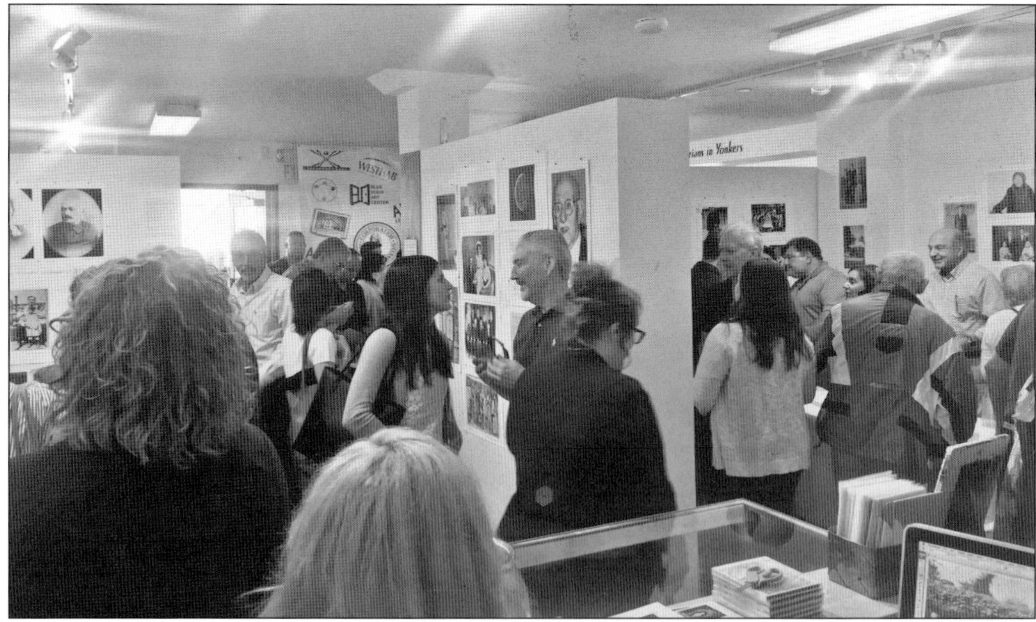

The Opening of the Assyrians in Yonkers Exhibit. Assyrians and local patrons are pictured at an exhibit at the Blue Door Gallery on Riverdale Avenue that celebrated the Yonkers Assyrian community. The opening of the exhibit on October 9, 2017, broke the gallery's record for the opening day of an exhibit. (Courtesy of Jacquie BabayiKunka.)

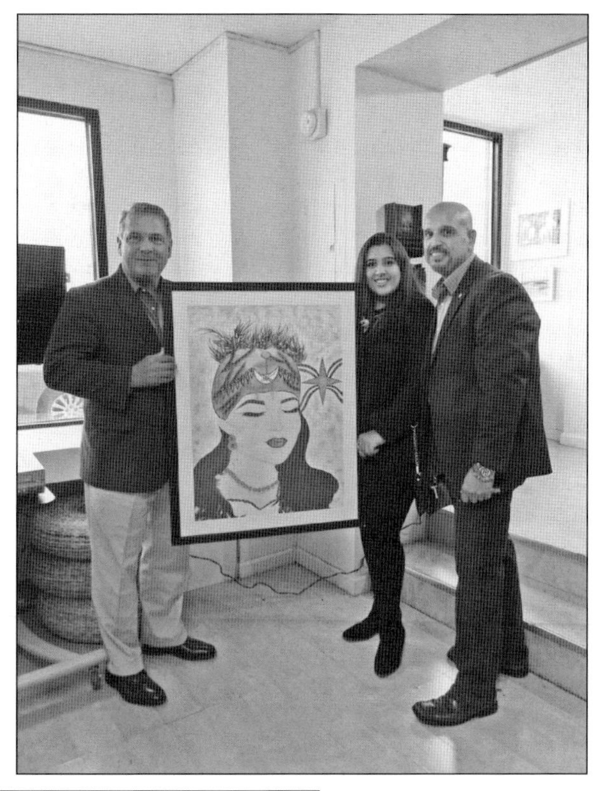

Serena Sarkiso's Painting, *An Assyrian Beauty*. Serena Sarkiso, a high school student, makes her contribution to the Assyrians in Yonkers exhibit. Pictured on October 9, 2017, with Mayor Mike Spano and her father, Fred Sarkiso, Serena stands proud of her heritage. (Courtesy of Jacquie BabayiKunka.)

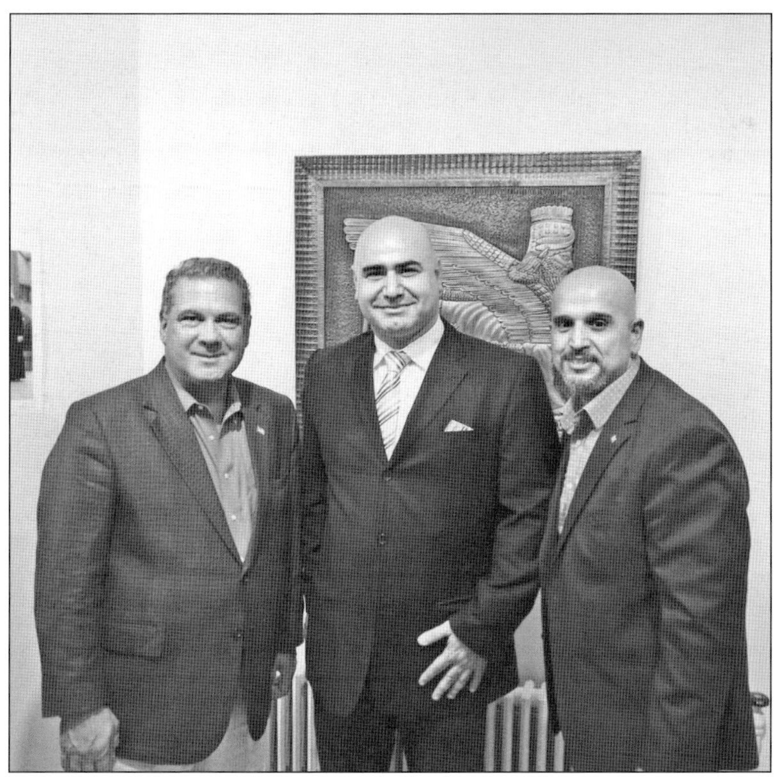

Lamassu in Copper. Pictured at the Blue Door Gallery on October 9, 2017, are (from left to right) Mayor Mike Spano, artist Haraj Lulu, and Fred Sarkiso, president of the Assyrian American Association. (Author's collection.)

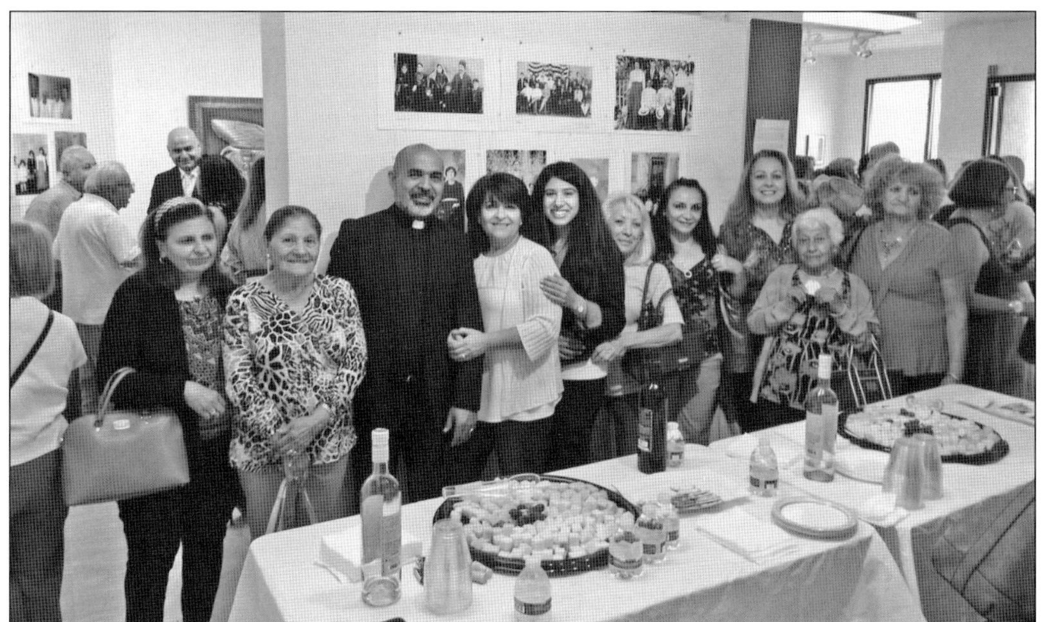

ART AND A CELEBRATION OF ASSYRIAN HERITAGE. Yonkers Assyrians gather to view the exhibit on opening day. From left to right are Rosa Shlimoun Gervargiz, Ana Constantine, Rev. Addai Francis, Jacquie BabayiKunka, Samara Brakhia, Valentine Mirza Shamoun, Janeet Yousif Francis, Josephine Eshoo, Ana David, and Daisy Tatari, on October 9, 2017. (Courtesy of Jacquie BabayiKunka.)

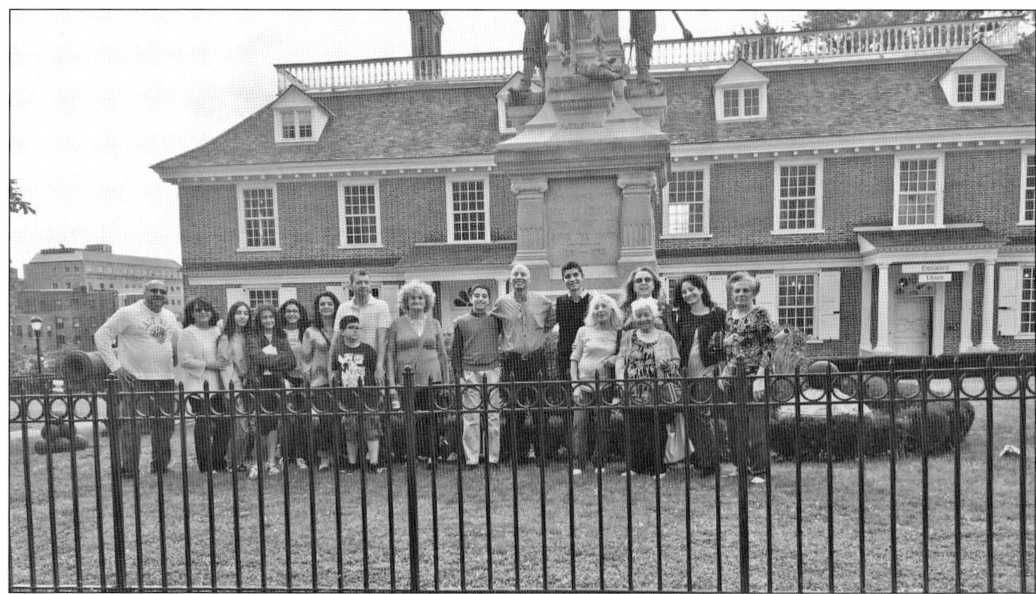

PHILIPSE HALL MANOR. The Assyrians in Yonkers exhibit featured a portion on immigration as part of a larger exhibit on Yonkers history at Philipse Hall Manor on Riverdale Avenue in Getty Square. This group of Mar Mari parishioners in front of the landmark are, from left to right, Joe Lazar, Jacquie BabayiKunka, Karizma Francis, Lara Lazar, Samantha Odishoo, Rita Odishoo, Sargon Odishoo, Andrew Odishoo (standing in front of his father), Daisy Tatari, Peter Multari, Ralph Multari, Matthew Multari, Valentine Shamoun and Ana David (in front), Josephine Eshoo, Nancy Mirza Multari, and Mary Oso. (Courtesy of Jacquie BabayiKunka.)

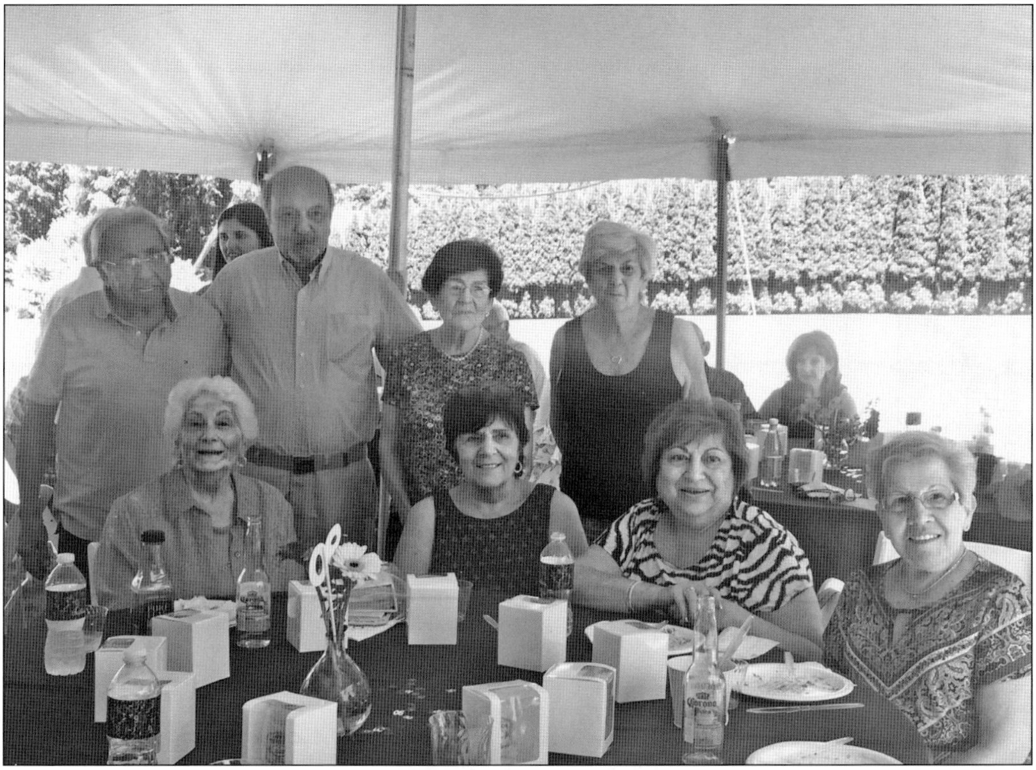

Billy Sargis's 90th Birthday Party. From left to right are (first row) Sue Nweeia, Barbara Ovanes Baba, Alice Aziz David, and Georgina Kerr; (second row) Billy Sargis, Darius Baba, Lilly Nweeia Sargis, and Lydia Benjamin Kambar in July 2018. (Author's collection.)

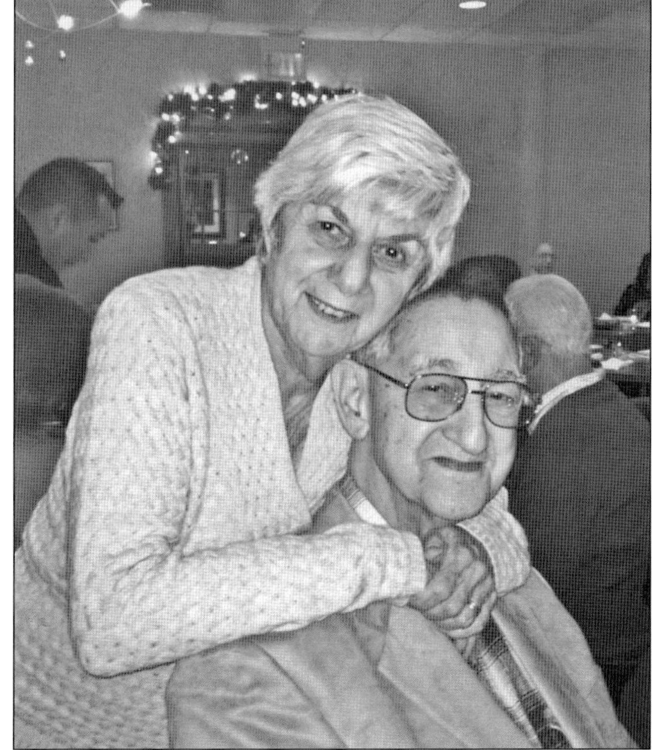

Lydia and William Kambar. Lydia and Bill Kambar are pictured at An American Bistro in Crestwood, New York, on January 20, 2014. (Author's collection.)